# Mergers

## What Can Go Wrong
## and How to Prevent It

Patrick A. Gaughan

WILEY

John Wiley & Sons, Inc.

Copyright © 2005 by John Wiley & Sons, Inc., Hoboken, New Jersey. All rights reserved.

Published simultaneously in Canada.

For general information on our other products and services, or technical support, please contact our Customer Care Department within the United States at 800-762-2974, outside the United States at 317-572-3993 or fax 317-572-4002.

Wiley also publishes its books in a variety of electronic formats. Some content that appears in print may not be available in electronic books.

For more information about Wiley products, visit our Web site at www.wiley.com.

*Library of Congress Cataloging-in-Publication Data:*

Gaughan, Patrick A.
    Mergers : what can go wrong and how to prevent it / Patrick A. Gaughan.
        p. cm.
    Includes index.
        ISBN-13    978-0-471-41900-6 (cloth)
        ISBN-10    0-471-41900-1 (cloth)
        1. Consolidation and merger of corporations.    I. Title.
    HD2746.5,M384 2005
    658.1'62—dc22                                                              2004025811

Printed in the United States of America

10 9 8 7 6 5 4 3 2 1

# Contents

# Preface

Now that we have had a few years to look back on some of the failed mergers and acquisitions of the recent fifth merger wave, we see that there is an abundant supply of poorly conceived deals. When the fourth merger wave ended in the late 1980s, much attention was paid to the reasons for the many failed transactions of that period. Some of those deals even resulted in the bankruptcy of the companies involved. At that time, many managers asserted that in the future they would not make the mistakes of some of their deal-oriented counterparts. Some of these deal-making managers attempted to blame overly aggressive investment bankers, who supposedly pushed companies into poorly conceived, short-term-oriented deals. While this may have been true on certain occasions, it is a poor explanation for a board of directors and its corporate management. In any event, it seemed that corporate culture started the 1990s with a determination to do better deals while avoiding failures. However, just one decade and one merger wave later, we had another supply of merger blunders—only they were larger and generated even greater losses for shareholders. Why do we seem to have trouble learning our merger lessons? Are companies making the same mistakes, or are the failures of the more recent merger period different from those of prior merger waves? Are a certain number of bad deals simply a by-product of an unprecedented high volume of M&As, of which a certain percentage will naturally be mistakes? In this book we explore the reasons for merger failures and try to discern the extent to which these failures are preventable.

Although the reasons for failed M&As appear to be many and varied, an alarming percentage seem to have one common element—hubris-filled CEOs who are unchecked by their boards. The penchant for ego-driven CEOs to want to build empires at the shareholders' expense will become obvious as readers go through the different chapters in this book. The material in these chapters will be supported by the abundant research that is available in this area. At the end of each chapter, a full case study explores specific failed deals. In addition, smaller mini-cases are featured throughout the book to ensure pragmatic applications of the various concepts that are discussed.

Readers may be somewhat surprised at the magnitude of the strategic errors and the extent to which shareholders paid for the losses caused by managers and allowed by boards. Some of the errors are so extreme that one title for this book that was lightheartedly considered was *CEOs Gone Wild*. However, the similarity of this title to that of a particular video series eliminated this as an option.

The subtitle of the book, *What Can Go Wrong and How to Prevent It,* implies that we do not consider the many deals that are successful. In fact, many deals turn out well, and we can certainly learn from these success stories. However, in this book we take the opportunity to examine some major merger failures and try to find common elements that are present in these various deals. Although a cursory review of many failed deals may point to a wide variety of factors without common elements, a closer examination will reveal that a troubling amount of failures can be attributed, in part or in whole, to CEO hubris that takes the place of well-designed corporate strategy. These out-of-control managers often are unchecked by their boards, which they sometimes dominate. Some CEOs work to influence their boards and may even partially control their makeup. It is not a surprise when we see that such boards rubber-stamp empire-building strategies that yield few benefits for shareholders and possibly even large losses.

What is even more troubling than the occasional deal failure is the fact that so many companies seem to not be able to learn from the mistakes of other managers who pursued failed deals even when their own companies were the ones involved in the failures. Some of the same companies that were involved in major blunders seem to go right on with the next mistake without pausing to learn from their troubled past. Sometimes boards change managers who engaged in prior failed deals, and the new managers proceed to make similar mistakes without being halted by their boards, even though both should know better. It is hoped that this book will draw attention to some of the sources of these failures so that managers and directors may avoid similar mistakes.

This book is designed for a diverse audience of those interested in this aspect of corporate strategy and finance. Such an audience should include general business readers but also corporate managers and members of boards of directors, as well as their various advisors including investment bankers, attorneys, consultants, and accountants. Although the material featured in some chapters is somewhat technical, an effort was made to present it in a nontechnical manner so that a broader group of readers can benefit from the material. Also, we occasionally approach the material in a lighthearted manner so that we can find a little humor in a situation that would only draw the ire of adversely affected investors. We hope that readers enjoy the material while also gaining from its content.

# 1

# Introduction to Mergers and Acquisitions

The field of mergers and acquisitions (M&As) has greatly expanded over the past quarter of a century. While M&As used to be somewhat more of a U.S. business phenomenon, this changed significantly in the 1990s, and now M&As are more commonly used by corporations throughout the world to expand and pursue other corporate goals. This was very much the case in the latest merger wave of the 1990s and early 2000s, where the numbers of deals in Europe were comparable to those in the United States. In addition, other markets, such as the Asian economies, also saw much M&A activity as well as other forms of corporate restructuring. Restructuring, sell-offs, and acquisitions become more common in Asia, where countries such as Japan and South Korea began the slow process of deregulating their economies in an effort to deal with economic declines experienced during that period.

In this book we will analyze how mergers and acquisitions can be used to further a corporation's goals. However, we will focus mainly on how M&As can be misused and why this occurs so often. We will see that flawed mergers and failed acquisitions are quite common and are not restricted to one time period. We will see that while we have had three merger booms in the United States over the past four decades, every decade featured many prominent merger failures. One characteristic of these failures is their similarity. It might seem reasonable that if several corporations had made certain prominent merger errors, then the rest of the corporate world would learn from such mistakes and not repeat them. This seems not to be the case. It is ironic, but we seem to be making some of the same merger mistakes—decade after decade. In this book we will discuss these errors and try to trace their source.

Before we begin such discussions, it is useful to establish a background in the field. For this reason we will have an initial discussion of the field of M&As that starts off with basic terminology and then goes on to provide an overview. We will start this review by highlighting some of the main laws that govern M&As in the United States. It is beyond the bounds of this book to provide a full review of the major laws in Europe and Asia. Fortunately, many of these are covered elsewhere.

Following our review of the regulatory framework of M&As, we will discuss some of the basic economics of M&As as well as provide an overview of the basic reasons why companies merge or acquire other companies. We will generally introduce these reasons in this chapter, but we will devote Chapter 2 to this issue.

In this initial chapter on M&As, we will also review leveraged transactions and buyouts. The role of debt financing, and the junk bond market in particular, and the private equity business will be covered along with the trends in leveraged deals. We will see that these were more popular in some time periods than in others. In the most recent merger wave, for example, we saw fewer of the larger leveraged buyouts than what we saw in the 1980s when M&As were booming to unprecedented levels.

Finally, we will review the trends in number of dollar value of M&As. We will do this from a historical perspective that focuses on the different merger waves we have had in the United States, but also elsewhere—where relevant. As part of this review, we will point out the differences between the merger waves. Each is distinct and reflects the changing economy in the United States.

## BACKGROUND AND TERMINOLOGY

A *merger* is a combination of two corporations in which only one corporation survives. The merged corporation typically ceases to exist. The acquirer gets the assets of the target but it must also assume its liabilities. Sometimes we have a combination of two companies that are of similar sizes and where both of the companies cease to exist following the deal and an entirely new company is created. This occurred in 1986 when UNISYS was formed through the combination of Burroughs and Sperry. However, in most cases, we have one surviving corporate entity and the other, a company we often refer to as the *target*, ceases to officially exist. This raises an important issue on the compilation of M&A statistics. Companies that compile data on merger statistics, such as those that are published in *Mergerstat Review*, usually treat the smaller company in a merger as the target and the larger one as the buyer even when they may report the deal as a merger between two companies.

Readers of literature of M&A will quickly notice that some terms are used differently in different contexts. This is actually not unique to M&As but generally applies to the use of the English language. Mergers and acquisitions are no different, although perhaps it is true to a greater extent in this field. One example is the term *takeover*. When one company acquires another, we could refer to this as a takeover. However, more often than not, when the term *takeover* is used, it refers to a hostile situation. This is where one company is attempting to acquire another against the will of the target company's management and board. This often is done through the use of a *tender offer*. We will discuss hostile takeovers and tender offers a little later in this chapter. Before doing that, let's continue with our general discussion of the terminology in the field of M&As.

## MERGER PROCESS

Most M&As are friendly deals in which two companies negotiate the terms of the deal. Depending on the size of the deal, this usually involves communications between senior management of the two companies, in which they try to work out the pricing and other terms of the deal. For public companies, once the terms of the deal have been agreed upon, they are presented to shareholders of the target company for their approval. Larger deals may sometimes require the approval of the shareholders of both companies. Once shareholders approve the deal, the process moves forward to a closing. Public companies have to do public filings for major corporate events, and the sale of the company is obviously one such event that warrants such a filing by the target.

In hostile deals, the takeover process is different. A different set of communications takes place between the target and bidder. Instead of direct contact, we have an odd communications process that involves attorneys and the courts. Bidders try to make appeals directly to shareholders as they seek to have them accept their own terms, often against the recommendations of management. Target companies may go to great lengths to avoid the takeover. Sometimes this process can go on for months, such as in the 2004 Oracle and People-Soft takeover battle.

## ECONOMIC CLASSIFICATIONS OF MERGERS AND ACQUISITIONS

Economic theory classifies mergers into three broad categories:

1. Horizontal
2. Vertical
3. Conglomerate

Horizontal mergers are combinations between two competitors. When Pfizer acquired Warner Lambert in 2000, the combination of these two pharmaceutical companies was a horizontal deal. The deal is an excellent example of the great value that can be derived from acquisitions, as Pfizer was able to acquire Lipitor as part of the package of products it gained when it acquired Warner Lambert. Lipitor, the leading anticholesterol drug, would become the top-selling drug in the world, with annual revenues in excess of $11 billion by 2004. This helped Pfizer maintain its position as the number-one pharmaceutical company in the world. This transaction was actually part of a series of horizontal combinations in which we saw the pharmaceutical industry consolidate. Such consolidations often occur when an industry is deregulated, although this was not the case for pharmaceuticals as it was for the banking industry. In banking this consolidation process has been going on for the past two decades. Regulatory strictures may prevent a combination that would otherwise occur among companies in an industry. Once deregulation happens, however, the artificial separations among companies may cease to exist, and the industry adjusts through a widespread combination of firms as they seek to move to a size and level of business activity that they believe is more efficient.

Increased horizontal mergers can affect the level of competition in an industry. Economic theory has shown us that competition normally benefits consumers. Competition usually results in lower prices and a greater output being put on the market relative to less competitive situations. As a result of this benefit to consumer welfare, most nations have laws that help prevent the domination of an industry by a few competitors. Such laws are referred to as *antitrust laws* in the United States. Outside the United States they are more clearly referred to as *competition policy*. Sometimes they may make exceptions to this policy if the regulators believe that special circumstances dictate it. We will discuss the laws that regulate the level of competition in an industry later in this chapter.

Sometimes industries consolidate in a series of horizontal transactions. An example has been the spate of horizontal M&As that has occurred in both the oil and pharmaceutical industries. Both industries have consolidated for somewhat different reasons. The mergers between oil companies, such as the merger between Exxon and Mobil in 1998, have provided some clear benefits in the form of economies of scale, which is a motive for M&As that we will discuss later in this chapter. The demonstration of such benefits, or even the suspicion that competitors who have pursued mergers are enjoying them, can set off a mini-wave of M&As in an industry. This was the case in the late 1990s and early 2000s as companies such as Conoco and Phillips, Texaco and Chevron merged following the Exxon-Mobil deal, which followed on the heels of the Amoco-BP merger and occurred at roughly the same time as the PetroFina-Total merger.

Vertical mergers are deals between companies that have a buyer and seller relationship with each other. In a vertical transaction, a company might acquire a supplier or another company closer in the distribution chain to consumers. The oil industry, for example, features many large vertically integrated companies, which explore for and extract oil but also refine and distribute fuel directly to consumers.

An example of a vertical transaction occurred in 1993 with the $6.6 billion merger between drug manufacturer Merck and Medco Containment Services—a company involved in the distribution of drugs. As with horizontal transactions, certain deals can set off a series of other copycat deals as competitors seek to respond to a perceived advantage that one company may have gotten by enhancing its distribution system. We already discussed this concept in the context of the oil industry. In the case of pharmaceuticals, Merck incorrectly thought it would acquire distribution-related advantages through its acquisition of Medco. Following the deal, competitors sought to do their own similar deals. In 1994 Eli Lilly bought PCS Health Systems for $4.1 billion, while Roche Holdings acquired Syntex Corp. for $5.3 billion. Merck was not good at foreseeing the ramifications of such vertical acquisitions in this industry and neither were the copycat competitors. They incorrectly believed that they would be able to enhance their distribution of drugs while gaining an advantage over competitors who might have reduced access to such distribution. The market and regulators did not accept such arrangements, so the deals were failures. The companies simply could not predict how their consumers and regulators in their own industry would react to such combinations.

Conglomerate deals are combinations of companies that do not have a business relationship with each other. That is, they do not have a buyer-seller relationship and they are not competitors. Conglomerates were popular in the 1960s, when antitrust enforcement prevented companies from easily engaging in horizontal or even vertical transactions. They still wanted to use M&As to facilitate their growth, and their own alternative was to buy companies with whom they did not have any business relationship. We will discuss this phenomena more when we review merger history. Also, we will discuss diversifying deals in general in Chapter 2 on merger strategies. We will find that while some types of diversifying mergers promote shareholder wealth, many do not. We will also see that even those companies that have demonstrated a special prowess for doing successful diversifying deals also do big flops as well. General Electric (GE) is a well-known diversified company or conglomerate, but even it failed when it acquired Kidder Peabody. Acquiring a brokerage firm proved to be too big a stretch for this diversified corporation that was used to marketing very different products. The assets of brokerage firms are really their brokers, human beings who walk in and out of the company every day. This is different from capital-intensive businesses, which utilize equipment that tends to stay in the same place you put it. With a brokerage firm, if you do not give the "asset" a sufficient bonus, it takes off to one of your competitors at the end of the year. If you are not used to dealing with such human assets, this may not be the acquisition for you. It wasn't for GE.

## REGULATORY FRAMEWORK OF MERGERS AND ACQUISITIONS

In the United States, three sets of laws regulate M&As: securities, antitrust, and state corporation laws. The developments of these laws have been an ongoing process as the business of M&As has evolved over time. In this section we will cover the highlights of some of the major laws.

### Securities Laws

In the United States, public companies—those that have sold shares to the public—are regulated by both federal and state securities laws. Although these laws regulate issuers of stock in many ways that are less relevant to M&As, they do contain specific sections that relate to such deals. Companies that engage in control transactions, of which an M&A would be considered such a transaction, have to make certain filings with the national governmental entity that regulates securities markets in the United States—the Securities and Exchange Commission (SEC). Securities laws require that with the occurrence of a significant event, including an M&A above a certain size, companies must file a Form 8K. This filing contains basic information on the transaction. In addition to this filing, when an entity is pursuing a tender offer, it must make certain filings with the SEC pursuant to the Williams Act. This law is primarily directed at the activities of companies that are seeking to pursue hostile deals.

The two most important laws in the history of U.S. securities regulation are the Securities Act of 1933 and the Securities Exchange Act of 1934. The 1933 Act required the registration of securities that were going to be offered to the public. This was passed in the wake of the stock market crash of 1929, when so many companies went bankrupt and their investors lost considerable sums. At this time investors had little access to relevant financial information on the companies that offered shares. The law was designed, in part, to provide greater disclosure, which small investors could use to assess the prospects for their investments in these public companies. The lawmakers' reasoning at that time was that individual investors would be better protected if companies were required to disclose such information with which the investors could make more informed decisions.

The Securities Act of 1934 added to the provisions of the 1933 Act but also established the federal enforcement agency that was charged with enforcing federal securities law—the Securities and Exchange Commission (SEC). Many of the securities and merger-related laws that have been enacted are amendments to the Securities Exchange Act. One major amendment to this law was the Williams Act, which regulated tender offers.

## Tender Offer Regulation

Tender offers, which are made directly to shareholders of target companies, were relatively unregulated until the Williams Act was passed in 1968. This act contains two sections that are relevant to the conduct of tender offers. The first is Section 13(d), which requires that if an entity, corporation, partnership, or individuals acquire 5% or more of a company's outstanding shares, it must file a Schedule 13D within 10 days of reaching the 5% threshold. The schedule features various financial data that are to be provided by the acquirers of the shares. This information includes the identity of the acquirer, its intentions, and other information, of which shareholders of the target company might want to be aware. Such information requires the acquirer to indicate the purpose of the transaction. If it intends to launch a hostile takeover of the company, it must say so. If the shares are being acquired for investment purposes, it must say so as well. This section of the law is important to shareholders who may not want to sell their shares if there is a bidder who is about to make an acquisition bid that would normally provide a takeover premium.

When a tender offer is made, the bidder must file a Schedule 14D, which also lists various information that the offerer must reveal. In addition to the identity of the bidder, the offerer must indicate the purpose of the transaction, the source of its financing, as well as other information that might be relevant to a target shareholder who wants to evaluate the transaction. Although the Williams Act regulates tender offers, ironically it actually does not define exactly what a tender offer is. This was done in court decisions that have interpreted that law. One such decision was rendered in *Wellman* v. *Dickinson*. In this case, the court set forth seven out of eight factors that later became known as the Eight Factor Test when another factor was added in a subsequent court decision. These are eight characteristics that an offer must have in order to be considered a tender offer requiring the filing of a Schedule 14D.[1] Hostile deals really become part of the fabric of corporate America in the 1980s, during a period that is known as the fourth merger wave. This time period and its characteristics will be discussed in detail in the next chapter.

Section 14(d) provides benefits to target company shareholders. It gives them more information that they can use to evaluate an offer. This is especially important in cases where the consideration is securities, such as shares in the bidder. Target company shareholders want to know that information so they can determine if the deal is in their interests. Section 14(d) requires that the bidder must wait 20 days before completing the purchase of the shares. During this time, shareholders may decide not to tender their shares to the bidder and may withdraw them even if they tendered them earlier in the 20-day time period. This time period is provided so that shareholders have time to fully consider the offer that has been presented to them and that is described in the materials submitted with the Schedule 14D. During that period, other bidders may come forward with competing bids, and this can have an effect on the length of the original offer period as under certain circumstances, depending on when during the 20-day time period a second or even third bids come, the total waiting period may be extended. Such extensions are designed to give shareholders time to evaluate both offers together.

## Insider Trading Laws

Various securities laws have been adopted to try to prevent insider trading. One is Rule 10b-5, which prohibits the use of fraud and deceit in the trading of securities. The passage of the Insider Trading Sanctions Act of 1984, however, specifically prevented the trading of securities based on insider information. Unfortunately, the exact definition of *inside information* was left murky by the law, and the process of coming up with a working definition of *inside information* and *insiders* evolved based on decisions in various cases brought alleging insider trading. However, the general concept behind the laws is that those who have access to inside information, which is not available to the average investors and which would affect the value of a security, should not be able to trade using such information unless it is first made available to the public. This does not mean that insiders, such as management and directors, cannot purchase shares in their own companies. Such purchases and sales have to be specifically disclosed, and there is a legal process for how such trading and disclosure should be conducted. Those who violate insider trading laws can face both criminal penalties and civil suits from investors.

In the 1980s, there were several prominent cases of corporate insiders, investment bankers, attorneys, and even newspaper reporters using inside information to trade for their own benefit. Information on a company that is about to be acquired can be valuable because takeover offers normally include a control premium, and shareholders may not want to sell shares in a company that is about to receive such an offer. Those who know about an impending but as-yet-undisclosed takeover offer may be tempted to buy shares from unsuspecting investors and gain this premium. This is why we have laws that try to prevent just that. Do the laws work? Laws never eliminate crime, but they raise the price of violating the rules. In doing so, the laws help level the playing field between those investors who have a preferential access to information that others do not have.

## ANTITRUST LAWS

In the United States, we call competition policy *antitrust policy*. This term was derived from the types of entities that were the focus of initial concerns about anticompetitive activity—trusts. These were the large business entities that came to dominate certain industries in the late 1800s. As part of this concern, the Sherman Antitrust Act was passed in 1890. This law has two main sections. Section One is designed to prevent the formation of monopolies and seeks to limit a company's ability to monopolize an industry. Section Two seeks to prevent combinations of companies from engaging in business activities that limit competition. The law was broad and initially had little impact on anticompetitive activities. It is ironic that the first great merger period, one that resulted in the formation of monopolies in various industries, took place after the passage of the law that was designed to prevent such actions. There are several reasons for the initial ineffectiveness of this law. One was that the law was so broad that many people did not think it was really enforceable. In addition, the Justice Department did not really have the resources to effectively enforce the law, especially since an unprecedented period of M&A activity took place soon after its passage, yet no additional resources were provided to the Justice Department to enable it to deal with the onslaught of new deals.

After this first merger wave came to an end, Congress sought to readdress competition policy in the United States. This led to the passage of some more laws regulating businesses. One of these was the Clayton Act of 1914. This law generally focused on competition policy, and it had a specific section, Section 7, which was designed to regulate anticompetitive mergers. At the same time, Congress also passed another law—the Federal Trade Commission Act, which established the Federal Trade Commission (FTC). The FTC was charged with enforcing the Federal Trade Commission Act but also is involved in enforcing our competition laws along with the Justice Department. Both governmental entities are involved in enforcing antitrust laws, and they tend to work together to ensure that one governmental entity enforces the laws in each particular case. This often means that one entity, say the FTC, focuses on certain industries while the Justice department handles others. The FTC had previously handled the competitive software industry, but when the U.S. government decided it was going to pursue action against Microsoft, it was decided that the Justice Department, which could command greater resources, would step forward and take over the matter.

One antitrust law that is also relevant to M&A is the Hart-Scott-Rodino Antitrust Improvements Act, which was passed in 1976. This law requires that companies involved in M&A transactions file data on sales and shipments with the Justice Department and FTC. Companies must receive prior approval from one of these regulatory bodies before being able to complete a deal. The purpose of the law is to prevent deals that might be anticompetitive from being consummated and having to be disassembled after the fact There has been criticism in recent years that the approval process is unnecessarily long and regulators have promised to work to eliminate unnecessary delays.

## STATE CORPORATION LAWS

Corporations are chartered by specific states. Being incorporated in a particular state means that the company must follow the laws of that state. However, companies may also have to adhere to laws of other states in which they do business. The most common state for companies to be incorporated in is the State of Delaware, which has made a small industry out of incorporating businesses and processing their legal claims in the State's court system. There has been much debate about why Delaware is the state of preference for companies. It cannot be fully explained by just tax differences or even the state's highly developed legal code. Other states, such as Nevada, have tried to attract away some of this business by copying the Delaware corporation laws, but this attempt has not been successful. At this point, part of the explanation lies in the fact that Delaware has been established as the preferred state, and that is difficult to change.

With respect to M&As, one major difference among states is their antitakeover laws. Many states adopted different antitakeover laws that made it more difficult for hostile bidders, especially those from outside a given state, to take over companies in that state. This was very popular in the 1980s, when hostile takeovers were the rage. Delaware actually lagged behind some of the other states, which had passed aggressive antitakeover laws as a result of lobbying pressures by potential target companies on state legislatures. Eventually Delaware passed a law in the midst of a takeover battle between Carl Icahn and Texaco, which actually was made retroactive to a date when Icahn's shareholdings would later be sufficient to be bound by this law. This underscores the role of potential target companies in passing such laws.

There are various types of antitakeover laws, and many states have sets of laws that embody several of the different types of restrictions. These include:

- *Fair price laws.* These laws require that all shareholders in tender offers receive what the law defines to be a fair price. The law includes some definition of a fair price, such as the highest price paid by the bidder for shares.

- *Business combination statutes.* These laws were designed to make leveraged takeovers that are dependent on sales of a target company's assets more difficult to complete. They tried to prevent unwanted bidders from taking full control of the target company's assets unless it acquires a minimum number of shares, such as 85%. If the shareholders or the board members decide that they do not want to be bound by the law, they can elect not to do so.

- *Control share provisions.* These laws require bidders to receive approvals from target company shareholders before they can acquire shares or use the voting rights associated with those shares.

- *Cash-out statutes.* These statutes require a bidder to purchase the shares of the shareholders whose stock may not have been purchased by a bidder whose purchases of target company stock may have provided it with an element of control in the company. This is designed to both prevent target shareholders from being unfairly treated by a controlling shareholder and to require that the bidder have sufficient financing to be able to afford to purchase these shares.

## HOSTILE TAKEOVERS

Hostile takeovers refer to the taking control of a corporation against the will of its management and/or directors. Taking over a company without the support of management and directors does not necessarily mean it is against the will of its shareholders. The way the takeover process works, shareholders usually do not get to express their views directly during a takeover battle and rely on management to do this for them. This is why having managers and directors who will live up to their fiduciary responsibilities is very important for the growth of shareholder wealth.

The main reason why a bidder pursues a hostile as opposed to a friendly takeover is that the deal is opposed by the target. Bidders usually want to do friendly deals because hostile deals typically are more expensive to complete. The greater expense comes from the fact that the bidding process may result in a higher premium because it may involve other bidders bidding the price up. It will also include costs such as additional investment bankers' fees and legal fees. Hostile deals also have less assurance that a deal would go through compared to friendly deals, which have a much higher percentage of completion.

One of the main tools used to complete a hostile takeover is the tender offer. This topic was discussed briefly while reviewing tender offer regulation. Tender offers are bids made directly to shareholders, bypassing management and the board of directors. If a company were pursuing a friendly deal, the logical place to start would be to contact the target company management. If this contact is rejected, then there are two other alternatives: (1) go to the board of directors or (2) go directly to shareholders. When bidders make an offer to the board of directors, this is sometimes referred to as a *bear hug*. It is mainly a hostile tactic because it carries with it the implied, and sometimes stated, threat that if the offer is not favorably received, the bidder will go directly to shareholders next.

If a friendly overture or a bear hug is not favorably responded to, then one of the next alternatives is a tender offer. Here the bidder communicates the terms of its offer directly to shareholders, hoping they will accept the deal. As discussed earlier, the Williams Act provides for specific regulations to which tender offers must adhere. Bidders are somewhat limited following the submission of the offer because they have the aforementioned 20-day waiting period that they must wait out before actually purchasing the shares—assuming shareholders find the offer sufficiently appealing to want to sell. During the 20-day offer period, other bidders may make offers. The first bidder may have put the target company *in play* and may then find itself in a bidding contest. Target company shareholders then get to consider both offers and possibly even others. This usually works to their advantage because they tend to receive higher premiums when there are multiple bids.

For bidders, however, it usually means they either will have to pay a higher price for the target or will have to drop out of the process. Shrewd bidders know where to draw the line and step back. Others, sometimes consumed by hubris, will bid on in an attempt to "win" the contest. Often what they end up winning is the "winner's curse," where they pay more than the company is worth. This was the case in 1988 when Robert Campeau, having already acquired Allied Stores, went on to make an offer for Federated, which would give him the largest department store chain in the world. Unfortunately for him, Macy's stepped into the bidding process, and Edward Finkelstein and Robert Campeau went head-to-head, increasing the premium until finally Campeau won out. The ultimate winning bid was $8.17 billion (equity, debt, and total fees paid), and the acquisition saddled the combined company with billions of dollars in new debt. We will discuss this takeover more in Chapter 4, but it is a great example of a bidder incorrectly estimating the value of a target and taking on more debt than it could service. Campeau was forced to file for Chapter 11 bankruptcy not that long after the "successful" completion of the takeover.

Hostile bidders have tried different means to thwart the requirements of the Williams Act. One way they have done this was through two-tiered tender offers, which provide preferential compensation to bidders who tender into the first tier of the offer—say the first 51% of all shares tendered. The 51% usually (but not always) gives the bidder control of the target, and the remaining 49% may be of less value. If this is the case, the bidder may seek to provide higher compensation for this percentage while offering lower compensation and maybe even different consideration for the remaining shares. Courts have found, however, that such offers are often "coercive" and work again the principles of the Williams Act. In such cases, they have been ruled illegal.

Another alternative to a tender offer is a proxy fight. This is where the bidder tries to use the corporate democracy process to garner enough votes to throw out the current board of directors and the managers they have selected. They would either try this at the next corporate election or call a special election. The *insurgent,* as such bidders are now called in this context, then presents its proposals and/or its slate of directors in opposition to the current group. This manner of taking over a company is costly and provides for an uncertain outcome. It is often unsuccessful, although success depends on how you define it. If the bidder is trying to bring about changes in the way the target company is run, this process often does accomplish that. If the goal, however, is to get shareholders to outright reject the current board and then go so far as to accept a bid for the company against management's recommendation, then this process often does not work. Bidders also find themselves having to expend significant sums for an outcome that often does not work in their favor—at least in the short run.

## TAKEOVER DEFENSE

The hostile takeover process is somewhat like a chess match, with the target company being pitted against the hostile bidder. During the fourth merger wave of the 1980s, the tactics and defenses deployed against hostile takeovers came to be greatly refined. Before the 1980s, the usual knee-jerk reaction of a target company when faced with an unwanted bid was to file a suit alleging antitrust violations. Today such a defense would usually be construed as weak and ineffective. However, in the 1960s and 1970s, when antitrust policy was much more stringent, especially during the 1960s, this was a much more credible response. At such times, if the antitrust lawsuit was not successful, then the bidder tried to pursue more friendly suitors and prepare a list of *white knights,* as such friendly suitors are referred. By the 1980s, when hostile bidders were initiating tender offers with increasing aggressiveness, targets began to catch up to bidders, and the arms race between bidders and targets took force in earnest. Targets enlisted the services of adept attorneys and investment bankers, who devised increasingly sophisticated takeover defenses.

There are two types of takeover defenses. *Preventive takeover defenses* are put in place in advance of any specific takeover bid. They are installed so that a bidder will not attempt a takeover. *Active takeover defenses* are deployed in the midst of a takeover battle where a bidder has made an offer for the company. Although there are a variety of both types of defenses, many of them are less effective than when they were initially created.

The most effective preventive takeover defense is a *poison pill.* Poison pills are also called *shareholders' rights plans.* Rights are short-term versions of warrants. Like warrants, they allow the holder to purchase securities at some specific price and under certain circumstances. Poison pills usually allow the rightsholders to purchase shares at half-price. This is usually worded as saying the holder can purchase $200 worth of stock for $100.

Poison pills are an effective defense because they make the costs of a takeover very expensive. If the bidder were to buy 100% of the outstanding shares, it would still have to honor the warrants held by former shareholders, who would then be able to purchase shares at half-price. Because this usually makes an acquisition cost prohibitive, bidders seek to negotiate with the target to get it to dismantle this defense. Sometimes the bidder makes direct appeals to shareholders, requesting them to take action so they can enjoy the premium it is offering and which management and the board may be preventing them from receiving. Target management and directors, however, may be using the protection provided by the poison pill to extract a suitable premium from the bidder. Once a satisfactory offer is received, they may then dismantle this defense, which can usually be done easily and at low cost to the target company.

Other types of preventive takeover defenses involve different amendments of the corporate charter. One such defense is a staggered board, which alters the elections of directors so that only a limited number of directors, such as one-third, come up for election at one time. If only one-third of the board could be elected at one time, then new controlling shareholders would have to wait for two elections before winning control of the board. This hinders bidders who make an investment in the target and then cannot make changes in the company for a period of time. Such changes may be a merger with the bidding company or the sales of assets, which might be used to help pay off debt the bidder incurred to finance the acquisition of the target's stock.

Other common corporate charter amendments are supermajority provisions, which require not just a simple majority but a higher percentage, before certain types of changes can be approved. If a pocket of shareholders will not vote with the bidder, such as managers and some employees who are worried about their jobs, then a bidder may not be able to get enough shares to enact the changes that it needs to take full control of the company.

Still other corporate charter changes include fair price provisions. These work similarly to fair price state corporation laws, except they are installed in the corporation's own bylaws. They require that bidders pay what they define as fair compensation for all shares that are purchased. It is especially focused on two-tiered bids, which seek to pay lower compensation to the back end of an offer. Fair price provisions are not considered a strong takeover defense.

Other corporate charter changes include dual capitalizations. These feature different classes of stock, which afford different voting rights and dividend entitlements to holders of the shares. They often involve one class of super voting rights stock, which usually pay very low dividends. These shares are usually distributed to all shareholders, but those who are interested in augmenting their control, such as managers, may retain it while others may accept a follow-up offer by the company to exchange these shares for regular voting and dividend-paying stock. The end result of such a stock offering/dividend distribution is that increased control is concentrated in the hands of shareholders who typically are more "loyal" to the corporation and who would be less likely to accept an offer from a hostile bidder. SEC and stock exchange rules limit the extent to which companies can issue and trade such shares.

Companies may also try to prevent a takeover by moving to a state that has stronger antitakeover laws than the state in which it may be incorporated. This often is not an effective defense. Many companies that have such concerns usually are already incorporated in a favorable state or are incorporated in Delaware, which has many attractive features in its antitakeover laws.

A target company can take several steps when it is the receipt of an unwanted bid. Drawing on the defense that has been used for many years, it could file a lawsuit. Unless there are important legal issues it could argue, this often is not enough to stop a takeover. It may, however, provide time, which may enable the target to mount other defenses. This may include selling to a more favored bidder — a white knight. It may also involve selling shares to a more friendly party. This can be done in advance of an offer or as an active defense. The buyer in such sales is referred to as a *white squire.*

During the 1980s, targets were more likely to try to greenmail the bidder to get it to go away and leave the company independent. *Greenmail,* which plays on the word *blackmail,* involves the payment to the bidder of a sufficient amount so that it retreats and does not continue with the takeover. Many changes have occurred since the mid-1980s, when this active defense was used more liberally. The changes include tax penalties on such payments as well as corporate charter amendments that companies have passed limiting their ability to pay greenmail. Greenmail is usually frowned on by shareholders who find their financial resources being used to prevent a bidder, who might be willing to pay a premium for their shares, from making a successful offer.

Greenmail is often accompanied by standstill agreements, whereby a bidder agrees to not purchase shares beyond some limit. In exchange for those agreements, the bidder receive certain compensation. We still see standstill agreements today for various reasons, and they are used independent of greenmail.

Targets may also restructure the company to make it less attractive to a bidder, or it may make some of the same changes that are being suggested by a bidder, thereby taking this recommendation away from the bidder. Restructuring the company may involve both asset sales and purchases. The company may also restructure its capitalization to increase its debt, making it more leveraged. Capital structure changes may have some impact by making the company less attractive and by reducing the amount of debt that can be raised by a bidder to finance the target's own takeover.

## LEVERAGED TRANSACTIONS

Leveraged deals are those that use debt to finance takeover. They are sometimes referred to as highly leveraged transactions (HLTs). One well-known version of HLTs is a leveraged buyout (LBO). An LBO is an acquisition that uses debt to buy the target's stock. When people refer to an LBO, however, they are often referring to a transaction in which a public company is bought using debt and then goes private. The largest LBO of all time was that of RJR Nabisco in 1988 for $24.8 billion. The company was bought by the well-known buyout firm of Kohlberg Kravis and Roberts (KKR). Although many of KKR's deals have been successes, this buyout was not part of that notable group. One of the problems it had, which LBOs in general have, is that the buyer takes on substantial debt, which leaves the company with a high degree of financial leverage. This carries with it all of the risk that high financial leverage imposes. This comes in the form of fixed charges for the increased debt service. Buyers of companies in leveraged transactions often plan on reducing this leverage with asset sales where the proceeds from those sales can be used to pay down the debt and reduce the debt service. They also try to implement cost structure changes and increased efficiencies, which will lower the company's overall costs and enable it to service the debt.

Buyers of companies in LBOs usually have a plan to reduce the debt over a period of time while they make various changes at the company. Many of these deal makers plan on doing a *reverse LBO* some time after the original LBO. In a reverse LBO, the private company that was bought out in the LBO goes public again. This can be done all at once or in stages, as it was done in the case of RJR Nabisco. In the RJR Nabisco deal, KKR sold percentages of the company to the public and used these proceeds to pay down the mountain of debt it had assumed. One of the reasons why this deal was not a success has to do with the budding contest that occurred as part of the buyout. RJR received a low-ball offer from a group led by then CEO Ross Johnson.[2] KKR entered the fray with its own offer, knowing that the Johnson group's offer was low. However, a bidding contest ensued, and KKR won, but it really bore the winner's curse.

Many LBOs are management buyouts (MBOs), which is what the Ross Johnson proposal was. As the name suggests, in a management buyout a management group acquires the company from the public shareholders. This is often an awkward situation because management are fiduciaries for shareholders and are charged with the responsibility of getting the best deal for them. However, it is in management's interests to pay the least amount for the company, which would mean a lower value for shareholders. Organizers of MBOs try to finesse this situation and seek to get outside opinions to substantiate the idea that shareholders are getting their full value for the company.

During the 1980s, there were many mega-LBOs featuring billion-dollar prices for public companies such as RJR Nabisco but also companies such as Seagate Technologies and Beatrice (see Exhibit 1.1). Many of these deals, as well as non-LBO acquisitions, were financed using funds raised through the sale of junk bonds. Marketers of junk bonds prefer to call them high-yield bonds. The bonds offer a high yield because they are more risky than other corporate bonds. The risk of the bond is assessed by rating agencies such as Standard & Poor's and Moody's. Under the Standard & Poor's system, AAA is the highest rating, AA is next, and so on. Bonds that receive a BB rating or worse are considered junk bonds. The name *junk bonds* is a poor one because these securities can pay attractive yields and be an important part of many investors' portfolios. Investors can combine them in diversified portfolios, thereby lowering their exposure to any one security, and enjoying impressive returns. However, because the agencies see greater risk in these corporate bonds as opposed to those to which they give a higher rating, the issuers have to offer a higher interest rate to investors to compensate them for assuming the relatively greater risk of these investments—hence the term *high yield*.

Exhibit 1.1    Top Ten LBO Deals

| Year Announced | Company Name | Purchase Price ($ millions) |
|---|---|---|
| 1988 | RJR Nabisco (tobacco and food giant) | 24,561.60 |
| 2000 | Seagate Technology Inc. (storage, retrieval, and data mgmt. products) | 11,661.60 |
| 1985 | Beatrice Cos. (diversified food and consumer products) | 5,361.60 |
| 1986 | Safeway Stores Inc. (supermarket chain) | 4,198.40 |
| 1987 | Borg-Warner Corp. (diversified manufacturing) | 3,798.60 |
| 1987 | Southland Corp. (convenience food stores) | 3,723.30 |
| 1986 | Owens-Illinois Inc. (packaging, financial services, nursing homes) | 3,631.90 |
| 1988 | Hospital Corp. of America (hospitals) | 3,602.10 |
| 1988 | Fort Howard Paper Corp. (paper products) | 3,574.20 |
| 1989 | NWA Inc. (airline) | 3,524.50 |

Source: Mergerstat Review, 2004.

The high-yield bond market provided some of the fuel for many of the megamergers and LBOs that occurred in the 1980s. When this market collapsed at the end of that decade, it helped end the fourth merger wave. We will discuss this interesting merger time period in the following section. Many of the companies that took on large amounts of debt during this period came to regret it shortly afterward when the economy slowed. Some of these companies were forced to file for bankruptcy. This put a damper on the junk-bond-financed merger and LBO market—one that it has not recovered from to date.

Ironically, after a sharp decline at the end of the 1980s, the junk bond market recovered and remains an important part of corporate finance. Now smaller, less well-known companies can tap into the capital that is available in the junk bond market. Before investment bankers such as Michael Milken helped pioneer the development of the original issue high-yield bond market, smaller companies did not have access to this huge capital market and were relegated to more restrictive financing sources such as bank loans. Although the junk bond market is alive and well in the 2000s, it does not play as prominent a role as it once did in the M&A market. Deals do not rely on this financing source as much, for reasons that will be discussed in the case study that follows the end of this chapter.

In the fifth merger wave of the 1990s and in the first half of the decade that followed, we still see many LBOs. However, they are different from the LBOs that were more common in the 1980s. One major difference is that they involve less debt and more equity. The companies that are bought in such deals tend to have less debt pressures and a greater likelihood of surviving the post-buyout period. A thriving *private equity market* has developed, and some of this capital finds its way into these types of deals. So we find that the whole LBO business has changed significantly over the past 20 years, but it is still very much alive, although in a different form.

## RESTRUCTURINGS

Mergers and acquisitions are but one form of corporate restructuring. However, while this is the focus of this book, other forms of restructuring can be related to M&As. One form of restructuring that is the opposite of M&As is sell-offs. In a *sell-off* a company sells part of itself to another entity. This can be done in several ways. The most common way is a divestiture, where a company simply sells off part of itself to another entity. However, downsizing can be accomplished in other ways, such as through spin-offs, where parts of a company are separated from the parent. Shares in the spun-off entity are given to shareholders of the parent company, who then become shareholders in two, as opposed to one, company. We discuss these types of transactions in Chapter 6 because they can be a way of reversing the error. Another way that a division of a parent company, perhaps one that was acquired in a deal that is now being viewed as a failure, can be separated from the parent company is through an equity carve out. Here shares in the divisions are offered to the market in a public offering. In Chapter 6 we discuss the shareholder wealth effects of these different types of transactions. However, we can point out now that, in general, the shareholder wealth effects of these various forms of downsizing tend to be positive. We will review the research, which convincingly shows this over an extended time period.

Another form of corporate restructuring on which we do not focus in this book but which is related to the world of M&As is restructuring in bankruptcy. Bankruptcy is not just an adverse event in a company's history that marks the end of the company. There are various forms of bankruptcy, and some of them are more of a tool of corporate finance where companies can make changes in their operations and financial structure and become a better company. Such restructurings can come through a Chapter 11 filing. The Chapter 11 filing refers to the part of the U.S. Bankruptcy Code that allows companies to receive protection from their creditors—an automatic stay. Other countries have bankruptcy laws that allow for restructuring, but many, such as Great Britain and Canada, are more restrictive on the debtor than the United States.

While operating under the protection of the bankruptcy court, the *debtor in possession,* as the company that did the Chapter 11 filing is called, prepares a reorganization plan, which may feature significant changes in the debtor company. These changes may provide for a different capital structure, one with less debt and more equity. It may also provide for asset sales, including sales of whole divisions, which supplies a cash infusion and which may be used to retire some of the debt that may have led to the bankruptcy.

In the 1990s, many of the companies that ate at the debt trough in the fourth merger wave, were forced to file for Chapter 11 protection. One of them was the Campeau Corporation which became a very different company after the company emerged from bankruptcy protection. As with most Chapter 11 reorganizations, the equity holders, which included the deal makers who dreamed up this highly leveraged acquisition, incurred significant losses as the market penalized them for their poor financial planning. Part of the focus of this book is to determine how such merger failures can be prevented. One of the options available for companies that have made poor deals is to proactively make some of the needed restructuring changes without having to go down the bankruptcy road. Sometimes, however, the situation is such that the pressure of the laws of the bankruptcy court is needed to force all relevant parties, including different groups of creditors who have different interests and motivations, to agree to go along with the proposed changes.

## REASONING FOR MERGERS AND ACQUISITIONS

Why do firms engage in M&As? There are many reasons, and the more often cited ones are reviewed in Chapter 2. The two most common ones are growth and synergy. That is, M&As are a way in which a company can grow at an accelerated rate. This type of growth is usually much faster than growth through internal development. So when a company sees an opportunity in the market that it could fulfill if it had the resources to do so, one way to reach this goal in some cases is to buy a company that can help meet this objective.

Synergy is also an often-cited motive for companies wanting to do deals. These synergies can come from reductions in costs as a result of a combination of two firms that have partially overlapping or redundant cost structures. Other sources of synergy can come from improved revenues that derive from the combination of the two companies. We will show that this source of synergy is often difficult to come by. It is much easier to talk about in advance of a deal than it is to actually make it come to pass.

Other motives or reasons for M&As include economic motives, such as the pursuit of economies of scale such as cost reductions from being a larger company. We will see that economies of scale are one of the more achievable forms of synergy, although even here many companies never achieve the synergistic gains talked about before the deal. Other economic motives include economies of scope, where a company may be able to offer a broader product line to its current customer base.

The reasons for M&As can be varied. We will review these motives and others that companies put forward to justify M&As. We will see that some types of deals are better than others for shareholders. For example, in many instances, mergers involving companies in different industries are often not well received in the market. However, deals that enhance a company's focus tend to be better received. We will also see that the market's initial reaction—something that is studied extensively by academic researchers—is often telling about the long-term effects of the change that is being implemented. Although some managers may not learn from prior similar events, the market seems to have a longer memory. It is sometimes fooled, but it seems that it is more on target than managers who seem to quickly forget where other managers, or even themselves, have gone wrong in the past.

## TRENDS IN MERGERS

Some volume of M&As always exist, but there have been several periods when a very high volume of deals was followed by a period of lower deal volume. These periods of intense M&A volume are referred to as *merger waves*. There have been five merger waves in the United States. The first merger wave occurred during the years 1897 to 1904. It featured many horizontal M&As. Many industries started the period in an unconcentrated state with many small firms operating. At the end of the period, many industries became much more concentrated, including some being near monopolies. This was ironic because the Sherman Act, as previously discussed, was specifically passed to prevent such an industry structure. The first wave ended when the economy and the market turned down. During the slow economy there was less pressure to do deals. This changed in the 1920s, when the economy started to boom. The vibrant economic conditions led to a second merger wave, which was concentrated during 1916 to 1929. This period featured many horizontal deals but also featured many vertical transactions. Deals were especially concentrated in specific industries. When the stock market collapsed in 1929 and the economy went into a prolonged and deep recession in the 1930s, the merger wave ended. We did not have another major merger period until the end of the 1960s.

The third merger wave was an interesting period in that it featured many conglomerate M&As, because of the intense antitrust enforcement of that time period. The Justice Department was aggressive in its opposition to M&As and saw many deals that would be immediately approved today as antitrust problems. For this reason, companies that were acquisition-minded were forced to do deals outside of their industry to avoid the wrath of the Justice Department and the FTC. Many large conglomerates, such as ITT, Gulf & Western, Teledyne, and Textron, were built during that period. While the 1960s featured a booming economy for much of the decade, the economy and the market turned down at the end of that period. Like the prior merger wave, it ended when the economic and financial pressures to expand subsided.

The 1970s featured a more modest number of M&As but did have many others forms of restructurings as companies, which may have been acquired during the third merger wave, were sold off as companies adjusted to the slower economic conditions and questioned some of the deals they had made when the economy was booming and their judgment may have been clouded by dreams of wealth that never materialized. As companies felt the economic pressures of a deep recession in the middle of the decade, they implemented management changes, and some of those changes helped bring about the various restructurings and sell-offs we saw during that period.

The 1980s proved to be the longest postwar economic expansion until we got to the following decade, which featured an even longer growth period. The 1980s provided the colorful fourth merger wave, which had many interested facets including the megamerger. This was the M&A in billion-dollar deals (see Exhibit 1.2). As noted earlier, some of these deals were highly levered and the fuel for these highly leveraged deals was provided by the junk bond market, which also boomed in response to the deal-related demand for this form of capital. The fourth wave also featured many hostile deals as companies, including major corporations, found themselves the target of unwanted suitors. Hostile deals certainly occurred before this period, but they were mainly bids by relatively smaller companies for other smaller companies. Before that period, it was unusual to hear of a hostile offer for large companies. It was even less common to have major reputable companies taking part in hostile takeovers. All of that changed in the late 1970s, and this set the stage for many of the hostile takeovers that occurred in the fourth merger wave.

Exhibit 1.2    Fourth Merger Wave

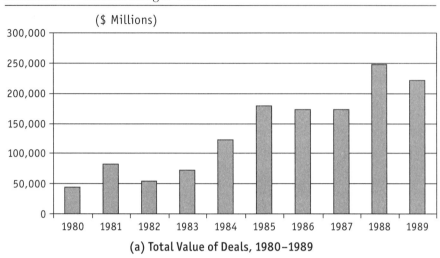

(a) Total Value of Deals, 1980–1989

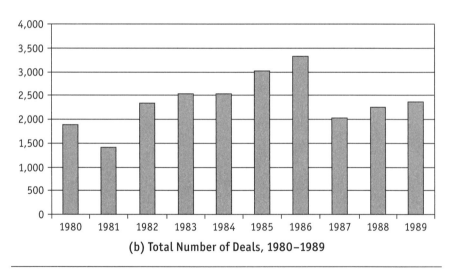

(b) Total Number of Deals, 1980–1989

*Source: Mergerstat Review, 2004.*

The fourth merger wave ended when the economy slowed at the end of the decade and the junk bond market collapsed, in part as a function of weak economic conditions but also as a result of specific problems with that market, including the indictment of Michael Milken and his investment bank—Drexel Burnham Lambert.

In the period 1990 to 1991, there was a mild recession, and the economy recovered slowly initially and then the rebound picked up steam. As with many prior expansions, companies looked to grow, and the fastest way to expand is to buy whole companies as opposed to building such a business internally. To some extent, this makes sense as expanding economic conditions create market opportunities that companies may need to react to quickly to take full advantage of. The problem occurs when dreams of economic riches cloud the judgment of management and it does not make the most enlightened decisions. Another problem with booming economic conditions is that they can mask poor management. Increased demand can lead to higher sales and profits even for some companies that are not that well managed. When this occurs, shareholders and the board may credit management with gains that they did not bring about. This may lead them to go along with acquisition proposals that they may not scrutinize carefully enough. Management may get a pass, so to speak, until, for some of the less astute managers, their acquisition schemes blow up in their face. For those who made well-thought-out deals, they may be able to advance the company and take advantage of competitive opportunities in the marketplace.

The fifth merger wave was precedent setting in terms of the total volume of mergers as well as the size of the deals that took place (see Exhibits 1.3 and 1.4). While many megamergers took place in the fourth wave, some of the deals that took place in the fifth wave made the fourth wave deals seem ordinary. In this book we will look at some of these leading deals and see that many of them were simply flops. Deals such as the AOL-Time Warner "merger of equals" were failures that left certain shareholders incensed. Others, such as the Warner Lambert acquisition by Pfizer or the merger between Exxon and Mobil, clearly were successes. The difference between successful and failed deals is the topic we will discuss throughout the rest of this book.

## CONCLUSION

The field of M&A is multifaceted with many different aspects. Companies engage in these deals for a variety of reasons, including to take advantage of synergies. These are situations where a combination of companies lead to a greater value than what would have occurred if the company remained independent. In addition to synergistic gains,

Exhibit 1.3      Fifth Merger Wave

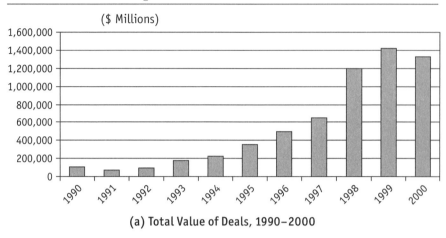

(a) Total Value of Deals, 1990–2000

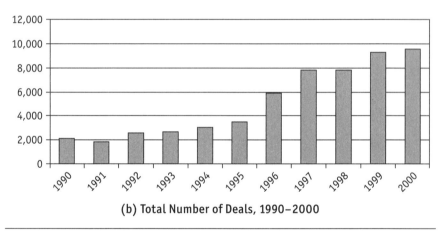

(b) Total Number of Deals, 1990–2000

*Source: Mergerstat Review, 2004.*

however, companies engage in M&A for other economic motives. These may come from the realization of economies of scale, such as what would occur in historical deals. Companies may also be able to lock up sources of supply to greater access to the market through vertical deals.

Mergers and acquisitions is just one form of restructuring. Other forms of restructuring include restructuring in bankruptcy. This is a more extreme situation where the company may not have performed well. Other forms of restructuring include sell-offs and spin-offs. There are various ways that a company can rid itself of a division in the business unit that no longer fits into its strategic plan. They may

Exhibit 1.4   Large Mergers and Acquisitions of the Fifth Merger Wave

| Announced Year | Effective Year | Acquirer | Target | Transaction Value ($ Billions) |
|---|---|---|---|---|
| Nov. 1999 | Jun. 2000 | Vodafone Air | Mannesman AG | $202.8 |
| Jan. 2000 | Jan. 2001 | America Online Inc. | Time Warner | $164.7 |
| Nov. 1999 | Jun. 2000 | Pfizer Inc. | Warner-Lambert Co. | $ 89.2 |
| Dec. 1998 | Nov. 1999 | Exxon Corp. | Mobil Corp. | $ 78.9 |
| Jan. 2000 | Dec. 2000 | Glaxo Wellcome PLC | SmithKline Beechman PLC | $ 76.0 |
| Apr. 1998 | Oct. 1998 | Travelers Group Inc. | Citicorp | $ 72.6 |
| May 1998 | Oct. 1999 | SBC Communications Inc. | Ameritech Corp. | $ 62.6 |
| Jan. 2000 | May 2000 | Shareholders | Nortel Networks Corp. | $ 61.7 |
| Apr. 1998 | Sep. 1998 | NationsBank Corp. | BankAmerica Corp. | $ 61.6 |
| Jan. 1999 | Jun. 1999 | Vodafone Group PLC | AirTouch Communications Inc. | $ 60.3 |

*Source:* Thomson Financial Securities Data.

do a divestiture or an equity carve-out or spin-off. We have devoted Chapter 6 to these types of restucturings because they often have positive shareholder wealth effects.

In the United States, M&As have occurred in waves or periods of intense activity. These waves have tended to occur in periods of economic expansion and have ended when the economy and the market have turned down. Each wave has distinct differences from the others. We have just completed the fifth merger wave—one that was truly international in its scope. The rest of this book is devoted to determining why many companies doing M&As do deals that are mistakes. In each of the major waves, mistakes were made. In some cases, it seems that we have learned from prior mistakes, but in others we seem to have forgotten our merger history and made some of the same mistakes. Some of the same companies, such as AT&T, have made major merger blunders in different merger waves.

## ENDNOTES

1. Wellman v. Dickinson lists seven factors. A subsequent court decision added the eighth factor.
2. For an excellent description of this colorful deal, see Bryan Burrough and John Helyar, *Barbarians at the Gate: The Rise and Fall of RJR Nabisco* (New York: Harper Trade, 1990).

# Case Study

# Lessons from the Failures of the Fourth Merger Wave

The fifth merger wave that recently ended provides many lessons on what can go wrong with M&As. However, this merger wave came on the heels of another precedent-setting merger period. It is useful to look back on some of the failure lessons we can derive from that period and see if we learned our lesson. Did we make some of the same mistakes in the 1990s that we made in the 1980s, or did we learn from them and make different mistakes? In this case study, we will review some of the more prominent merger failures from the 1980s and see what lessons still have to be learned from those mistakes and which ones have helped us avoid errors.

## FOURTH MERGER WAVE FAILURE LESSONS

Each wave has its set of failures and successes. Sometimes we focus too much on the failures because they tend to generate losses for shareholders and can create a big outcry regarding who is to blame. The fourth wave was notable for certain types of deals. We saw more hostile deals, particularly megamergers by large reputable companies.

Many of the deals gave rise to bidding contests, and the winners sometimes got stuck with the winner's curse, having overpaid for the target companies. This was the case in the infamous takeover of Federated Stores by Campeau. Campeau made two major mistakes in that takeover. First and most fundamentally, he overpaid for the target. He got into a bidding contest and would not back out when the price got too high. He stayed in the contest and ended up overpaying. He was not the first corporate buyer to overpay for an asset. However, the fact that he did so on such a grand scale, combined with the fact that he had to declare bankruptcy so soon after the takeover makes him and his takeover a leading failure from that period. The second mistake that Campeau made and that we also hope to learn from is that he borrowed heavily to finance a pricey acquisition. His heavy borrowing put great pressure on the company's cash flows, and this pressure could not be alleviated by asset sales. The high leverage of the deal raised its risk level. He did not have an equity cushion to give him some breathing room in case the markets weakened, as they did. So with the Campeau deal, we had two major lessons:

1. Beware of overpaying, especially if you are in a bidding contest.
2. Beware of using too much debt to finance a pricey acquisition.

Did the markets learn from not just this particular case of overpaying and taking on too much debt but many others that occurred during that heady period? The answer appears that they did—at least at the beginning of the fifth merger wave. When the merger business started to heat up in 1994 and the economic expansion of the 1990s started to pick up steam, companies were leery of relying on debt to finance their acquisitions. Many capital providers were burned by some of the highly leveraged transactions of the fourth merger wave, and they were reluctant to duplicate prior mistakes. In that sense, a learning process had occurred, and the recently learned lessons from the fourth merger wave were not lost on capital providers and deal makers.

## SHORT-TERM ORIENTATION OF FINANCIAL, NOT STRATEGIC, DEALS

Another lesson that was painfully taught to some corporations was to be leery of overly aggressive deal makers who are seeking quick gains and have a short-term focus. Many of the deals, for example, that Drexel Burnham Lambert, but also other major investment banks, were involved in were motivated by the pursuit of high profits from deal making without sufficient care for the long-term health of their investment banking clients. The money from such deal work was so good that it was too hard to resist. Deal makers promoted some transactions purely with a short-term focus to realize fees and having little strategic purpose. Where did the companies go wrong? There was plenty of blame to go around, but much of it has to be laid at the feet of the management and directors of the companies that willingly went along with these proposals. It is not unusual for management to receive deal proposals from bankers, but management has to critically analyze the strategic purpose of the proposed deals and reject those that do not fit its strategy. Management has to have a strategy and should only do deals if they fit their plans, not change the strategy as deals come along. Here again, investment bankers may have appealed to CEO hubris, and this may have led management to make decisions that were not in shareholders' best interests.

Investment bankers had a prominent role in the 1980s, and there were many "Masters of the Universe" running around. Some were arrogant and had an all-knowing air about them. In some cases, they clearly intimidated management of client companies. Given the prominence of hostile deals, certain companies went along with investment bankers, promoting hostile takeovers lest they become the target of their own banker's hostile ambitions. When many of these deals came with mountains of high-yield debt, companies and their shareholders were left holding the bag, for management and their advisors' takeover schemes.

Many corporations were burned from doing deals that were so eagerly recommended by investment bankers. As many companies rebounded from some of their failed deals of the fourth merger wave, they sought to regain full control of their growth strategy. In the fifth merger wave, management assumed the driving role for deals—as should be their normal place. Investment bankers were brought in to assist in specific aspects of deals and were sometimes asked to leave M&A meetings when their presentations on the financing and other aspects of their work were finished. This was an important and needed change in order for the corporate governance process to work properly.

Our discussion of management losing control of the process in the fourth merger wave and investment bankers assuming too large a role is a generalization and applies more to the small percentage of failed deals than it applies to corporations in general. For many corporations, management being in charge of the process was always the norm. However, as we consider that our discussion is on the subset of deals that failed, not a discussion of all types of takeovers of the fourth wave, we can see how those deals that involved management losing control of the process will more often fall into the merger failure category.

In the fifth merger wave, there seemed to be fewer instances of failures because of management's loss of control of the deal-making process and investment bankers being too aggressive in promoting short-term-oriented deals. This is not to say that we did not have an overabundance of failures in the fifth wave. We did, but fewer of them can be blamed on investment bankers. In the fifth wave, we seem to have had more cases of overaggressive and hubris-filled managers making mistakes than overaggressive investment bankers.

## AGGRESSIVE USE OF LEVERAGE

When the fifth merger wave took hold, we saw a very different management orientation at play. The failure of many of the highly leveraged takeovers of the fourth wave in the recessionary economy that followed left many deal makers with "black eyes." It is truly ironic that many of the deal makers quickly switched into doing bankruptcy work as opposed to doing acquisitions. During the post–fourth wave period, many deal makers helped finance sales of acquisitions as companies needed to downsize to relieve the combined pressure of weak economic demand with high debt service pressures. Money could now be made with asset sales and other restructuring-related work as well as securities sales to try to arrange different capital structures for companies that found themselves too highly leveraged from the fourth wave period. Investment bankers made money by helping companies load up on debt in the fourth merger wave and later helped them restructure this debt and have a less leveraged capital structure in the 1990s. Many helped companies acquire other businesses in leveraged acquisitions and then other, or sometimes the same, investment bankers helped them sell off the prior acquisitions that brought with them debt that they could not service.

A related change in the fifth merger wave that was based on lessons of the fourth wave was that the mega-LBO disappeared. Gone from the landscape was the RJR-Nabisco-type deal. This $24.8 billion buyout of a food and tobacco giant did not do well for its chief architect—Kolhberg Kravis and Roberts. The deal came toward the end of the fourth merger wave and followed some other mega-LBOs such as the Beatrice buyout. However, RJR Nabisco was far larger than any other LBO, and it was a problem for the buyers for years to come. When the markets turned down as we moved into the 1990–1991 recession, the demand for debt issued by acquirers greatly declined. Investment banks had trouble financing highly leveraged transactions (HLTs) of all types as the market worried about the ability of companies to service high debt levels. Such companies were ill prepared to handle a weak economic climate such as what ensued right after the end of the fourth wave. The lesson, which was underscored by the bankruptcy of many of these debt-laden companies, was not lost both on corporations that would contemplate deals as well as on capital providers and their middlemen—investment bankers. There was an all-around reluctance on the part of both demanders and suppliers of capital to assume or provide high debt levels to finance deals. This was the case for the megadeals as mega-LBOs disappeared from the landscape. However, this did not mean that the LBO disappeared. In fact, after a short hiatus, we started to see an increased number of LBOs, but they were clearly different from many of the LBOs in the 1980s. The LBOs of the fifth merger wave featured more equity and less debt. Gone were the megabuyouts, but there were still plenty of LBOs. They just were smaller deals and often were less debt laden (see Exhibit A).

## CORPORATE GOVERNANCE AND USE OF ANTITAKEOVER DEFENSES

Another major change from the fourth merger wave was that there was a greater focus on the importance of corporate governance. The role of the board of directors became more important in ensuring

**Exhibit A**

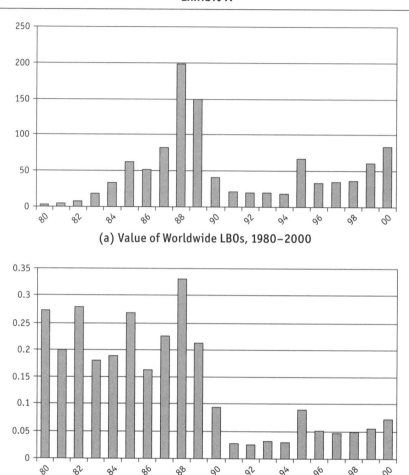

(a) Value of Worldwide LBOs, 1980–2000

(b) Average Value of Worldwide LBOs, 1980–2000

*Source:* Thomson Financial Securities Data.

that shareholder sights were protected and that management ran
the company in a manner that promoted gains in their stock values.
There were more instances of antitakeover defenses being challenged. Unfortunately, the heightened corporate governance did
not become pronounced until the end of the fifth wave, and even
then was more focused on the prevention of accounting fraud than
on the optimal growth and acquisition strategy. From a governance
perspective, we learned from the fourth merger wave that the

indiscriminant use of antitakeover defenses, especially when deployed by underperforming and entrenched managers, should be avoided. However, directors have not really gone so far as to become sufficiently active in their scrutiny of proposed deals as they should be. Perhaps by the sixth merger wave we will be sufficiently aware to make sure that we do not repeat the mistakes of the fifth wave, while also sufficiently mindful of the errors of prior waves so that we do not repeat those either.

# 2

Merger Strategy:
Why Do Firms Merge?

In this chapter we will explore the different reasons why companies expand through M&As. We will consider the different expansion strategies that are available to companies and try to discern why some choose M&As as the best way to achieve these goals. It will be seen that companies may merge and acquire other firms for several possible reasons. In the case of a failed merger, it is important to determine if companies combined for the wrong reasons and if this could be an explanation for why certain deals did not live up to their expectations. Many different reasons are cited to justify M&As. Some deals cite more than one reason for the transaction, and it is sometimes difficult to establish what the real goals were. Sometimes the stated goals are not the true goals. Fortunately, we have benchmarks and yardsticks to measure corporate performance, and when companies fail to perform up to an expected level, we can begin the search for the reason. In cases of large M&As, the deals themselves may be the reason.

We will see that some motives for M&As are more commendable than others. For example, no bidder would say that the reason it is doing a deal is managerial hubris. However, as we will see later in this chapter, this motive plays a major role in some deal failures. Other motives, such as synergy, are often cited as a reason for deals, but the market's adverse reaction to bidders' claims of possibly synergies shows that it is skeptical of the likelihood that such gains will be realized.

After we review the various reasons or motives for deals, we will then attempt to relate them to the success rate of the transactions. Are certain motives or reasons for pursuing deals more likely to result in successes or failures? The answer is complex, but we will explore its various aspects.

## GROWTH

To state that the goal of a merger or acquisition is to enhance growth seems to be a relatively straightforward statement, but even this statement can be somewhat ambiguous and interpreted in different ways. The main difference is whether growth refers to revenue growth or sheer size, or to growth in profitability. The two goals may be very different. For example, it could be that the optimal size of a company, defined as the one that creates the greatest profits, could be well below the size that is consistent with generation of the greatest revenues. Economists have long debated this issue within the context of determining what is the objective function of managers. This is an economist's way of cryptically saying something very straightforward: "What should be the main goal of management: profit maximization or revenue maximization?"

Using an economic framework, Exhibit 2.1 demonstrates this point. In this Exhibit, $x^*$ is the optimal output—the one where marginal revenues equal marginal costs. This is the profit-maximizing output level for the company. It is the point on the graph where the gap between total revenues and total costs is the greatest. However, a CEO might not be satisfied with being at that size ($x^*$). There is often a good relationship between firm size and executive compensation. This creates an incentive for management to grow to a larger level,

Exhibit 2.1   Total Cost, Total Revenues, and Profit Functions

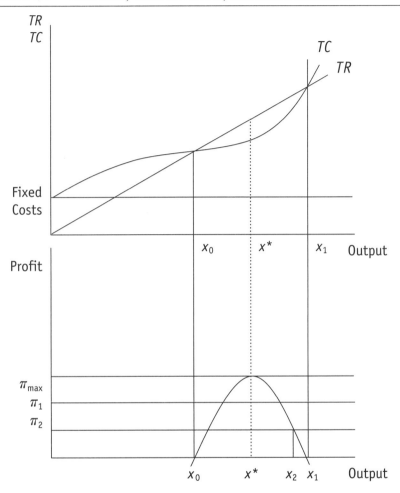

to be "as big as they can be" while enjoying the higher levels of compensation and perquisites along with the psychic benefits of being the CEO of a larger "empire." Management may choose to produce a higher output level, say $X_2$, which may generate a lower profit level but one which may be consistent with the average for the industry. This is not as high as the profits it could enjoy at $X^*$, but it may serve management's personal goals. If the average rate of return for the industry is one that is consistent with output level $q^*$, management might decide to produce at this output level. It is difficult for shareholders to throw out management for poor performance if they are generating profits consistent with industry averages. What we have is a situation where managers are trading off the benefits of shareholders for those of their own interests. It is a classic Berle and Means agency theory situation where the agents, the management put in place by directors, along with the directors themselves, are pursuing their own interests along with those of shareholders.[1]

This discussion points out that pursuing growth as a goal in and of itself may not necessarily be in the shareholders' interest. When managerial self-interest and hubris come into play, we need to take a harder look at the growth strategy. More appropriate growth refers to increasing profits and returns to shareholders.

## EXAMPLES OF GROWTH AS AN INAPPROPRIATE GOAL

Growth that facilitates the payment of dividends and the maximization of shareholder values is certainly a valid goal to pursue. Growth that is motivated by goals other than the maximization of shareholder wealth is questionable. As discussed previously, there is normally a good relationship between company size and the compensation of a CEO. Coming with the direct compensation are usually a whole host of perks. Some have taken the pursuit of perks to an extreme, and perhaps the most glaring example of that is Tyco and the perks and extravagance enjoyed by its CEO, Dennis Kozlowski. These perks and expenditures were the focus of a criminal lawsuit in which Kozlowski was the defendant.

It is also important to note that some managers are better at growing a business than at managing one. They may excel at using M&As to fuel rapid growth, but this may be the extent of their abilities. The case of WorldCom is a classic example. Bernie Ebbers amazed the market by being able to rapidly transform LDDS, a small telecommunications reseller, into one of the largest telecommunications companies in the world. He built this telecom empire through deal after deal. Unfortunately, this was his only proven ability, and he was unable to be an effective manager of a large telecommunications company. It is difficult for a manager to recognize this weakness and step aside when the company then needs a different set of skills that he or she may not possess. Once again, ego and hubris play a role. This is a time when the board of directors needs to recognize the changing needs of the company and step in to make the difficult but necessary changes that have to be made. However, when the board has a close relationship with the CEO, this may also prove to be difficult to accomplish. Nonetheless, it is the board's responsibility to recognize when growth through deals has provided sufficient benefits and when growth through deal making should stop or pause, while the company pursues other forms of growth or better integrates prior acquisitions. With an impartial and diligent board, this may be possible. With a board that has a close relationship with the CEO or that is not sufficiently diligent, the deal making may be allowed to continue until the situation explodes. This is what happened at World-Com—a company that became the focus of the the largest bankruptcy in U.S. history.

## USING M&AS TO ACHIEVE GROWTH

Companies can grow in two broad ways: (1) through internal expansion and (2) through M&As. Internal expansion, sometimes referred to as *organic growth,* can be slower and presents its own risks. If a company perceives a window of opportunity, such as an unexploited market opportunity, it may not be able to pursue slower growth through internal expansion. If this is the case, then an acquisition or merger with another company may enable it to take advantage of this situation. A merger or acquisition can enable a company to more quickly respond to perceived opportunities in the marketplace. With a merger or acquisition, a company is able to acquire a ready-made business operation rather than have to develop it from the ground up. The pursuit of this type of growth can be worthwhile, but when a bidder is pursuing growth for its own sake, then problems can arise.

## M&AS IN A SLOW-GROWTH INDUSTRY AS A WAY TO ACHIEVE GROWTH

Industry growth is influenced by a wide variety of factors, such as the ups and downs of the economy. However, as an industry grows it may become mature, and unless major innovation occurs, the pace of growth can slow. For example, in the 1980s, the slow growth in the electronics industry was reversed by the development and marketing of the videocassette recorder (VCR), which gave the industry a jolt forward. However, with the proliferation of long-lasting VCRs in households, the industry was left waiting for the next innovation while companies sought to cannibalize market share from each other in this then-stagnant industry. A similar growth stagnation process occurred in the flavor and fragrance industry in the 1990s. This industry's mergers are discussed in a case study that follows.

Companies in slow-growth businesses sometimes try to deal with the problem of meager growth by merging with or acquiring competitors. This can sometimes be a lot easier than creating an innovative new product that will propel the growth trend forward. It is sometimes easier to simply focus on a vulnerable competitor and acquire it. This vulnerability can come from a low profit/earnings (P/E) ratio for the target because the company may be trading at a comparatively low price as a result of the market's assessment of its growth. Although the bidder may also have a low P/E, sometimes bidders act as though they have an inelastic demand for target companies and are willing to offer more of their shares or more cash for vulnerable targets. The merger or acquisition may create the *appearance* of growth. It is important to understand that this growth is different from the growth that is achieved through coming up with innovative products that give the firm an advantage over competitors and may even expand the boundaries of the industry.

When a company acquires growth through M&As, the growth has been paid for by premiums given to target company shareholders. The bidder may then have a greater share of a slow-growth industry if that is the nature of the industry. If the deal helps insulate the bidder from cutthroat prices and other forms of competition in a manner that does not draw the wrath of antitrust regulators, then it may be able to improve margins. Is this really realistic? Will the remaining competitors really not be able to respond to an attempt to raise prices? If the bidder is able to achieve increased prices and can combine these gains with economies of scale, then margins may be further improved. Each of these sources of gains can be a valid strategy. However,

## ATTEMPTING TO ACHIEVE GROWTH IN A
## SLOW-GROWTH INDUSTRY THROUGH M&AS

The flavor and fragrance industry at first seems like an odd combination of chemicals that are used to make fragrances worn on the outside of one's body but that cannot be consumed and flavors that are used in a wide variety of food products. However, the businesses and the process of developing products in this industry are actually somewhat similar, although the marketing of the products focuses on two different markets.

In September 2000, International Flavor and Fragrances (IFF) announced that it was buying Bush Boake Allen, another large company in this industry. IFF paid $48.50 per share in an all-cash deal valued at $970 million. The deal was not that warmly received by investors at the time it was announced because it was anticipated that it would dilute earnings. In addition, IFF also announced that it was cutting its dividend while also pursuing a stock buy-back program. The company also announced that it was embarking on a restructuring program designed to reduce costs. Cutting a dividend and engaging in a cost restructuring program normally do not occur at the same time a company announces that it is acquiring one of its major rivals. Nonetheless, IFF's CEO at that time, Richard Goldstein, announced that the deal and related programs were "an opportunity to reinvent ourselves." Specifically with respect to the acquisition, he stated that it would help IFF refocus on higher-margin products in growth areas while also providing cost efficiencies equal to $35 million.[a] The acquisition of Bush Boake Allen would enable the combined company to be the number-one company in *both* the flavor and fragrance businesses.

Before the acquisition of Bush Boake Allen, IFF's sales had stagnated at around the $1.4 billion level, and because of the slow-growth nature of the industry, the company was unable to achieve meaningful sales growth. As Exhibits A and B show, the deal quickly enabled IFF to move to the approximately $1.8 billion level—a jump up from its $1.4 premerger level. However, the growth in sales, improvement in profitability, and realization of cost efficiencies were not very noticeable in the postmerger period.

Interestingly enough, the acquisition by IFF was an expansion into a business of which it was already the leader and which it knew well. In

**Exhibit A**
International Flavors and Fragrances, Inc.
Financial Data

| Year | Total Revenue | % Change | Gross Profit | Gross Margin | Net Profit | Net Margin |
|------|---------------|----------|--------------|--------------|------------|------------|
| 1999 | 1439.5 | 2.29% | 633.1 | 44% | 162.0 | 11% |
| 2000 | 1462.8 | 1.62% | 631.1 | 43% | 123.0 | 8% |
| 2001 | 1843.8 | 26.05% | 780.3 | 42% | 116.0 | 6% |
| 2002 | 1809.2 | −1.88% | 773.4 | 43% | 175.9 | 10% |
| 2003 | 1901.5 | 5.10% | 809.1 | 43% | 172.6 | 9% |
| 2004 | 2033.7 | 6.95% | 873.4 | 43% | 196.1 | 10% |

*Source: www.marketguide.com* and 1999 Annual Report.

**Exhibit B**
International Flavors and Fragrances, Inc.
Revenue and Net Income Trends

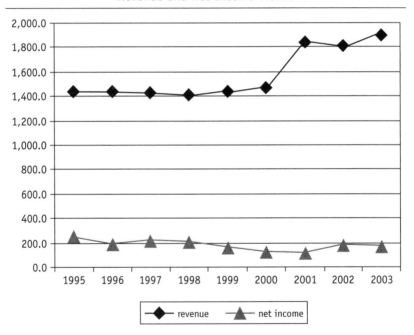

addition, having competed directly with Bush Boake, it knew this company fairly well, so it was not moving into an unknown area by any means. Sixty-eight percent of Bush Boake was owned by International Paper, which was selling off Bush Boake as part of an effort to refocus and expand its core business. International Paper had just bought Champion Paper and was pursuing a refocusing strategy and eliminating noncore assets.

The IFF–Bush Boake deal is also instructive in deflating CEO deal speak when they oversell the merits of a deal to investors. Goldstein described, "the acquisition of Bush Boake Allen as a *catalyst to accelerate change (and) an opportunity for us to reinvent ourselves.*" He later went on to say, "our actions will be comprehensive and swift."[b] The lukewarm response to the deal by the market seemed to be its way of saying, "Please tone it down and give us a break." We should not be critical of the CEO for his blustery comments. You want an energetic CEO who will strive to achieve the most for shareholders, but we may just need to deflate some of what CEOs say when trying to objectively evaluate what they really can accomplish.

As we look back now several years after the merger, we can arrive at some assessment of its success. We also have to consider that the postacquisition period was a weak economy, and it would be expected that performance would be less stellar during such periods. Nonetheless, we should not attribute all of the weakness in the combined company's performance to mere economic weakness. As we look at Exhibit A, we see that after an initial jump up in revenues, IFF's revenue growth resumed at its slow premerger pace. While its CEO railed about what a wonderful impact the deal with Bush Boake would have, it is difficult to see any positive effects in profitability during the postmerger period. Exhibit A shows that both the gross margin and the net margin declined following the deal. The acquisition of Bush Boake Allen did not provide all of the overstated gains that IFF's ambitious CEO asserted to the market. The company was in a slow-growth business before the deal, and it was a bigger part of a slow-growth industry after the deal.

The merger did not change the industry. This does not mean it was not a good deal. Certainly, it was better than many of the mergers that companies engage in when they try to escape the doldrums of the slow-growth pattern in their industry by trying to move into a business that they do not fully understand. At least IFF knew the business well, being the industry leader, and it also knew its target as well. It understood what it was getting when it pursued the deal, and the postmerger performance reveals a pattern that is reasonable and should have been expected. In sum, the deal was somewhat beneficial if one approaches it with reasonable expectations and discounts the deal bravado that often comes out at the time of the announcement from the participants.

a. Martin Sikora, "International Flavors Buys Bush Boake," *Mergers and Acquisitions Journal* (November 1, 2000).
b. Andrew Edgecliffe-Johnson, "IFF in Dollars $1 Billion Acquisition of Smaller Rival," *Financial Times* (September 26, 2000).

it is useful to keep in mind that unless the company is able to come up with important innovations, it is a simply a larger part of a slow-growth industry. Once it moves to the higher revenue level, it may possibly still be on a similar slow-growth path.

## Comment on Growth

It is almost taken as a truism that all companies should pursue growth. Growth is good, and somehow a lack of growth, the maintenance of one's position in a given industry, is taken to be bad and a sign of poor management. Because M&As can be a fast way to grow, companies often make deals to enable them to grow faster than they otherwise would. However, in some cases, the basic premise is flawed. It is not always best to pursue growth. Sometimes a company may have reached its most efficient size, and growing will make it less efficient. Maybe a company has pursued all of the best opportunities it has available, and to pursue others will generate lower returns with shareholders' capital than what they could realize if the capital were released to them in the form of dividends and stock buy-backs. Sometimes it is better for a company to maintain its position while it still actively seeks better opportunities but resists pursuing returns that do not meet an appropriate hurdle rate.

In addition to assessing the position of the company and the impact of the growth on the company's profitability, we also need to assess the motives of the managers who are proposing the growth-oriented acquisitions. Are they suggesting the deals for the shareholders' benefits or their own? We have already discussed how the literature in this area suggests that managers may pursue revenue growth over profit growth.[2] Others have suggested that junior managers may propose acquisitions to help further their own careers, even though they may not necessarily be in the best interests of shareholders.[3]

In sum, when evaluating growth, we need to know if growth in and of itself is desirable. To some this may be a shocking question, but it still needs to be asked. We also need to question the motives of managers who are advocating the growth-orienting M&As. Each situation is different, and we need to investigate the facts of each particular situation.

## Size as a Possible Valid Goal: Being the Number-One or Number-Two Company in an Industry

Being big for the sake of being big and attaining this size to receive greater compensation and psychic rewards for management is clearly an inappropriate goal. However, being the leader or at least the number-two company in an industry can provide a company with advantages over smaller rivals that such smaller competitors might find it difficult to overcome. Sometimes being even number three or four creates such disadvantages that it hinders companies so much that they cannot effectively compete. If this is the case, then the pursuit of growth that allows a company to achieve this threshold size may be a valid objective. If a merger or acquisition is the most efficient way to achieve this goal, as opposed to internal growth, then such deals, if priced properly, *may* be appropriate goals.

The goal of being in the leading number-one or number-two position in any business it enters was part of the acquisition philosophy pursued by General Electric (GE). GE is a serial acquirer that annually acquires many companies while also selling off those that no longer fit into its business model. GE tends to only want leading companies as part of its conglomerate. A target did not necessarily have to be in the number-one or number-two position at the time it was acquired by GE. Given the many financial and managerial resources that GE has, it can help an ambitious company quickly move up to a leadership position in its industry. GE's management philosophy was that being in that position gives a company distinct advantages over its rivals who find themselves in a disadvantageous position. If after reasonable efforts and the application of necessary resources, the acquired company is not able to attain a leader position in the industry, GE often considers divesting the business and using the freed-up resources to invest in other business units that have such a dominant position. Jack Welch, the former CEO of GE, applied the number-one or number-two model with a "fix, sell, or close" strategy.[4]

One example of how GE applied its fix, sell, or close business was its sale of its central air-conditioning business to Trane in 1982. Although GE was in many different businesses, with air-conditioning only a small part of the overall company, Trane was a dominant player in its industry, with air-conditioning being its main focus. The GE air-conditioning operations had only a 10% market share, and the business was just not profitable. This business involves manufacturers working with various contractors who install systems for purchasers. The dominant companies in the market worked with the best and strongest contractors, while GE, a huge conglomerate, was only a marginal player in this business and, therefore, tended to work with weaker contractors. Unfortunately, the performance of these contractors reflects on the manufacturer, and when consumers complain about performance, they contact GE even when the problem is the fault of its contractors. Welch sold off this business and used the $135 million in cash it received, an amount that did not impress the market, to finance other deals.

In applying the number-one or number-two strategy, Welch and GE showed that no part of a business should be immune from the pressure of being a leader. For years, GE was known to many consumers by its major and small appliances businesses. Welch never liked this business, which was vulnerable to competition from foreign, low-cost manufacturers, while U.S. small appliance manufacturers operated relatively high-cost manufacturing facilities. He saw that over time their position would erode while the upside potential was limited. To him there was little to gain by staying in that business and potentially a lot to lose. When he was approached by Black & Decker in 1983 with an attractive offer to sell, he gladly left the industry and again used freed-up resources to pursue more attractive sectors.

A recent example of companies that merged in part to move into the number-one and number-two rank in an industry was the 2004 merger between J.P. Morgan Chase and Bank One. As the name shows, J.P. Morgan Chase was the product of the merger between J.P. Morgan and Chase Manhattan Bank in September 2000. That merger was not regarded as a great success, partly because of weakness in the investment banking business, which caused many J.P. Morgan managers to leave the company in 2000. That left a managerial void that J.P. Morgan sought to correct in 2004 by merging with Bank One. We will discuss the management issues related to this merger later in this chapter.

In 2004 the combined J.P. Morgan Chase merged with Bank One. There are two ways we can rank banks: (1) total deposits and (2) total assets. Before the merger, J.P. Morgan was third in total deposits and total assets behind both Bank of America and Citigroup. Bank One was sixth in deposits and assets behind these banks as well as Wells Fargo and Wachovia (see Exhibit 2.2). After the merger, the combined J.P. Morgan and Bank One became number two in the U.S. banking industry.

There is no rule that being number one or number two will lead to success. For example, it could be the case that the industry is in decline and the merger of two large competitors, which resulted in the combined entity being either number one or two, is a defensive measure designed to arrest the decline. It could be that this combination might improve the lot of the merged firms relative to smaller rivals, but it does not necessarily imply that the merged companies will enjoy success as measured by the performance of companies outside of the industry. As we saw in the IFF case study, the combined entity may still be in the same declining industry and is just a larger part of it. The business cannot be at a stage where it is *commoditized,* where many rivals make a similar product or market a similar service and there is no ability to command a good profit margin. So another key part of the number-one or number-two strategy is to make sure that the markets we are talking about are *growth* markets. By being in that dominant position in a growth market, the leaders may be able to extract disproportionate rewards from that growth.

Exhibit 2.2    J.P. Morgan Chase and Bank One Merger

### (a) Largest U.S. Bank Acquisitions

| Acquirer | Target | Value of Deal ($ billions) |
|---|---|---|
| Travelers | Citicorp | 72.6 |
| NationsBank | BankAmerica | 61.6 |
| J.P. Morgan Chase | Bank One | 58.0* |
| Bank of America | FleetBoston | 48.0* |
| Norwest | Wells Fargo | 34.4 |
| Chase Manhattan | J.P. Morgan | 33.6 |
| Bank One | First Chicago | 29.6 |
| Firstar Corp. | U.S. Bancorp | 21.1 |
| First Union | CoreStates | 17.1 |
| Fleet Financial | BankBoston | 15.9 |

*Based on closing share prices the day before the announcement.

### (b) Post-Acquisition Banking Rank

**Ranked by Deposits, $ Billions as of June 30**

| | |
|---|---|
| Bank of America* | 552.1 |
| New J.P. Morgan Chase | 490.2 |
| Citigroup | 447.9 |
| J.P. Morgan Chase | 318.2 |
| Wells Fargo | 230.9 |
| Wachovia | 203.8 |
| Bank One | 172.0 |
| U.S. Bancorp | 126.3 |
| Washington Mutual | 114.3 |
| SunTrust Banks | 77.3 |

**Ranked By Assets, $ Billions as of June 30**

| | |
|---|---|
| Citigroup | 1,187.0 |
| New J.P. Morgan Chase | 1,102.1 |
| Bank of America* | 966.4 |
| J.P. Morgan Chase | 802.6 |
| Wells Fargo | 369.6 |
| Wachovia | 364.3 |
| Bank One | 299.5 |
| Washington Mutual | 241.9 |
| U.S. Bancorp | 194.9 |
| National City | 123.4 |

*After merger of Bank of America and FleetBoston is completed.

## CISCO: SERIAL ACQUIRER PURSUING GROWTH IN A RAPIDLY CHANGING INDUSTRY

Cisco shares with GE the distinction of being a serial acquirer — a company that engages in many acquisitions — one after the other. We devote a large part of this book talking about what certain acquirers do wrong and perhaps not enough time is devoted to companies that have demonstrated success in the M&A business. One such company is Cisco. This does not mean that it cannot do its own merger flops. It is just that its success in many deals has been impressive.

Cisco is a leader in the networking industry. Led by John Chambers, it sought to become in networking what Microsoft was for PCs and what IBM was at one time in the mainframe business. In 1993, the year when it did its first acquisition, Cisco was the leader in routers, however, other technology was competing with them. When large clients asked for different technological solutions such as switching and asynchronous transfer mode (ATM) technology, Cisco became worried that it would be marketing yesterday's technology in the very near future. It needed to stay on the forefront of technological change and Chambers decided that the best way to do that was through a series of acquisitions of smaller, technologically innovative companies.

Cisco started down the acquisition path through its acquisition of Sunnyvale, California start-up, Crescendo, a marketer of switch technology. The market was not very keen on this deal, one in which Cisco paid a hefty premium. However, Chambers believed he understood this business and its whirlwind evolution better than the market or the media. Cisco's revenues began to jump and the market came to accept Chamber's prior deal but by now he was surging ahead with other acquisitions that he hoped would give him a further technological edge. In 1994 he acquired Kalpana, an Ethernet switch maker, and Lightstream, an ATM switch maker. In 1996 Cisco did its largest deal yet with the acquisition of StrataCom for $4 billion. This was followed by an even larger acquisition — Cerent in 1999 for $6.9 billion.

At its peak Cisco acquired one or two companies a month. Most of the deals were not multibillion dollar transactions. They were relatively smaller companies that Cisco readily assimilated into its corporate culture. Some had even likened Cisco to the Star Trek Borg characters. While Cisco was good at acquisitions, it slowed its buying frenzy when the Internet boom turned down toward the end of the fifth merger wave. Some criticized the company for not responding quicker to the changing nature of the slowing market. This was a great adjustment which the company eventually was able to achieve but not without some financial pain. However, there can be no denying the fact that Cisco was able to achieve leadership in its field through serial acquisitions of many smaller companies that gave it technological capabilities that allowed it to stay in the forefront of a rapidly changing industry.

## SYNERGY

Another often-cited term in M&As is synergy. While the term *synergy* is often associated with the physical sciences, it has actually become a bit overused in the field of M&As as the reason (if not the excuse) for doing deals. In the physical sciences, synergy refers to the type of reactions that occur when two substances or factors combine to produce a greater effect together than what the sum of the two operating independently could account for. For example, a synergistic reaction occurs in chemistry when two chemicals combine to produce a more potent total reaction than the sum of their separate effects. Simply stated, synergy refers to the phenomenon of $2 + 2 = 5$. In mergers, this translates into the ability of a corporate combination to be more profitable than the individual profits of the firms that were combined.

The anticipation of synergistic benefits provides incentives for companies to incur the expenses of the acquisition process and still pay a premium over market value to target shareholders. Synergy may allow the combined firm to appear to have a positive *net acquisition value* (NAV):

$$NAV = V_{AB} - [V_A + V_B]$$

where

$V_{AB} =$ the combined value of the two firms
$V_A \ \ =$ value of $A$ on its own value
$V_B \ \ =$ value of $B$ on its own
$E \ \ \ =$ expenses of the acquisition process                    (2.1)

Reorganizing equation 2.1, we get:

$$NAV = [V_{AB} - (V_A + V_B)] - E \qquad (2.2)$$

The term in the brackets is the synergistic effect. This effect must be greater than $E$ to justify going forward with the merger. If the bracketed term is not greater than the sum of $E$, then the bidding firm will have overpaid for the target.

Synergy is sometimes categorized into two types: (1) operating and (2) financial. *Operating synergy* refers to the efficiency gains or operating economies that are derived in horizontal or vertical mergers. *Revenue-enhancing synergy* is the ability of a combined entity to realize more revenues than what the individual companies would have if they remained independent. *Financial synergy* refers to the possibility that the cost of capital can be lowered by combining one or more companies.

## Operating Synergy

Operating synergy often comes from a reduction in costs that results from a corporate combination. These cost reductions may result from *economies of scale*. This is an economic term that refers to the reductions in per-unit costs that result from an increase in the size or scale of a company's operations. It is easier to envision scale economies by considering manufacturing businesses that have a physical plant and equipment that is leveraged to realize increases in output without corresponding increases in inputs and the costs that they command.

Manufacturing firms often incur high per-unit costs when they produce low levels of output, because the fixed costs of operating their manufacturing facilities are spread out over relatively low levels of output. As the output levels rise, the per-unit costs decline. This is sometimes referred to as *spreading overhead*. Some of the other sources of these gains arise from increased specialization of labor and management as well as the more efficient use of capital equipment, which might not be possible at low output levels. This phenomenon continues for a certain range of output, after which per-unit costs may rise as the firm incurs diseconomies of scale. Diseconomies of scale may arise as the firm experiences higher costs and other problems associated with coordinating a larger-scale operation. The extent to which diseconomies of scale exist is a topic of dispute to many economists. Some cite as evidence the continued growth of large, multinational companies, such as Exxon and General Motors. These firms have exhibited extended periods of growth while still paying stockholders an acceptable return on equity. Others contend that such firms would be able to provide stockholders a higher rate of return if they were smaller, more efficient companies.

Exhibit 2.3, which depicts scale economies and diseconomies, around an optimal output level occurs where per-unit costs are at a minimum. This implies that an expansion through the horizontal acquisition of a competitor may increase the size of the acquiring firm's operation and lower per-unit costs. It is important to note, however, that while economic theory shows the output level where per-unit costs are lowest, this is not necessarily the optimal output for the firm to produce. This optimal output ($q^*$) is determined by the interaction between marginal costs and marginal revenues. This is shown in Exhibit 2.4.

One business that has witnessed many M&As is the cruise industry. Larger cruise lines are able to effectively leverage national television, radio, and print advertising campaigns where they are able to offer a large number of ships and beds to the market. These sizable costs are then spread out over a large number of berths, lowering the per-berth cost of such advertising. In the early 1980s, the cruise industry featured several smaller cruise lines, some of which could not afford to engage in such marketing. Since they had a smaller number of ships and cabins to sell, their ability to compete with the larger cruise lines was limited. In addition, the administrative costs of having a reservation system, billing, and other administrative services also could not be spread out over a large number of cabins to lower their costs. A consolidation in the industry began to occur to address this issue.

One of the interesting aspects of this consolidation is that it even featured the M&A of upper-end cruise lines by larger, lower-priced, more mass-market companies. For example, Seabourne, one of the higher-priced luxury cruise lines with smaller ships, was acquired by Carnival, which is a lower-priced, mass-market cruise line that features lower prices and very large ships. Nonetheless, in doing acquisitions such as this, Carnival obviously thought it would benefit by

Exhibit 2.3    Economies of Scale: U-Shaped Average Cost Curve

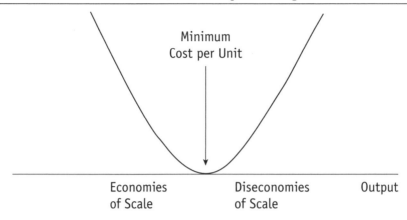

Minimum
Cost per Unit

Economies          Diseconomies          Output
of Scale            of Scale

Exhibit 2.4    Optimal Output: $MR = MC$ Showing $AC$

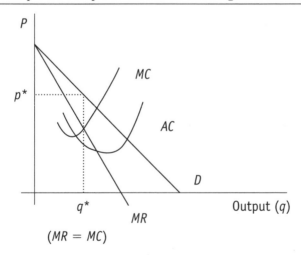

being able to market from its common base of activities a full range of price offerings. Carnival made sure that customers were able to clearly differentiate between the products by keeping Seaborne somewhat separate, and its marketing was largely targeted to its upper-end consumers, while Carnival engaged in more mass-market marketing.

The industry further consolidated in the 1990s and 2000s, and in 2001, Princess, owned by P&O Lines, was acquired by Carnival Cruises in a takeover battle with Royal Caribbean. The takeover battle for Princess was long and difficult as neither Carnival or Royal Caribbean wanted the other cruise line to gain control of Princess which itself was a major player in that industry. The winner of the contest would be the leader in the industry and Royal Caribbean fought hard to avoid ceding this dominant position to its arch rival. However, Carnival was not be to denied and eventually was able to add Princess, a mid-market cruise line, to its diverse cruise offerings.

The capital demands of some industries can be so great that even large companies are forced to join forces and pool their capital resources. The pharmaceutical industry is a case in point. As a result of the many technological advances, particularly those involving genetic research, drug companies scrambled in the 1990s to use this new technology to develop new products before their competitors. The financial requirements of effective research rose significantly. Moreover, as the drug pipeline at larger pharmaceutical companies began to dry up, larger drug firms looked to the acquisition of smaller competitors to fill this void. The industry further consolidated by large drug manufacturers merging with each other. Although many of these deals have provided benefits, it is debatable if they have really solved the problem of developing new drugs.

---

### ACHIEVING ECONOMIES OF SCALE IN
### THE EXXON–MOBIL MERGER

The merger of Exxon and Mobil, two of the largest U.S.-based oil companies in the world, formed one of the largest companies in the world. One of the lessons of this successful merger is that when you know the industry well, you may be better able to predict when economies of scale will be realized. Both of these merger partners knew the industry and had a good concept of what costs were redundant and what could be eliminated without a loss of market share. When companies are in different industries, it is sometimes difficult to predict just what costs can be reduced or eliminated without having an adverse effect on the company. However, when two well-established companies are in a similar position in the same industry, each merger partner has a good knowledge of the other's business because it is so much like its own. It is interesting to note that in advance of the deal, the companies jointly stated that they anticipated they would be able to save $3.8 billion. In a contrast with so many deals that did not work out, the combined Exxon/Mobil later informed the markets that the actual savings from the merger exceeded the anticipated amount by about 20%.

The success of the merger between Exxon and Mobil led to a spate of copycat mergers between Arco and BP and Texaco and Chevron. The competitors in this industry wanted to combine, in part to realize some of the same savings that Exxon and Mobil realized.

The Exxon–Mobil merger was not implemented just to enjoy economies of scale. Not unlike the dilemma of pharmaceutical companies that found their drug pipeline dwindling without sufficient replacement products on the horizon, these two petroleum giants also faced declining reserves and formidable competitors with large reserves. For Exxon, much of its production was concentrated in the United States and the North Sea. However, these reserves, while large, were in a gradual state of decline. One of the problems that both of these companies faced was that many of the newer sources of reserves were controlled by newer powers in the world oil industry, such as Russia, and these competitors were reluctant to part with the reserves on terms that were favorable to companies like Exxon and Mobil.

The combination of Exxon and Mobil was part of an overall international consolidation in the oil industry that featured the combination of many oil giants. At around the same time that Exxon and Mobil were planning their megadeal, several of their larger competitors were doing the same. In December 1998, the large French petroleum giant, Total, announced that it was merging with the large Belgian oil company PetroFina. The combined company, TotalFina, then successfully completed a hostile bid for Elf Acquitaine, a former state-owned company.

It was not just Exxon and Mobil that were responding to the merger of oil giants around the world. Other U.S. companies responded to the changes in the industry in the same manner (see Exhibit A). BP has already been mentioned, which is BP Amoco, itself a merger between British Petroleum and Amoco. This combined company then acquired Arco in April 1999. Ironically, in this deal, the Federal Trade Commission required the combined entity to sell its Cushing Oklahoma operations in Oklahoma and its Alaska oil operations, and Phillips Petroleum became the buyer. This situation is also instructive because it is another way that companies, even companies outside of deals, can profit from mergers. Here Phillips was able to acquire petroleum resources by merely waiting observantly on the sidelines and stepping up at the right moment when an opportunity arose. Mergers and acquisitions can create opportunities for industry competitors if they are patient.

**Exhibit A**
Oil Industry Mergers

| Date Announced | Acquirer | Target | Value of Transaction ($ Millions) |
|---|---|---|---|
| 12/1/1998 | Exxon Corp | Mobil Corp | 78,945.79 |
| 7/5/1999 | Total Fina SA | Elf Aquitaine | 50,070.05 |
| 8/11/1998 | British Petroleum Co PLC | Amoco Corp | 48,174.09 |
| 1/18/1998 | El Paso Energy Corp | Coastal Corp | 16,006.38 |
| 4/22/2003 | Yukosneftegaz | Sibneft | 13,615.23 |
| 4/29/1999 | Repsol SA | YPF SA | 13,151.70 |
| 4/22/2002 | National Grid Group PLC | Lattice Group PLC | 9,377.63 |
| 8/18/2000 | Transocean Sedco Forex Inc | R&B Falcon Corp | 9,091.49 |
| 3/22/2000 | Shareholders | Lattice Group PLC (BG Group) | 8,515.95 |
| 2/28/2000 | NiSource Inc | Columbia Energy Group | 8,500.54 |

*Source:* Thomson Financial Securities Data.

## Revenue-Enhancing Synergy

Revenue-enhancing synergies are those combinations that increase the ability of the combined entity to generate revenues. That is, after a corporate combination, if the corporation has an increase in its revenues that is beyond what is accomplished by merely adding together the revenues of the merger partners, then perhaps revenue-enhancing synergies explain the gain. Of the two types of synergy, operating and revenue enhancing, the latter is the most difficult to achieve. It is easier to try to use cost-cutting techniques and to find areas of overlapping business that can be eliminated, thereby cutting costs. It is often much more difficult to find ways that two merged companies can combine and generate greater revenues than they would have as two separate companies. This is one of the real challenges of M&As, and this is what CEOs and senior management get paid handsomely for. Unfortunately, many do not succeed in this task and are thus relegated to accounting-oriented exercises in cost reduction while failing in their attempts to truly increase revenue growth in a way that more than offsets the costs of the deal.

An example of how revenue-enhancing mergers can occur is when Company A merges with Company B, which produces products that A's customers want but A does not produce. If the same can be said in reverse, that B's customers want products that A makes but B does not currently provide, there may be a basis for each company

---

### REVENUE-ENHANCING SYNERGIES

Revenue-enhancing synergies are often talked about in advance of M&As, but cases where this is actually achieved over an extended period are much less frequently encountered. One such successful case appears to be the 2002 acquisition by Northrop Grumman of TRW, both defense industry contractors. Northrop Grumman was formed with the merger of Northrop and Grumman, each defense industry companies with specialties in aircraft. They combined in 1994 when the defense industry started to consolidate and the U.S. defense budget began to be curtailed. The collapse of the Soviet Union helped make this defense contraction a U.S.–European phenomena that contracted the industry internationally, not just in the United States. This began to change in the 1990s, and Northrop Grumman began to look to enhance its capabilities — especially those that related to more high tech weaponry. Buyers of military equipment were looking more for greater high tech capabilities and somewhat less for tanks and other more standard vehicles that had been mainstays of armies.

Both Northrop Grumman and TRW had previously not focused on large high-tech defense projects because they believed they lacked some of the capabilities of other large defense firms, such as Boeing, Raytheon, and Lockheed Martin. However, shortly after they combined, Northrop made a successful bid for the Kinetic Energy Interceptor, a Star Wars–type antimissile interceptor.[a] The combination helped earn the combined company a new $4.5 billion contract — a deal they would never have pursued had it not been for their newly combined capabilities.

Northrop Grumman did not stop with its merger between these two major defense contractors. It recognized that if the company was going to be successful in the rapidly changing defense business, it needed to change with the way the military was changing. High-tech weaponry would become an increasingly important part of each component of the defense industry. If the company was going to be successful, it needed to continually expand its capabilities. It responded to these changes with an M&A program that preceded the acquisition of TRW. Over the 10 years before the TRW transaction, it bought 16 different defense companies, including Litton Industries and Newport News Shipbuilding. These deals made Northrop the largest shipbuilder for the U.S. Navy. The synergies between Northrop and the newly acquired shipbuilding divisions immediately became apparent in the types of ships that Northrop began building to meet the Navy's changing needs. Northrop was already well known for its successful Stealth B-2 bomber, which can evade traditional energy radar-detection defenses to deal offensive blows far away. The Navy also sought similar stealth capabilities for its ships that can less easily use speed to evade detection and missile attacks. Northrop responded to this need by contracting with the U.S. Navy to build a stealth destroyer. The contract to build the DD (X) stealth destroyer would bring in $1.4 billion for the company's Mississippi shipbuilding division. The ship would draw on not just Northrop's stealth design capabilities but would also integrate new high-tech weapon capabilities that combined low-noise propulsion systems and motors as well as advanced 155-millimeter guns that would fire 12 satellite-guided shells per minute for up to a 100-mile distance.[b] In order to construct such a floating high-tech ship, the company needed diverse design and construction capabilities that only a company that had acquired the many different companies that Northrop had acquired would be capable of providing. Without this range of capabilities, the company would either lose the contract to another more diverse company or have to share the lucrative work with other contractors. Instead, Northrop won the DD (X) destroyer contract and retained in-house a much larger percentage of the work.

---

a. Christopher Plummer, "Northrop's Heavy Artillery," *BusinessWeek* (March 8, 2004): 52–54.
b. Ibid.

being able to leverage its own customer base by doing such a deal. A merger or acquisition may be the best way that Company A can take advantage of the relationships it has forged with its customer base. If its customers are loyal and have been asking for these additional products, then perhaps there is a good basis for believing that the greater sales could be achieved by simply acquiring this capability. The process seems simple, but as the saying goes, "There may be many a slip between the cup and the lip."

Unfortunately, companies make an erroneous assumption that their customers would prefer buying other products from them that they are currently buying from other companies. The acquirer needs to have a sound basis for the belief that its current customers would truly be interested in buying the additional products in question from them. Many times the only basis for this belief is the imagination of the acquirer's management that fails to truly understand the factors that determine its customer's purchases—especially those that relate to the contemplated products. This was the basis for the flawed diversification strategy of Sears when it expanded aggressively into the real estate and securities brokerage business. Sears thought that it could leverage the fact that it had a large and somewhat loyal customer base. Its management thought that these same customers would want to buy various other products from them—products that they normally bought in very different venues. In retrospect, this strategy was clearly flawed if not outright silly. Armed with hindsight, it is hard to fathom why Sears ever thought it could have successfully pursued such a diversifying acquisition strategy.

## MERGER GAINS: OPERATING SYNERGY OR REVENUE ENHANCEMENTS—CASE OF BANKING INDUSTRY

The high volume of mergers in the banking industry over the past two decades has provided a fertile ground for research on the source of gains from mergers in acquisitions. Some research that has focused on the acquisition performance of merged banks has found little value in such deals.[5] Steven Piloff's study of 48 banking mergers over the period 1982–1991 found little change in performance measures and cumulative abnormal returns following mergers. Others have surmised that banking mergers are more motivated by managerial hubris than by the pursuit of financial gains that would embrace shareholder wealth.[6] Houston, James, and Ryngaert analyzed a sample of 64 large bank acquisitions (those over $400 million in value) over the period 1985–1996.[7] Consistent with the findings of the bulk of the research on merger gains, they found that total gains from M&As were positive, while gains for bidders were negative with target gains being positive. Specifically, they found that average gains over a five-day window that started four days before the takeover announcement averaged 1.86%, while bidder abnormal returns were –3.47% and target abnormal returns were 20.8%. These values are not unusual and consistent with prior research. However, Houston, James, and Ryngaert researched the source of the gains and divided their sample into deals that had significant geographical overlap and those that did not. They found that combined overall returns were higher for the overlap sample compared to the subsample that did not feature such an overlap. In addition, they found that bidder returns were less negative for the overlap group (−2.69%) compared to the nonoverlap group (−4.4%), while target gains were higher for overlap (24.6%) compared to the nonoverlap sample (16.17). They theorized that the greater gains from the overlap of transactions presented greater opportunities for branch consolidation as well as other cost savings from consolidating operations when there is greater geographical overlap.

The higher gains from geographical overlap support operating synergies as a source of merger gains. Houston, James, and Ryngaert did not find evidence of revenue enhancements being related to the announcement gains. They also found that management's estimates of gains were typically overestimated. This study also confirms the fact that cost economies are much easier to realize than revenue-enhancing synergies. The market knows this and tends to discount management's statements about such revenue enhancements because it knows that it is much easier for management to talk about achieving these gains than it is to actual do so.

## Other Sources of Synergy

While cost-based and revenue-enhancing synergies are two of the most commonly cited sources of synergy, others may be relevant depending on the particular circumstances.

*Tax-Based Synergies.*    Sometimes a target may have certain unexploited tax benefits that can be utilized by a buyer. For example, a company may have net operating losses (NOLs), which can be transferred to a buyer through an acquisition of the target. These NOLs may enable the target to offset profits it would otherwise have to pay taxes on. It may be possible for the NOLs to be carried forward and provide tax benefits for a certain defined time period. It is ironic, but losses that a target company may have sustained in the past may actually be a source of value for it in an acquisition. Other sources of tax-based gains may be depreciation tax shields, which may come from a step-up in the basis of the target's assets following an acquisition.

Tax-based synergies can play a significant role in M&As. For example, Kmart had $3.8 billion in tax credits in 2004 based on prior losses this troubled retail giant had incurred. These tax benefits played a role in Kmart's offer for Sears as the tax credits could shield some of the combined company's profits following the merger. By having such credits, Kmart could help the combined company realize greater profits for Sears' business than what Sears could derive on its own. It is ironic that Kmart's prior financial difficulties could form the basis for a buying advantage when it made a bid for Sears.

*Financial Synergies.*    When a target company has certain growth opportunities that it would like to pursue but where it is hampered by an insufficient access to capital, one way this problem may be alleviated is with a merger with a company that has better access to capital but that may not have the same profit-making opportunities as the target. This is sometimes the basis for acquisitions of smaller companies by larger bidders. The key question here is if the target really has access to those opportunities, why does the market not recognize this and provide the capital. Perhaps the market is willing to provide the capital, but given the target's size and perhaps track record, the cost of capital for the target would be too high and would diminish much of the profitability. One solution could be to merger with an acquirer that has access to capital at better rates.

A situation somewhat similar to the scenario described in the previous paragraph occurred with the 1995 acquisition of McCaw Cellular by AT&T. McCaw wanted to build a national cellular telephone business, and while it was moving in that direction, it was hampered in getting access to sufficient capital it would need to fund this aggressive expansion. Creating such a national telecommunications network is a capital-intensive exercise, and competitive pressures required McCaw to accomplish this task quickly and efficiently. AT&T was the most established name in the telecommunications business (although not in the cellular side of the business) and had access to capital and attractive rates. McCaw had a debt rating of CCC, while AT&T's debt rating was AA. In a combination like this, the bidder may experience some deterioration in its overall rating while the merger enables the combined company to access capital markets at far lower rates than what the target would have been able to receive.

*Another Comment on Synergy.*   Synergistic benefits are usually easier to realize when the businesses are similar. When the businesses are in the same or closely related fields, then it is more likely that the parties understand each other's business and can better evaluate how realistic the proposed synergies are. Acquisitions into other industries, such as conglomerate acquisitions, have a much lower prospect of producing synergistic benefits than acquisitions within one's own industry. Horizontal combinations have a greater likelihood of producing synergies, such as cost-based synergies. Vertical deals may allow better access to markets or supplies but may not provide any real synergies. Combinations that are within the company's market may be more likely to provide synergies than market extension deals. An example would be a merger of two banks that provide service in the same market. They may be able to close some branches and service the same market with a smaller number of branches and, therefore, lower cost. Market extension bank mergers that expand the geographical banking network may provide a national banking network for customers, which is a benefit but a different type of benefit than synergistic gains that go more quickly to the bottom line.

## Synergy and the Internalization Hypothesis

A related view of a source of synergy in M&As is what is known as the *internalization hypothesis*. This is where a given target has certain assets, such as intangible assets of a brand name or know-how, which may be of benefit to the acquirer. A larger acquirer with greater capabilities than the target, such as a large multinational firm or a computer networking giant, such as Cisco, could enable the capabilities of the target to reach a far larger market. When M&As provide synergistic gains, research has shown that the target normally received the bulk of these gains in the form of shareholders returns, whereas event studies fail to show the acquirer benefiting much from such synergistic gains.[8] This may be because of the high premium a target may extract from the bidder as well as the market skepticism that the bidder will really realize the synergies. However, a sample of 225 foreign acquisitions of U.S. firms over the period 1979–1990 found that when a basis for real synergies existed, such as when the target had valuable intangible assets or impressive R&D capabilities, both the target and the acquirer gained. We will discuss this study further later in this chapter when we discuss M&As that are motivated by a desire to enhance a bidder's R&D capabilities.

## INDUSTRY CLUSTERING

The term *industry clustering* refers to deals tending to occur within the same industry category as opposed to cross-industry transactions. The phenomena of industry clustering began in the 1970s and contrasts with the 1960s—the third merger wave. During that period companies were constrained by antitrust enforcement from doing many deals within their own industry. As discussed in Chapter 1, they then tried to expand by buying companies outside of their own industries. This gave rise to the name of this period—the Conglomerate Era. Once the enforcement stance changed, companies began to pursue more deals within their own industry and fewer outside of their industry boundaries.

The phenomena of industry clustering has been documented by several researchers. Mitchell and Mulherin showed this phenomena applied to the fourth merger wave.[9] Andrade and Stafford showed it over a longer period: 1970–1994.[10] Industry clustering contrasts with diversification, which is a strategy companies pursue far less frequently than deals within companies' own industries.

When M&A patterns that have occurred in the United States are reviewed, we notice that the number of deals do not continue smoothly but tend to be concentrated in clusters and exhibit wavelike patterns.

In Chapter 1, we noted certain patterns in these clusters or waves. For example, the first wave of the late 1800s was noted for the formation of monopolies, the wave of the 1920s oligopolies, the late 1960s conglomerates, and the fourth wave of the 1980s was noted for its hostile takeovers as well as other characteristics. The fifth wave seems to show more strategic deals and fewer short-term purely financial plays. Looking back on the fifth wave and comparing it with the fourth wave, we can note some common features in these two periods that initially seemed to be more different than similar. One common feature of these two waves is that many of the deals tended to be concentrated or clustered in specific industries. These industries, in turn, often were those that underwent significant deregulation—what some researchers have referred to as *shocks*—a term more often utilized in macroeconomic theory to refer to systemic changes that affect the overall level of economic activity. In the context of M&A research, industry shocks are defined as any factor that changes the industry structure. Shocks can include deregulation but also technological innovation as well as changing supply and demand conditions.

Mitchell and Mulherin tried to empirically determine if industry shocks played a significant role in the pace of takeovers. As part of their research, they looked at the volume of takeovers by industry and sought to determine if there were industry-specific differences in the rate of takeover and restructuring activity. They focused on the fourth merger wave and found that the bulk of takeovers in a given industry tended to be clustered together over a relatively short time period. These takeovers, in turn, tended to be related to various shocks such as economic shocks but also other shocks such as deregulation.

Competitive pressures can force companies to merge with one another when size and scope of product offerings give companies an advantage over one another. This was the case in banking when following deregulation, banks began to merge with and acquire one another. They sought to be able to offer a national and international banking network, and M&As were a far quicker way to do this than international expansion. Exhibit 2.5 shows the leading banking industry mergers after the combination of J. P. Morgan Chase and Bank One at the beginning of 2004.

Exhibit 2.5  Largest Bank Mergers and Acquisitions as of 2004

| Date Announced | Acquirer | Target | Value of Transaction ($ Millions) |
|---|---|---|---|
| 4/6/1998 | Travelers Group, Inc. | Citicorp | 72,558.18 |
| 4/13/1998 | NationsBank Corp, Charlotte, NC | BankAmerica Corp | 61,633.40 |
| 1/14/2004 | J.P. Morgan Chase & Co. | Bank One Corp, Chicago, IL | 58,760.64 |
| 10/27/2003 | Bank of America Corp. | FleetBoston Financial Corp, MA | 49,260.63 |
| 10/13/1999 | Sumitomo Bank Ltd | Sakura Bank Ltd | 45,494.36 |
| 8/20/1999 | Fuji Bank Ltd | Dai-Ichi Kangyo Bank Ltd | 40,096.63 |
| 11/29/1999 | Royal Bank of Scotland Group | National Westminster Bank PLC | 38,524.65 |
| 6/8/1998 | Norwest Corp., Minneapolis, MN | Wells Fargo Capital C | 34,325.64 |
| 8/20/1999 | Fuji Bank Ltd | Industrial Bank of Japan Ltd | 30,759.61 |
| 4/13/1998 | BANC ONE Corp., Columbus, Ohio | First Chicago NBD Corp | 29,616.04 |

*Source:* Thomson Financial Securities Data and *The New York Times* (January 15, 2004): C8.

## DEREGULATION

When one looks for reasons for the rising volume of mergers within any given industry, deregulation consistently comes up as a major important factor. As noted earlier, in the research literature this is referred to as a shock. Deregulation potentially creates new opportunities for companies as deals that were previously impossible if the prior state of regulation prevented such transactions. Classic examples are the deregulation of the power utility, trucking, airline, and banking industries. In banking, various laws, such as the Garn-St. Germain Act and the Financial Services Modernization Act, changed the structure of the industry by allowing mergers across state lines.[11] This set in motion a process of consolidation throughout the United States and even internationally. That process continues as of this writing.

Andrade, Mitchell, and Stafford have traced the deregulation of the following industries to the various dates shown in Exhibit 2.6.[12]

## IMPROVED MANAGEMENT HYPOTHESIS

Improved management can be a reasonable motive for acquisitions by large companies with deep layers of managerial skills when the target is a company that lacks such resources. As smaller companies grow, they have an increased need for a broader range of managerial expertise and depth. A larger company may be able to provide such managerial depth and may already have in place the management structure to meet the company's future needs. It takes a greater degree of managerial sophistication to run a larger company than what is necessary for smaller businesses.

There are instances in which two larger companies merge and access to the management of one of the companies is cited as a motive for the deal. This was one of the motives cited in the aforementioned $60 billion 2004 merger between J. P. Morgan and Bank One. The deal combined the New York money market center–based J. P. Morgan with Bank One, which has a very strong consumer banking network in the Midwest as well as a strong credit card portfolio, both of which J. P. Morgan lacked. The combined bank would have 2,300 branches and $1.1 trillion in assets—just behind Citibank at $1.2 trillion.[13] Bank One did not have a major New York presence or the international reputation of the venerable J. P. Morgan, so the merger had significant potential benefits for both banks. The deal, however, also brought to the combined entity the future leadership of Jamie Dimon, who was Bank One's chairman and CEO and, as part of the deal, would become the successor to the then-current J. P. Morgan chief William Harrison in two years after the deal.[14] It is ironic that Jamie Dimon would come to head a bank that would rival Citigroup because he was reported to have been ousted by Citigroup by his longtime mentor, Sanford I. Weill.[15] However, Dimon had learned many lessons from Weill's leadership in cost cutting and corporate restructuring as he led Citigroup to a preeminent position

Exhibit 2.6    Dates of Deregulation of Certain Industries

| Deregulated Industry | Year of Deregulation |
|---|---|
| Airlines | 1973 |
| Broadcasting | 1984 and 1996 |
| Entertainment | 1984 |
| Natural Gas | 1978 |
| Trucking | 1980 |
| Banks and Thrifts | 1994 |
| Utilities | 1992 |
| Telecommunications | 1996 |

in the industry. J. P. Morgan knew that it would need managerial leadership of that sort to compete head-on with Citigroup and other banking giants like Bank of America. This was but one of various assets it would get by merging with Bank One. In addition to getting Dimon, J. P. Morgan also gained the top management team that Dimon assembled after he left Citigroup. Dimon's top five managers, such as Heidi Miller who was CFO at Bank One and would be head of Treasury at J. P. Morgan, were placed in specific leadership positions at the combined bank.[16]

Mergers and acquisitions also may serve as a process whereby management is changed. It is not unusual to have an acquirer change management of the target company after a takeover. One has to keep in mind, however, that an acquisition is a costly process that includes costs that go well beyond just the immediate deal expenses. They include integration costs, which are often hard to measure but can be significant. Most large companies have access to the same market for management talent. Like many other markets, a robust industry of middlemen or brokers of talent, executive search firms, exists. If a company wants to change its management, it can more easily do that by the board of directors deciding to do so and employing a search firm to compile a new management team. Theoretically, this new management team should be able to bring about necessary changes in the running of the business that an acquirer could; however, it does not always work that way. Management of poorly performing companies can sometimes stay in power longer than is prudent, and boards are not always as diligent as they should be in ensuring that the business has the best management available. When this process is sluggish, the market usually continues to function relatively efficiently, and the market value of the company will decline, creating an opportunity for companies with more skilled managers to buy the less-well-managed target.

The Martin and McConnell study lent support to the improved management hypothesis.[17] They examined a sample of 253 successful tender offer takeovers that were completed during the period 1958 through 1984. They focused on what they called *disciplinary takeovers*, which are deals where the top management is removed shortly after the acquisition is completed. When management stayed in place, they considered the deals nondisciplinary. They then compared the cumulative industry-adjusted returns over various time periods, such as four years and two years before the takeover for the disciplinary sample with that of the nondisciplinary group. Their results were striking. They found that the cumulative industry-adjusted returns for the disciplinary sample was a statistically significant $-15.38\%$, whereas it was $+4.35$ and not statistically significant for the nondisciplinary group. We can conclude that as far as their sample is concerned, the disciplinary group performed significantly worse than its industry peers, while the nondisciplinary group was not statistically different from the industry.

The Martin and McConnell research supports the view that the market works to weed out bad managers whose companies underperform in the market. These companies become vulnerable to hostile takeovers by bidders who often quickly remove the underperforming managers. In a sense, the market is doing what the board should be doing: making sure that underperforming managers are removed and replaced by others who hopefully will do better. As Mitchell and Lehn have also shown, when the bidders continue to underperform, they also become the targets of takeovers.[18]

In Chapter 3 we will analyze some research studies on the returns to bidder and target from takeovers, which lends some support to the improved management hypothesis. One study by Lang, Stulz, and Walking and another by Searves showed that returns to bidders are higher when bidders have higher q ratios and when targets have lower q ratios.[19] We will discuss q ratios in Chapter 4, where we will see that it is a proxy for management performance and their utilization of the assets they have at their disposal. The research studies show that merger gains are greater when a better-managed bidder takes over less-well-managed targets. Both studies lend support to the improved management hypothesis and imply that when such management-based differences are not present, the gains from takeovers will be a lot less.

M&As can be a process that changes poor managers. However, it is a costly one that is pursued when the board of directors is not doing its job. It could change poorly performing managers at much lower costs than what would be incurred to have this change brought about through a merger or acquisition. Only when the board is not doing its job does the M&A process serve as the next best alternative.

## HUBRIS HYPOTHESIS OF TAKEOVERS

No discussion of merger successes and failures, but especially failures, would be complete without an exploration of the hubris hypothesis of takeovers. This hypothesis was first proposed by Richard Roll.[20] He considered the role that hubris, or managerial pride, played in explaining takeover activity. This theory implies that managers engage in M&As for their own personal reasons and that this is their primary motive, and the economic gains of the company they are managing are secondary to this personal motive.

Roll used this hypothesis to explain why managers might pay a premium for a firm that the market has already correctly valued. Managers superimpose their own valuation over that of an objectively determined market valuation. Roll's position is that managerial pride makes managers believe that their valuation is superior to that of the market. Implicit in this theory is an underlying conviction that the market is efficient and can provide the best indicator of the value of a firm. Some, however, would argue that there are many instances of market inefficiency or irrationality and that this creates an opportunity for astute managers to utilize their own valuation methodologies, which they might contend are superior to that of the market. As evidence in support of this hypothesis, Roll draws on a wide body of research studies. This evidence is described in the following section. When we consider some of the colossal merger failures of the fourth and fifth waves, we have to conclude that hubris, as opposed to cold objective analysis, played an important role in some of these misguided deals. However, in order to try to identify the specific role that hubris played in such deals, we need to come up with more exact empirical criteria.

## Expected Empirical Evidence of Hubris in Mergers

Roll states that if the hubris hypothesis explains takeovers, then the following should occur for those takeovers that are motivated by hubris:

- *The stock price of the acquiring firm should fall after the market becomes aware of the takeover bid.* This should occur because the takeover is not in the best interests of the acquiring firm's stockholders and does not represent an efficient allocation of their wealth.

- *The stock price of the target firm should increase with the bid for control.* This should occur because the acquiring firm is not only going to pay a premium but also may pay a premium in excess of the value of the target.

- *The combined effect of the rising value of the target and the falling value of the acquiring firm should be negative.* This takes into account the costs of completing the takeover process.

In Chapter 3 we explore the shareholder wealth effects of M&A announcements as they relate to acquirers and targets. We do this on both a short-term basis and from a long-term perspective. Because a significant part of Chapter 3 is devoted to this issue, we will not pursue the results of such research at length here. However, we can point out that in large part, the short- and long-term research findings tend to support the applicability of the hubris hypothesis in many M&As. Studies do show that targets generally receive a premium for their shares. Markets also tend to either be neutral or react negatively with regard to bidders when they announce acquisitions. When they react negatively, they are, in effect, saying that they do not agree with the bidder's valuation and its claimed ability to derive sufficient value from the acquisition to be able to justify the premium that is being offered. In order to pay such a premium, the bidder often has to be able to extract greater value from the target than it can generate for itself. Sometimes, when there are realizable synergies, this may be a reasonable expectation. Other times, the basis for the premium is speculative, and the deal is a mistake. Bidders need to be cognizant of the market's valuation and recognize that it results from an objective process. The market regularly values and revalues the shares of a company in light of the available public (and sometimes private) information. We will now focus on a few of the studies that support the hubris hypothesis.

## Research Evidence Supporting the Hubris Hypothesis

There has been a quarter of a century of merger research, which can in various ways shed light on the role that hubris plays in M&As. From this body of research we find that several studies show that the acquiring firm's announcement of the takeover results in a decline in the value of the acquirer's stock. Dodd found statistically significant negative returns to the acquirer following the announcement of the planned takeover.[21] Other studies have demonstrated similar findings.[22] However, not all studies support this conclusion. Paul Asquith failed to find a consistent pattern of declining stock prices following the announcement of a takeover.[23]

A body of research supports the hubris hypothesis of takeovers. Some of the relevant studies are discussed in Chapters 3 and 4. Various studies have shown that acquirers tend to realize few gains at the announcement of a proposed merger or acquisition, whereas targets tend to do well. Other studies support the concept of bidder management overpaying for targets. Some of these studies explore the motives for this overpayment and they tend to support the role that hubris plays. One recent study by Moeller et al. showed that larger firms, which might reasonably be run by hubris-filled managers, tend to offer higher premiums and are more likely to complete a takeover than their smaller counterparts.[24]

Research from the field of management also seems to support the hubris hypothesis.[25] Using a sample of 106 large acquisitions, Hayward and Hambrick found CEO hubris positively associated with the size of premiums paid. Their study was especially interesting in that they tried to derive quantitative measures that would reflect psychological factors that might, in turn, reflect hubris. They measured hubris with variables such as the company's recent performance and CEO self-importance (as reflected by media praise and compensation relative to the second-highest paid executive). The study also considered independent variables such as CEO inexperience, as measured by years in that position, along with board vigilance, as measured by the number of inside versus outside directors. The interaction of these variables is depicted in Exhibit 2.7.

It is noteworthy to notice the role that the board of directors plays in Exhibit 2.7. The board in its role as overseer of management's decisions has the opportunity to prevent CEO hubris from manifesting itself in overly expensive acquisition premiums. CEO hubris and ego is not necessarily bad because it can serve as an important motivator for management to strive to be successful. The board must keep such hubris in check. However, when the board is dominated by the hubris-laden CEO, it does not serve its stopgap function.

Roll did not intend the hubris hypothesis to explain all takeovers. He merely proposed that an important human element enters takeovers when individuals are interacting and negotiating the purchase

**Exhibit 2.7    Hubris-Related Determinants of Merger Premiums**

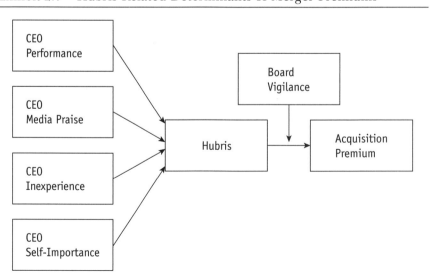

of a company. Management's acquisition of a target may be motivated purely by a desire to maximize stockholder wealth. However, other motives may include a desire to enter a target's industry or to become "the largest firm in the business." The extent to which these motives may play a role will vary from takeover to takeover. It is therefore of some interest that much evidence does support the hubris hypothesis. Surely the questionably high premiums paid for some firms, such as Federated Stores and RJR Nabisco, imply some element of hubris. The fact that Campeau Corporation was forced to declare bankruptcy not long after the acquisition of Federated lends support to the view that it overpaid in the highly leveraged deal.

## WINNER'S CURSE AND THE HUBRIS HYPOTHESIS

A related concept to the hubris hypothesis is the winner's curse of mergers. The winner's curse is certainly not exclusive to the field of M&As. It is even more apparent in the field of professional sports, where teams bid for high-priced free agents such as in baseball, football, basketball, and hockey. Players and their agents set the teams against each other in a bidding contest. The winner of the contest is the one who bids the highest price for the free agent. One of the most glaring cases of the winner's curse was the bidding contest for the highly paid shortstop Alex Rodriguez. The contest was won by the Texas Rangers, who gave Rodriguez a record-setting contract that other wiser bidders such as the New York Mets felt was too expensive relative to the value one player in that position could provide. The Rangers came to agree with that assessment as they finished in last place and could not afford all-important pitchers who are crucial to the success of a baseball team. After admitting its error, Texas ended up trading Rodriguez to the New York Yankees but still had to agree to pay some of the salary it contracted to pay him over the length of his long contract.

The parallels between the winner's curse of free agents in sports and companies in M&As are apparent. Auction model theory has long recognized that when various economic actors are bidding for an asset, or in this case a company, the one who wins the contest is the one who assigns the highest valuation to the target. If we assume that there is a range or distribution of values with the "correct" or most accurate one, possibly somewhere toward the middle of the distribution, then the winner may be the one with the highest end of the distribution. This is depicted in Exhibit 2.8, which assumes for convenience a smooth normal distribution.

What is the source of the winner's curse? It is twofold. First, it is an inaccurate valuation process, which results in too high a value. If this is the source of the problem, it means that the bidder does not know how to accurately value the target and arrives at an overestimate of the firm's value. This inaccurate valuation does not mean that the bidder does not know the proper methods of valuation, although that certainly could be the case. If the bidder does not know how to value the target, then there are many consultants available to assist with this process. However, while those consultants may utilize sophisticated valuation models, the assumptions, such as cash flow growth rates and discount rates, may be too optimistic and, if so, may result in an overvaluation of the target. This error may come from simply insufficient knowledge about the target. This could be a result of not knowing the specific industry, such as in the case of cross-industry deals. Robert Hansen discussed such a failure from a lack of accurate information on the target's business.[26] Presumably, this information is possessed by the target but not the bidder. The target has the information necessary to determine its accurate value, but the bidder does not. The target is then able to determine if the

Exhibit 2.8    Normally Distributed Valuations

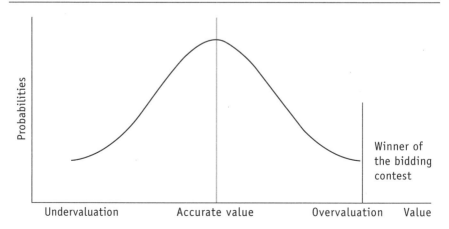

bidder's offer is high and if it can sell itself for a value that is greater than its real worth. This process does not mean to imply that the target is purposefully deceiving the bidder, although that could certainly happen. It just may be the case that the target simply knows its own business and its potential better than the bidder. Certainly this was the case in AT&T's acquisition of TCI—a deal discussed later in this book. The bidder may believe that the target has a greater potential than what the target believes. Sometimes this may be an accurate view and sometimes it may be flawed. When it is flawed, we may have a case of the winner's curse.

Another source of the winner's curse problem may occur when the bidder starts off with an accurate valuation and knows the limit to what it should pay. However, hubris or other human emotional elements may come into play as a bidder may simply not want to lose. If sellers know that the individuals they are dealing with are susceptible to such weaknesses, they may play on them so that emotion overtakes objective valuation and a higher price is paid for the target than what it is worth. The 1988 bidding contest between Robert Campeau and Campeau Corporation and Macy's for the famous department store chain Federated Stores is a classic example of such ego-motivated overbidding. Campeau did not want to lose and would not back down from Macy's aggressive effort to acquire the department store chain. Campeau upped the price based on dangerous leveraging of the company and taking on burdensome debt that the company quickly realized it could not service.

What can be done to limit the role of hubris and to prevent the winner's curse? There may be a few solutions to this problem. The most obvious one is to not put CEOs in place who are filled with hubris and susceptible to the winner's curse. While it is also obvious, one way to know this is to look at the CEO's prior deals. If they were losers, then it may be the case that hubris and the winner's curse may possibly have been a reason. As obvious as this may seem, it is amazing how many companies engage in repeated flawed deals. Daimler Benz, which acquired entire companies and stakes in companies that were failures, was undaunted in going ahead with the Chrysler acquisition, even though its deal-making track record was highly questionable. Its prior M&A busts of Freightliner and its acquisition of a significant stake in Mitsubishi gave it no pause as it rolled on to pursue another even more ambitious deal with its acquisition of Chrysler Corporation. The role of hubris seemed to have played a major role in this deal as Daimler's hard-driving CEO, Jurgen Schrempp, overpowered what checks and balances were in place and barreled on to do a deal that cost shareholders much value.

## CROSS-INDUSTRY DEALS AND HUBRIS

When the bidder is in the same business as the target, it may know what the target is capable of generating and may even know the reason why it is not achieving all that it should. However, when the bidder is in a very different business from the target, it may think it knows how to solve the target's problems, but this can be a mistake. Alternately, it may think that the target is so valuable, but this assumption may be flawed. One test that should be applied in cases of cross-industry acquisitions where the bidder is offering a significant premium is to ask the question, "Why haven't other companies in the industry made a bid for the target and offered such a premium?" If there are good answers, such as antitrust restrictions that would prevent this, then this deal may still be acceptable. If, however, there are no obvious prohibitions on an acquisition, and several companies with the financial wherewithal in the same industry have exhibited no desire to acquire the target, then the cross-industry bidder may need to step back from the deal and revisit its merits, especially in light of the premium it is paying. Boards of bidders contemplating cross-industry deals need to make sure there are realizable synergies from the combination and that there will not be significant unforeseen integration costs. In such transactions bidders may be well served by bringing in outside consultants who they believes will render an objective review of the deal. While it is an obvious point, the board needs to also make sure that these consultants are familiar with the track record of such cross-industry deals.

### Diversification

Diversification through acquisitions involves doing deals outside of one's industry. If a company is considering pursuing growth through M&As, there are two directions it can go: (1) buy or merge with companies in its own industry or (2) go outside the boundaries of its industry. The advantage of buying companies in your own industry is that this is probably a field the buyer knows well—or at least probably better than other industries. However, if the buyer's business is doing poorly, sometimes the attractive alternative is to go into other industries that show higher returns. The question that management has to answer for shareholders is: 'Is the acquisition, and therefore the investment of resources in another field, really in the shareholders' interests?' Couldn't shareholders do this themselves? For example, was the mega-acquisition of Conoco by DuPont in 1981 really in the interests of shareholders? If you are in the chemical and plastics business, does the petroleum industry really present synergies? Apparently not, as DuPont eventually spun off the oil company in 1998. The obvious question arises: Why did it take DuPont nearly two decades to come to that realization?

When we consider shareholders' interests, we have to realize that if a potential bidder is in one industry and is considering making an investment in another, the bidder's own shareholders can easily make such an investment at relatively low costs. The reason they are shareholders in the bidder's industry is based on their assessment of the costs and benefits of an investment in that particular industry. They may already have investments in the other industry, or they may not think the cost-benefits of investments in that sector are worthwhile. Individual investors can each structure their portfolios as they wish, and management of a company is not really doing shareholders a favor when they restructure shareholders' investments for them. When considered from a portfolio theory perspective, diversifying mergers are tough to justify. Some companies, such as General Electric, have been able to successfully manage diversification programs, but they are the exception rather than the rule. Those that tried to follow in their footsteps, such as Tyco, have not fared as well.

## Diversification to Enter More Profitable Industries

If a company realizes that the returns in its industry are below those of other industries, it might consider acquisitions in other more profitable industries as a way of trying to achieve the returns available in those industries. One possible scenario is that the acquirer's industry is mature and competition is high, while innovations are not sufficient to spark higher returns. If management is considering such a diversification strategy, it has to keep in mind the basic economics of competitive markets. As new entrants are attracted to an industry in search of higher returns, competitive forces heat up, and this often drives down returns. This is basic Economics 101 and is shown in simple supply-and-demand curves. As the supply curve shifts out with the movement of new entrants into an industry, competitive pressures will naturally tend to drive prices downward, and with them, profitability and shareholder returns (see Exhibit 2.9).

When an acquirer enters an industry seeking better profit opportunities, there is no assurance that those gains will be there when it completes the deal and has successfully integrated the target.[27] Competitive pressures bring about a movement toward the long-term equalization of rates of return across industries. Clearly, this does not mean that the rates of return in all industries at any moment in time are equal. The forces of competition that move industries to have equal returns are offset by opposing forces, such as industrial development, that cause industries to have varying rates of return. Those above-average return industries that do not have imposing barriers to entry will experience declining returns until they reach the cross-industry average.

Economic theory implies that only those industries with barriers to entry will be able to maintain long-term above-average returns. This implies that a diversification program to enter more profitable industries will not be successful in the long term. Therefore, when a company is considering diversifying acquisitions seeking higher returns, at a minimum, bidders need to consider the ease of entry. If entry is easy, then it will be just as easy for other companies to

Exhibit 2.9   Price Effects with Increasing Supply

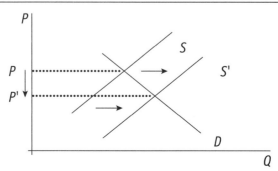

enter as well. Are there other vulnerable targets that other potential bidders could acquire? The bidder needs to think several steps ahead and not assume that the industry will remain static and that the only changes are going to be the ones brought about by the bidder.

## International Diversification

As the world has become a more globalized marketplace, companies have increasingly looked across their own borders to other markets as a source of expansion opportunities. They have also realized that, to the extent that other markets have a different pattern of variation in demand, they could possibly lower their risk profile by moving into markets elsewhere in the world. International diversification is both an expansion strategy as well as a possible means of diversifying away corporate risks. Which one is more relevant depends on the particular company and industry. The fact that companies respond to such motives can be seen in the increased volume of international and cross-border deals we have seen in recent years, particularly in the fifth merger wave.

When we examine the characteristics of these deals, we see that cross-border transactions tend to be more related than mergers within a given country. That is, there is evidence that when companies expand across their borders, they generally do not do so to move into industries that are very different from their main area of focus. One major exception was Vivendi, where Jean-Marie Meissner apparently decided that being a French water company was too boring when he could be running an international media and telecom empire. Fortunately, this is not the norm. More cross-border deals are like the DaimlerChrysler deals in the sense that they are related businesses.

The same arguments that work against using M&As to achieve diversification also apply to cross-border M&As. There have long been arguments that international diversification can provide some benefits to stockholders.[28] The real issue is whether the benefits that a corporation can attempt to realize can be better achieved by shareholders themselves when they assemble their portfolio—and at a fraction of the cost. Given the development of international investment markets and the proliferation of international mutual funds, investors can assemble whatever mix of international equity and

## SEARS ROEBUCK'S DIVERSIFICATION STRATEGY

In 1992 Sears Roebuck and Co. announced that it was ending its costly diversification strategy and would be selling off its financial services operations. In order to understand the company and its decision to enter the financial services business, it helps to know a little of its history and how it got to be one of the leading retail merchants in the United States. The company was formed in 1886 by Alvah Roebuck and Richard Sears. At the turn of the twentieth century, the company formed a financial services division that would handle some of the credit needs of customers seeking to purchase products from Sears. As it built its retail empire, the company continued to move further into financial services. In the 1930s, it started an insurance division, Allstate, which marketed automobile insurance. In the 1950s, the company formed Sears Roebuck Acceptance Corporation, which focused on short-term financial management for the company. It also began its own credit card operation at that time. So when we say Sears Roebuck's movement into financial services in the 1980s was part of a diversification strategy, it is important to keep in mind that this was not a totally new area for the company. However, the part of the financial services business that it moved into in the 1980s was different from that with which it had been previously involved. With the exception of automobile insurance, the other parts of its financial services business were complementary to its retail operations. For example, credit cards could enhance credit sales to its customers, especially those who might not be eligible for credit from other companies.

However, the movement into automobile insurance was a move away from its core operations. This was not the only initial move away from core activities. The company moved into mutual fund operations and purchased California Financial Corporation, a large savings and loan company. The moves demonstrated a tendency on the part of Sears to move away from its core businesses. In later years it would take this tendency and move it to a new level.

The seeds of the movement away from its core businesses can partially be traced to weaknesses in its retail operation, which were related to the difficulties Sears had in competing with Wal-Mart. Sears was losing ground to other retail rivals who were willing to use aggressive price competition to attract customers away from Sears while weakening the margins of the retail giant. At a point like this, the company can move in two different directions: fix the problem or invest resources elsewhere by trying to find a more attractive business. Sears took the latter route, and it proved to be a failure.

In 1981 Sears bought Coldwell Banker, the largest real estate brokerage company in the United States, for $175 million in stock and cash. It then purchased Dean Witter Reynolds, a large securities brokerage company, for $600 million in stock and cash. These deals were acquisitions of leading companies in their respective businesses. What were the gains that Sears saw? That is, how could Sears sell real estate and securities more advantageously than these two companies? Remember that when one acquires a target company, you are usually paying a value that reflects their projected profitability and cash flow–generating capability. So unless you bring something new to the table, such as by realizing valuable synergies, you may not be able to justify paying the acquisition premium. Sears saw such synergies through taking advantage of its large retail network and regular customer base to sell them new products—homes and stocks, and maybe a bond or two.

The Sears strategy is not a new one. It goes by several names, and some would say it is based on cross-selling the acquirers and target products and services to their respective customer bases. Sears had a large network of retail stores throughout the United States and a regular flow of customers. However, to put the strategy in perspective, consider a hypothetical discussion between two Sears customers. Say, for example, a husband is going to Sears to buy some lawn-mowing equipment. Or perhaps a wife is going to Sears for a new dishwasher (excuse the sexist nature of this example). One spouse says to the other, "Hi, honey, I'm off to Sears to buy that new lawn mower/dishwasher." The spouse responds, "Oh, great, but could you pick me up a house while you're there? And how about 100 shares of IBM as well?" While somewhat humorous, the absurdity of this exchange underscores the flaws in Sears' strategy. These products simply do not go together, and when that is the case, it does not matter if you are one of the biggest retailers in the world—you are not going to make this combination work.

Sears' management was convinced that the strategy would be successful. The market thought otherwise. In particular, institutional investors, who typically command a majority of the shares of most large public companies, questioned Sears' strategy as well as its inability to solve the woes of the retail business. Finally, after intense pressure from in-stitutional investors, who clearly saw that the strategy was not work-ing, Sears decided to spin off Dean Witter and Coldwell Banker in 1992 and refocused its efforts back onto its core business that had contin-ued to decline over the prior decade. In that same year Wal-Mart passed Sears in total sales. Wal-Mart was not distracted by poorly conceived deals and used Sears acquisition problems to surpass the distracted Sears. When Sears refocused it began to capitalize on its strengths and started to grow again. However, it was not until 2003 that it finally came to the realization that its credit card business was also a drain and sold it to Citigroup.

Gillan, Kensinger, and Martin described the insurrection brought about by institutional investors, which were led by Robert Monks of the LENS fund.[a] Sears was a case of an entrenched management team that also dominated the board of directors. Management held almost a ma-jority of the board seats, and some of the board members sat on different boards together. The close relationship between management and the board did not facilitate objectivity. Management was not responsive to dissent by its shareholders, particularly knowledgeable institutional investors.

The lesson from the failed Sears diversification strategy is threefold. First, just because you are good at one business does not mean that you can extend the assets and managerial resources of your organization to another very different business. The second lesson is that forays into more exciting business categories in which you have not demonstrated any expertise can be expensive and a losing proposition. It is often better to simply stay with the same old boring business that you are good at and learn ways to improve your performance. It is much easier to make small but meaningful improvements in a business in which you have established success than to move to a totally different business area. The third lesson is that so often the one-stop shop does not work. If customers are not of a mindset to buy products from you that they normally do not associate with your business, then adding such business activities may not work. You may be doing the customers a favor they do not want.

In 2004 Sears still lagged behind Wal-Mart along with another retail giant—Kmart. Kmart, fresh from its Chapter 11 bankruptcy, made an offer for Sears. Sears had 1,100 stores while Kmart had 1,504 stores. It is too early to tell if this combination will be profitable but we do know that it is a merger of two companies in similar segments of the same industry that has to be an advantage over some of its prior deals.

a. Stuart Gillan, John W. Kensinger, and John Martin, "Value Creation and Corporate Diversification," *Journal of Financial Economics* 56, no. 1 (January 2000): 103–137.

fixed-income investments they want. So the question also arises with international M&As just as it did with our general discussion of diversification: What benefits are management providing to shareholders if they are acquiring other international companies to diversify their business? If management's argument is that they are engaging in cross-border deals to grow the company faster and reach out to new markets for their products, then that is probably a reasonable motive in many cases. If, however, they are doing deals to achieve some level of international diversification, then this may be a questionable motive. One has to also recognize that cross-border deals done to achieve growth may, as a side benefit, provide some diversification benefits, but this should be a side benefit and not a reason for the deal.

Studies have looked at how diversification discounts varied across country boundaries. One such study was conducted by Faiver, Houston, and Maranjo, who looked at 8,000 companies that operated in 35 different countries.[29] They found that, to the extent that such a diversification discount exists, it varied depending on the country. They concluded that diversified companies have their own internal capital markets and may be able to use the resources of its combined corporate entities to provide capital to its component entities when needed. When a country's capital markets were such that a diversified entity provided better access to capital, then the diversified discount was less and possibly zero. When the capital markets were more developed, and thus the internal capital market provided by the diversified company was less valuable, the diversification discount was greater.[30]

## Research on the Valuation Effects
## of Diversification Strategies

Berger and Ofek examined a large sample of companies over the period 1986–1991. They found that firms that pursued a diversification strategy experienced a loss of value between 13% and 15%.[31] They also found that firm size was not a factor affecting the results. It applied to larger firms just as it applied to smaller ones. However, the extent of the diversification did play a role. That is, the adverse results that they found varied depending on how far out of their industries the diversifying acquirers went. When the diversification was limited to *related* industries, the adverse effects were less. Berger and Ofek investigated the returns of the diversified divisions and compared them to the straight-line operations of the diversified entity. These diversified divisions were shown to exhibit performance below that of the undiversified business segments.

The results of Berger and Ofek were supported by other research by Robert Comment and Gregg Jarrell. They reviewed a large sample of exchange-listed companies over the period 1978–1989.[32] They showed that increased focus or specialization within industry boundaries promoted the goals of shareholder maximization. They did not find evidence that acquirers truly benefit from such diversification programs. Moreover, there does not seem to be a basis for believing that when diversified targets are brought under the umbrella of a larger corporation with more financial resources, they are better off.

Another way to analyze the valuation effects of diversification is to try to measure the diversification discount. This is the difference between the market value of a diversified company compared to the value that its individual divisions would command on the market if they were separate corporate entities. The studies usually used market multiples to value the different corporate divisions and then compared the combined value with the market value of the diversified company. These studies have generally concluded that diversified companies trade at a diversification discount in the range of 8% to 15%.[33] This has led many of these researchers to conclude that diversification destroys value. Not all studies, however, support the diversification discount.

Some research indicates that the components of such diversified companies may have already included a discount to their value before they even became part of the diversified entity. Still other research fails to find any diversification discount. One is forced to conclude that diversification may destroy value, but some companies, such as General Electric and 3M, may be so well managed that they are able to overcome the challenges of managing a diversified entity and may be able to extract synergies from being diversified. It is also important to bear in mind that what is true at one moment in time or over one market period may not be true at other times. Companies may do well as a diversified entity, but the market or management may change, and this may not be true indefinitely. For example, in the years to come, will GE do as well as it had under the leadership of Jack Welch? Or does the company have in place a management system that will persist over various different managements?

## DIVERSIFICATION AND CEO COMPENSATION

If diversification adds little, and possibly detracts from firm value, then the market should not reward CEOs who promote such strategies. Boards should probably not allow CEOs to go ahead with diversifying M&As if the effect is going to be that they cause shareholders to lose. If, however, the companies go ahead and pursue such deals, and if, on average, they reduce shareholder value, then CEOs should be penalized with lower compensation. There seems to be some evidence that this actually occurs. One study by Rose and Shepard analyzed the relationship between CEO compensation and firm diversification over the period 1985–1990.[34] They did find that a firm that operates in two or more lines of business averaged 13% higher compensation than CEOs in just one business line. These aggregate data imply that there is a diversification premium where CEOs benefit from pursuing such a strategy. However, when they looked at CEOs who pursued a diversification strategy and traced the relationship between increases in diversification and change in compensation over a period of time, they found an inverse relationship. CEOs who increased a company's range of business operations personally lost money from the strategy. This implies that corporate governance was sluggish and did not act quickly enough to stop the diversification strategy from being implemented but did at least penalize the CEO after the fact. It is hoped that directors can learn from this observation and prevent the strategy that caused shareholders to lose money. However, as we will see in the next section, things are not so simple and clear cut, and there may be some forms of diversification that directors should recommend.

## DIVERSIFICATION THAT DOES SEEM TO WORK BETTER: RELATED DIVERSIFICATION

Not all types of diversified acquisitions are the same. Some types, such as related diversification, seem to do better than nonrelated diversifications. This theory was supported by Morck, Shleifer, and Vishny's study of 326 acquisitions over the period 1975–1987.[35] They found that the market punished companies that engaged in unrelated acquisitions through a loss of their market value. Related diversifications, however, fared better. These results are intuitive: It is more likely that a company knows businesses closer to its own than those that are more different.

Another form of diversification that also seems to work better is when the various companies in the diversified entity have valuable information-based assets. Such companies may be better able to transfer their knowledge and intellectual property if they are within the same corporate framework and do not need to worry about the value of these assets being misappropriated by unaffiliated entities. This seems to be why a study by Morck and Yeung showed that diversification provides greater benefits when both the target and the acquirers are in information-intensive industries.[36]

If the track record of related diversifications is better than unrelated, then how do we define *related*? This is not that obvious and, unfortunately, is open to interpretation. If it is misinterpreted, it can result in losses for shareholders. One such example was LVMH's fifth merger wave expansion strategy. LVMH (i.e., Louis Vuitton, Moet, and Hennessy), led by its flamboyant CEO Bernard Arnault, seems to define "related" as anything that deals with luxury. The company went on an acquisition binge that focused on a wide variety of companies that marketed products or services to upper end customers. This led them to acquire such major brand names as Chaumet jewelry, Dom Perignon (part of Moet), Fendi, Givenchy, Donna Karan, Loewe leather goods, Sephora, TAG Heuer, Thomas Pink shirts, and Veuve Cliquot champagne. The company became a clearinghouse for luxury products, but the combination of the variety of acquired

## 3M: ANATOMY OF A SUCCESSFUL CONGLOMERATE

When the discussion centers on conglomerates and the discussers seek to point out a conglomerate that has been a resounding success, the name General Electric (GE) almost immediately comes to mind. During the successful reign of CEO Jack Welch, GE used an aggressive M&A, but also divestiture, program to buy companies in several different industry sectors while greatly increasing shareholder value. However, 3M is too often unmentioned in such discussions. This company has also amassed great shareholder value while being a true conglomerate. While Jack Welch is a household name, Jim McNerney, 3M's CEO, is far less known; however, McNerney can trace his roots to Welch as he was actually a candidate to replace Welch but was passed over. Instead, while 3M was a successful conglomerate before McNerney became its CEO, he continued its impressive growth.

The 3M Corporation was formerly known as the Minnesota Mining and Manufacturing Company. While 3M may be better known to consumers for its famous Scotch tape and Post-it Notes, it manufacturers and markets a far broader range of products. As Exhibit A shows, the company has seven main divisions.

The largest and most profitable segment of 3M's business is health care. As Exhibit B shows, this segment constitutes approximately $4 billion in total revenues and an impressive $1 billion in operating profit. The health care segment markets medical and surgical supplies. This field, in general, is a high-growth area, especially in light of the aging population along with the fact that this sector is more resistant to the cyclical variation of the economy.

3M has enjoyed good growth in the total market value of its shares. While this is true, it is not clear if shareholders truly benefit by having

**Exhibit A**
3M Revenue and Operating Income by Segment

| Segment | Revenue ($ Billions) | Operating Income ($ Millions) |
|---|---|---|
| Consumer and Office Products | 2.61 | 460 |
| Healthcare | 4.00 | 1,003 |
| Safety, Security, and Protection Services | 1.93 | 437 |
| Industrial | 3.35 | 458 |
| Display and Graphics | 2.96 | 885 |
| Electro and Communication | 1.82 | 255 |
| Transportation | 1.54 | 389 |

*Source:* 3M Annual Report 2004.

**Exhibit B**

### 3M Net Sales by Segment

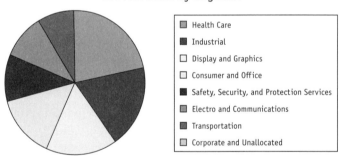

### 3M Operating Income by Segment

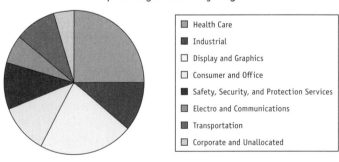

*Source:* 3M Annual Report 2004.

such a diverse mix of businesses under one corporate roof. Are there really important synergies between the health care segment and the electrical and communications segments? Would shareholders be better off if some of these divisions were sold off? Would they perform better on their own, or do they derive significant benefits by being part of the 3M Corporation? If 3M were to sell off some of its less related segments and use the proceeds to expand into what it might consider its more core businesses, would its shareholder returns be greater? These are complex questions, but given that 3M has chosen not to do so, we have to conclude that its management does not believe that this would be the best strategy for the company. Given also that the company has performed fairly well, management may be able to make a good argument that there are synergies across its diversified corporate structure and that it is realizing solid gains for shareholders. While management can say this, it is harder to argue that a more focused business would generate even greater gains.

companies provided few, if any, synergies. Many of the acquired brands (e.g., Fendi and Donna Karan), while major international brands, generated few profits. In November 1999 LVMH stretched the luxury-related connection by buying fine art auctioneer Phillips De Pury & Luxembourgh for $115 million. However, in doing so Arnault violated several rules of merger success. First, he acquired a company that was a distant third behind Sotheby's and Christies. Second, he stretched the definition of related so far there were no possibly synergies. Last, he acquired a company that needed a large cash infusion with little potential for it to be recouped. Like many other failed deals, CEO Arnault went unchecked by his directors, and shareholders paid the price. Clearly, defining "related" as any luxury good was a faulty strategy. Relatedness is a subjective concept and the more narrow the definition is, the more likely the deal will be successful.

## MERGING TO ACHIEVE GREATER MARKET POWER

*Market power* is defined in economies as the ability to raise price above the competitive price.[28] Market power implies that a company has a greater chance of enjoying profits for a period of time as opposed to more competitive business, where competitive forces pressure prices down to a level where participants in the industry earn only what economists term a *normal return*. This is a return consistent with the opportunity costs of the resources being used in the industry and not a return that allows for extranormal profits. Various factors influence the ability of a company to enjoy extranormal returns, but barriers to entry are very important to the long-term staying power of extranormal profits. Markets are not static, and the presence of extranormal profits attracts new entrants. The availability of vulnerable targets in an industry with above-average profits can attract well-financed bidders to enter the industry.

One measure of market power is the Lerner Index, developed by the economist Abba Lerner of the City University of New York. It measures the gap between price and marginal costs as it relates to price:

$$\text{Lerner Index} = (P - MC)/P$$

where

$P$  = price
$MC$ = marginal cost

The greater the gap between price and marginal costs, the greater the degree of market power. The ability to maintain price above marginal cost is a function of several factors, such as product differentiation, the existence of barriers to entry, number of competitors, and market share. The more unique the product or service, the more it is differentiated from its competitors, the greater the opportunities for market power. The fewer the competitors, the less likely there will be competitive pressures to lower price down to the level of marginal costs. However, it is important to bear in mind that the existence of barriers to entry is directly related to the number of competitors. The higher the returns in a given industry, the greater the attraction it has to potential competitors. Therefore, when considering the number of competitors, we should also try to consider potential competitors as well as current competitors—to the extent that this is possible. One can be assured, however, that even if you cannot get a concrete fix on the number of potential competitors, the higher the profit level in an industry, the more likely it is that there are potential competitors out there, and the higher the barriers to entry need to be to maintain the profit levels.

It is also important to bear in mind that merely having market or monopoly power does not ensure that there will even be profits. A company could be a monopolist in an industry that is losing money. The key is the relationship between revenues and costs at the profit-maximizing level of output. Exhibit 2.10(a) depicts a hypothetical situation in which a monopolist earns a profit with average costs (AC) above price, whereas Exhibit 2.10(b) is a situation in which a company loses money and average costs are greater than price. Given the way the curves are drawn, there is no output level at which this company—a company that is the only producer of the product and has no competition—earns a profit.

## DO FIRMS REALLY MERGE TO ACHIEVE MARKET POWER?

There is support for the view that companies merge to increase their monopoly power. Much of the evidence that elucidates this question is indirect. One study was done by Robert S. Stillman in 1983 as part of his doctoral thesis at the University of California in Los Angeles. In a relatively small sample of 11 mergers, he noticed that the stock prices of competitors failed to respond when the deals were announced.[38] His analysis looked at the value of the shares of companies in the industry where the merger took place. If the deals, however, did add to the market power of companies in the industry, one might expect some reaction based on the ability of the current participants to move prices to a level above marginal costs. In his sample of 11 mergers that were challenged on antitrust grounds under Section 7 of the Clayton Act, he found no statistically significant abnormal returns for 9 of the 11 mergers found. Of the other two, one showed positive abnormal returns and the other showed ambiguous results. These results fail to support the view that firms merge in an effort to seek monopoly power.

A similar study, also based on a doctoral thesis, was conducted by B. Epsen Eckbo, who looked at a larger sample of 126 horizontal

Exhibit 2.10     Relationship between Revenues and Costs
               at the Profit-Maximizing Level of Output

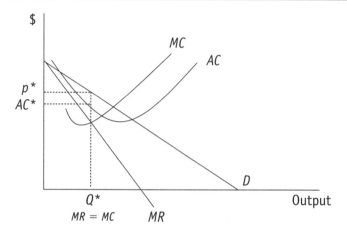

**(a) Profit Earned with Average Costs (*AC*) Below Price**

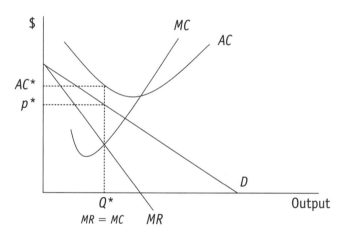

**(b) Profit Lost with Average Costs (*AC*) Above Price**

and vertical mergers in the manufacturing and mining industries.[39]
About half of this sample was horizontal mergers. In these deals,
there were an average of 15 rivals in each industry category. If the
market power hypothesis delineated earlier was valid, then negative
abnormal returns would be observed for firms in industries that had
announced mergers that were challenged on antitrust grounds. The
reasoning is that the merger is less likely when there is an antitrust

challenge. When challenges take place, negative abnormal returns should be associated with the announcement of the challenge. Eckbo found statistically insignificant abnormal returns. The study also showed that firms initially showed positive and statistically significant abnormal returns when the mergers were first announced but failed to show a negative response after the complaint was filed.

Like Stillman's results, Eckbo's research does not support the belief that firms merge to enjoy increases in market power. Curiously, Eckbo's results reveal that "stockholders of bidder and target firms in challenged (horizontal) mergers earn larger abnormal returns than do the corresponding firms in unchallenged mergers."[40] Eckbo concludes that the gains found in mergers are not related to increases in market power but rather are motivated by factors such as efficiency gains.

While the Stillman and Eckbo studies of the early 1980s provide little support for the pursuit of market power as a motive for M&As, more recent research implies that market power may be a motive for some deals. Specifically, Kim and Singal found that mergers in the airline industry during the late 1980s resulted in higher prices on routes served by merging firms compared to a control group of routes that were not involved in control transactions.[41] Some critics of deregulation have cited the unfettered ability of previously regulated competitors to merge and the subsequent increase in airfares as an example of failure of deregulation. Their study took into account many factors such as the existence of financially distressed firms as well as possible premerger excess supply and any postmerger quality improvements. Even after all of these factors were taken into account, they showed that market power and its associated price increases dominated any postmerger efficiency effects to result in a welfare loss. It should be noted that nowadays this industry has changed significantly, and some of the larger companies that may have derived market power from mergers have had difficulty being profitable. Smaller and more nimble competitors, such as Southwest and JetBlue, have been able to aggressively use price competition and better service to rapidly gain market share in selected markets and did so profitably. So we see that to the extent that the larger consolidated companies achieved market power through M&As, as long as the barriers to entry are not too formidable, new entrants may enter the industry and erode the gains a merged company may temporarily achieve.

Looking back at the research in this area, it appears that in some instances and in certain industries, such as the airline industry, the pursuit of market power through horizontal M&As *may* be one reason why some firms merge. This result is intuitive because it helps explain why companies may pay a premium over market value to buy rivals. If they can achieve market power, the present value of the post-transaction gains may offset the initial deal costs. However, companies contemplating such a strategy have to realize that such acquired market power may not be long lasting—depending on other economic factors such as the presence of barriers to entry. Long-term projections of market power–related merger gains may not be reasonable because economic rents derived through the achievement of acquired market power may be short lived.

## MERGING TO ACHIEVE THE BENEFITS OF VERTICAL INTEGRATION

Vertical integration refers to corporate movements that move either toward a source of supply (backward integration) or toward the market (forward integration). For example, most of the large petroleum companies are vertically integrated to varying degrees. So when a petroleum company owns its own oil fields and oil exploration companies while also refining its own oil and finally operating a retail gasoline sales network, such a company is vertically integrated. Being vertically integrated can provide certain obvious benefits. Having a captive source of supply may help prevent shortages or situations where supplies are only available at unpredictable and sometimes prohibitive prices. Having one's own retail network can also ensure that the company's products are able to get to the ultimate customer reliably. Thus being vertically integrated may provide competitive advantages and present greater profit opportunities while also being a risk-reduction tool. However, having these vertically integrated benefits comes at a price. The vertically integrated company may not excel at all of these different levels of operation. It may have to pay a high price for some of the components of this vertically integrated operation. These are decisions that a nonvertically integrated company has to make. Are the benefits of being vertically integrated through M&As worth the costs of such transactions? Can these benefits also be achieved through joint ventures and strategic alliance at a fraction of the costs of a complete acquisition? Such questions have to be answered on a case-by-case basis.

---

## BOISE CASCADE'S 2003 ACQUISITION OF OFFICEMAX

The acquisition of OfficeMax by Boise Cascade is an example of a vertical transaction, although it also represents an expansion into a related business in which Boise Cascade was already involved. Boise Cascade is headquartered in Boise, Idaho, and is best known for its involvement in the paper business. It operated five paper and pulp mills, two paper-covering facilities, and various paper distribution facilities as well as other corrugated container plants. The company was formed in a 1957 merger of the Boise Payette Lumber Company and the Cascade Lumber Company. However, in recent years, it shifted from being more of a manufacturer of paper products to being a distributor of office products. The movement from being a manufacturer of paper to selling paper to business and residential consumers is an example of a vertical movement. Before the acquisition of Office Max, office supplies constituted $3.5 billion of Boise Cascade's annual sales of $7.4 billion. The acquisition of the third largest office supply chain in the United States, Office Max, with almost 1,000 stores nationwide, was expected to double the size of Boise Cascade's office supply business to approximately $8.3 billion.[a]

The vertical move into the office supply business presented certain advantages to Boise Cascade. The paper business is cyclical, and the company believed that the office supply business provided some insulation from the ups and downs of the paper business. With this acquisition, the company became even more of an office supply company and less of a paper manufacturer and distributor. This raised speculation that the company might eventually sell off some or all of its paper business and concentrate more on the office supply business. The paper business had not generated great results for shareholders, and the company had been looking more and more at the office supply business for its future. The addition of OfficeMax now made Boise Cascade a more significant player in the office supply business. The vertical acquisition also allowed the company more of an internal distribution outlet to the eventual consumer of some of its paper products.

After Boise Cascade solidified its position in the office supply business by buying OfficeMax, it then completed its movement out of the paper manufacturing business by selling those assets, including its name, to Madison Dearborn Partners for $3.7 billion in July 2004. Boise CEO George Harad had been moving the company in this direction since he took the reins of the company in 1994. Since then he had closed some of the company's pulp mills and limited their production of paper products while enhancing its paper and office products distribution network.[b] The market has responded favorably to these moves.

---

a. Tara Craft, "Boise Cascade Boxes up OfficeMax," *Daily Deal* (July 15, 2003).
b. Claudia H. Deutsch, "Boise Cascade to Sell Assets to Madison for $3.7 Billion," *New York Times* (July 27, 2004): 12.

## SPECIAL CASES OF MERGERS MOTIVATED BY SPECIFIC NEEDS

In the remainder of this chapter, we discuss merger strategies that are based on specific motives or needs that companies may have. These needs are often based on specific circumstances that affect the companies or their industries. For example, we talk about the needs of pharmaceutical companies to make up for lack of products and insufficient productive research and development. However, while the discussion is specific to certain industries, it has many parallels to other industries. In addition, other situations that are discussed are mergers based on distributional needs.

### M&As to Acquire Products: Deals Instead of R&D

Productive research and development is a most important part of the future success of many corporations, but it is especially important for pharmaceutical companies. The R&D process has become costly and slow. Research has shown that the cost of developing a new drug now takes an average of 10 years and costs approximately $800 million.[42] The benefit of having successful R&D, however, is that products developed may be able to maintain protection for many years through patent laws. However, once the patent protection expires and the products have to compete against generics, sales and profits can decline dramatically. One of the answers of some pharmaceutical companies to an insufficient drug pipeline was to merge with other pharmaceutical companies. This was apparent in the fifth merger wave—a period that featured many megamergers among some of the world's largest drug companies. One such deal was the $73 billion megamerger between Glaxo Welcome and SmithKline Beecham. The strength of this merger was to combine the R&D efforts of these two large pharmaceutical companies. This deal put pressure on their competitors in this world of increasingly costly R&D efforts. Other companies such as Pfizer responded by outbidding American Home Products (now called Wyeth) in its efforts to acquire Warner Lambert. American Home Products was weighed down by its burdensome litigation liabilities and could not keep up with Pfizer's aggressive bidding, which earned it Warner Lambert for a price of $89 billion.

There is evidence that international acquisitions that are motivated by a desire to achieve synergies through enhanced R&D capabilities provide significant gains. Eun et al. showed that the source of some of the positive shareholder effects for Japanese acquirers of U.S. targets came from the R&D capabilities of the American companies.[43] These R&D resources were an important source of the gains that both target and bidders experienced.

It is not clear whether mergers and acquisitions in pursuit of acquired R&D have really been fruitful. While the pharmaceutical industry was a major industry player in the fifth merger wave, the various combinations of larger drug companies have not borne significant fruit in the form of introduction of many new drugs. For Pfizer, getting Warner Lambert was a boon. However, most of the deals failed to provide such bountiful gains. We have had a major consolidation in this industry yet the problem of slow and infrequent drug development continues. M&A is not the answer. While drug research and development itself has changed significantly over time and smaller companies may not be able to compete with some aspects of the modern drug R&D process, some of the newer consolidated drug companies are not yet showing significantly improved performance.

## M&As to Improve Distribution

A company can develop and manufacture a high-quality product but may not succeed sufficiently because of a weak distribution system. Distribution includes physical distribution, such as components of shipping and delivery, but more important it refers to the whole network through which a company provides the product to consumers. Included here is the all-important sales function. One alternative is to acquire another firm that is in the distribution business or is a competitor that is strong in this area. This is the alternative to internal development of a better distribution system. Such deals are a form of vertical integration. However, given the specialized nature of the deals and the importance they can have in the success of a company, we discuss them separately.

When a company decides to expand into distribution or to enhance its current distribution system, it needs to make sure that this form of expansion is the best use of the resources that are applied to the merger. For example, in the soft drinks business, many companies have decided that distribution was not nearly as profitable as the manufacture and marketing of the product. Many of these companies have decided to leave this business segment and sold their route system and even the whole bottling processes to their distributors. This allows the makers of the product to fully enjoy the value of their brand name while allowing others to pursue the part of the overall marketing and distribution process to others.

It is important to make sure that the company you are thinking of acquiring can really deliver the distribution benefits you anticipate. As obvious as this may seem, the failed mergers between Merck and Medco are an example of a deal that was supposed to enhance the distribution of Merck's drugs into the hands of consumers. This acquisition, which was discussed earlier, was based on a failed strategy for how drug distributors could provide such services to an acquirer relative to other companies that the market felt it was obligated to distribute on an even-field basis. Once again, failed conceptualization of how the deal would work help lead to this failure.

It is important for companies that are contemplating a merger or acquisition as a means of ensuring or enhancing their distribution to realize that there are sometimes other ways to achieve this goal. Sometimes long-term agreements with distributors can be the answer. Another may be a joint venture, which achieves some of the same goals that could be achieved through an outright acquisition. Pepsi reached a similar decision in 1997 when it concluded that it did not need to own fast-food restaurants outright to ensure that its soft drinks would be sold there. Pepsi was happy with its returns from the soft drink business and was not impressed by the returns from the fast-food business. Pepsi had an established brand name that was second only to the lofty Coca-Cola. The fast-food business, however, was highly competitive and sometimes did not provide the returns that Pepsi was interested in achieving. Its solution was to spin off its fast-food businesses. This included combining restaurants such as the Pizza Hut, Taco Bell, and Kentucky Fried Chicken chains into an entity by the name of Tricon Global Restaurants. Pepsi had previously acquired these chains in part to lock up distribution of its Pepsi and related drinks at these important distribution channels. We have to bear in mind that if it did not do so, then these channels could have become aligned with Coke, leaving Pepsi out in the cold. Pepsi's solution was to acquire the businesses. This expensive proposition required Pepsi to invest considerable capital in the restaurant business—a business it really did not want to be in. Its ultimate solution was to spin off the businesses while also reaching a long-term agreement with the umbrella entity for all three of them, which required the restaurants to still serve as an outlet for the Pepsi brand. In doing so, Pepsi was eventually able to leave that business and focus on what it did best—market major brands of soft drinks.

## CONCLUSION

It is clear that companies merge for a variety of reasons. The most fundamental one is to achieve more rapid growth. Sometimes the fastest way to achieve growth is through a merger or an acquisition with another company. The choice is between internal expansion versus an acquisition of another company. M&As can enable a company to grow faster than through internal expansion. However, this enhanced growth may come at a price—the premium that the bidder has to pay to acquire control of the target. It is not obvious, however, that this cost is higher than the cost of going the internal expansion route. Both avenues contain subtle costs, some of which are only known with the passage of time.

Another often-cited motive is synergy, which can come in two main forms: operating synergies and revenue-enhancing synergies. Operating synergies usually refer to corporate combinations that allow the combined entity to achieve efficiency gains such as lower average costs of some types. Revenue-enhancing synergies allow the combined entity to realize greater revenues than the individual unmerged companies could achieve on their own. Of the two types of synergies, revenue-enhancing synergies are the most difficult to achieve, and most acquirers tend to focus on operating synergies by instituting postmerger cost-cutting programs. Before the merger, acquirers may assert that they plan on achieving revenue enhancements by means of the merger. However, part of the negative reaction that the market registers when bidders announce proposed acquisitions may be explained by its skepticism with respect to such revenue enhancements.

Several other factors can explain why companies choose to merge with one another. Some of these are what may be referred to as the economic motives: diversification, merging to achieve market power, and merging to be a vertically integrated company. Being diversified may help insulate a company from the volatility that may be present in some aspects of its business. Although this is a benefit, a company contemplating doing this has to determine if the costs of doing this at the corporate level are outweighed by the fact that the company's shareholders can readily achieve such diversification within their own investment portfolio at a comparably modest and individually specific cost. Research studies have not painted a favorable picture of diversification benefits, but certain types of these transactions, related diversifications, seem to provide some positive benefits.

Market power, the ability to be able to raise price above a competitive level, is sometimes pursued as a motive for a merger or an acquisition. No meaningful research evidence has shown that companies generally pursue this goal. However, some instances, such as the airline industry, seem to indicate that market power may have played a role in some of the deals in that industry which has consolidated so much. The fact that many of the large companies that were formed partially through many mergers are not profitable and have been losing market share to smaller, more profitable rivals, underscores the fact that any market power gains may be short lived, assuming they even exist at all.

Companies do merge with and acquire other companies to become vertically integrated. Vertical transaction may help a company move toward its sources of supply, *backward integration*, or toward the market, *forward integration*. These deals are a kind of insurance policy whereby a company ensures itself of a dependable source of supply or that it will have dependable access to the market. Whether this is the most cost-effective way of achieving these benefits is another issue.

Companies merge for other specialized reasons, depending on the circumstances. For example, with the drug pipeline declining at some major pharmaceutical companies, some of the acquirers of other companies sought to enhance their R&D programs. Unfortunately, it appears that many of the heralded merger failures of the fourth and fifth merger waves can be attributed to nothing other than managerial hubris. This allowed companies to pay hefty premiums for targets that, in retrospect, were not worth the costs of the deal.

## ENDNOTES

1. Adolf A. Berle and Gardiner C. Means, *The Modern Corporation & Private Property* (New Brunswick, NJ: Transaction Books, 2003).
2. William J. Baumol, *Business Behavior, Value and Growth* (New York: McMillian, 1959).
3. Gordon Donaldson, *Managing Corporate Wealth* (New York: Praeger, 1984).
4. Jack Welch and John A. Byrne, *Jack* (New York: Warner Business Books, 2001), pp. 108–113.
5. Steven J. Piloff, "Performance Changes and Shareholder Wealth Creation Associated with Mergers of Publicly Trading Banking Institutions," *Journal of Money, Credit and Banking* 28 (1996): 294–310.
6. G. Gorton and R. Rosen, "Corporate Control, Portfolio Choice and the Decline of Banking," *Journal of Finance* 50, no. 5 (1995): 1377–1420.

7. Joel Houston, Christopher James, and Michael Ryngaert, "Where Do Merger Gains Comes From? Bank Mergers From the Perspective of Insiders and Outsiders," *Journal of Financial Economics* 60 (2001): 285–331.

8. Michael Bradley, Anand Desai, and Kim E. Man, "Synergistic Gains from Corporate Acquisitions and Their Division Between Shareholders and Acquiring Firms," *Journal of Financial Economics* 21 (1988): 3–40.

9. Mark Mitchell and J. Harold Mulherin, "The Impact of Industry Shocks on Takeover and Restructuring Activity," *Journal of Financial Economics* 41 (1996): 193–229.

10. Gregor Andrade and Erik Stafford, "Investigating the Economic Role in Mergers," *Journal of Corporate Finance* (2004): 1–36.

11. Jeff Madura, *Financial Markets and Institutions* (New York: Thompson Financial, 2003), pp. 516–521.

12. Gregor Andrade, Mark Mitchell, and Erik Stafford, *Journal of Economic Perspectives* (Spring 2001): 103–120.

13. Andrew Ross Sorkin, "$58 Billion Deal to Unite 2 Giants of U.S. Banking," *The New York Times* (January 15, 2004): 1.

14. Peter Moreira and Heidi Moore, "J.P. Morgan to Acquire Bank One for $60 B," *The Daily Deal* 11, no. 9 (January 15, 2004).

15. Landon Thomas, Jr. "An Outcast from Citigroup Will Inherit the Leadership of a Mergerd Global Rival," *The New York Times* (January 15, 2004): C1.

16. Emily Thornton and Joseph Weber, "A Made to Order Megamerger: Bank One Will Supply J.P. Morgan Chase with the Top Talent It Needed," *BusinessWeek* (January 26, 2004): 48.

17. Kenneth Martin and John J. McConnell, "Corporate Performance, Corporate Takeovers and Management Takeover," *Journal of Finance* 46, no. 2 (June 1991): 671–687.

18. Mark L. Mitchell and Kenneth Lehn, "Do Bad Bidders Become Good Targets?" *Journal of Political Economy* 98, no. 2 (1990): 372–398.

19. Larry Lang, Rene M. Stulz, and Ralph A. Walking, "Managerial Performance, Tobins q and the Gains From Unsuccessful Takeovers," *Journal of Financial Economics* 24 (1989): 137–154; and Henri Servaes, "Tobins q and the Gains from Takeovers," *Journal of Finance* 46, no. 1 (March 1991): 409–419.

20. Richard Roll, "The Hubris Hypothesis of Corporate Takeovers," *Journal of Business* 59, no. 2 (April 1986): 197–216.

21. P. Dodd, "Merger Proposals, Managerial Discretion and Stockholder Wealth," *Journal of Financial Economics* 8 (June 1980): 105, 138.

22. C.E. Eger, "An Empirical Test of the Redistribution Effect of Mergers," *Journal of Financial and Quantitative Analysis* 18 (December 1983): 547–572.

23. Paul Asquith, "Merger Bids, Uncertainty and Stockholder Returns," *Journal of Financial Economics* 11 (April 1983): 51–83.

24. Sara Moeller, Frederik P. Schlingemann and Rene Stulz, "Firm Size and the Gains from Acquisitions," *Journal of Financial Economics* 73 (2004): 201–228.

25. Mathew L.A. Hayward and Donald C. Hambrick, "Explaining Premiums Paid for Large Acquisitions: Evidence of CEO Hubris," *Administrative Science Quarterly* 42, no. 1 (1997): 103–127.

26. Robert G. Hansen, "A Theory for the Choice of Exchange Medium in Mergers and Acquisitions," *Journal of Business* 60 (January 1987): 75–95.

27. Michael Gort, "Diversification, Mergers and Profits," *The Corporate Merger* (Chicago: University of Chicago Press, 1974), p. 38.

28. Michael Adler and Michael Dumas, "International Portfolio Choice and Corporation Finance: A Synthesis," *Journal of Finance* (June 1983).

29. L. Faiver, J. F. Houston, and A. Naranjo, "Capital Market Development, Integration, Legal Systems, and the Value of Corporate Diversification: A Cross-Country Analysis," University of Florida Working Paper, April 1999.

30. As with so much of research in corporate finance, however, some opposing evidence fails to support this view. Studies that compared developed with undeveloped markets failed to find support for the internal capital markets view of diversification discounts.

31. P.G. Berger and E. Ofek, "Diversification's Effect on Firm Value," *Journal of Financial Economics* 37, no. 1 (January 1995): 39–65.

32. Robert Comment and Gregg Jarrell, "Corporate Focus and Stock Returns," *Journal of Financial Economics* 37, no. 1 (January 1995): 67–87.

33. Owen Lamont and Christopher Polk, "Does Diversification Destroy Value: Evidence from the Industry Shocks," *Journal of Financial Economics* 63 (2002): 51–77.

34. Nancy L. Rose and Andrea Shepard, "Firm Diversification and CEO Compensation: Managerial Ability or Executive Entrenchment," *Rand Journal of Economics* 28, no. 3 (Autumn 1997): 489–514.

35. Randall Morck, Andrei Shleifer, and Robert Vishny, "Do Managerial Objectives Drive Bad Acquisitions," *Journal of Finance* 45, no. 1 (March 1990): 31–48.

36. R.M. Morck and B. Yeung, "Why Investors Sometimes Value Size and Diversification: The Internalization Theory on Synergy," University of Alberta Working Paper, 1997.

37. Dennis W. Carlton and Jeffrey M. Perloff, Modern Industrial Organization, 4th ed. (New York: Pearson Addison Wesley, 2005), pp. 642–643.

38. Robert S. Stillman, "Examining Antitrust Policy Towards Mergers," Ph.D. dissertation, University of California at Los Angeles, 1983. This dissertation was later published in the *Journal of Financial Economics* 11, no. 1 (April 1983): 225–240.

39. B. Epsen Eckbo, "Horizontal Mergers, Collusion and Stockholder Wealth," *Journal of Financial Economics* 11, no. 1 (April 1983): 241–273.

40. Ibid.

41. E. Han Kim and Vijay Singal, "Mergers and Market Power: Evidence from the Airline Industry," *American Economic Review* 83, no. 3 (June 1993): 549–569.

42. "Why Do Prescription Drugs Cost So Much?," Pharmaceutical Research and Manufacturers of America, Washington, D.C., June 2000.

43. Cheol Eun, Richard Kolodny, and Carl Scheraga, "Cross Border Acquisitions and Shareholder Wealth: Test of the Synergy and Internalization Hypothsis," *Journal of Banking and Finance* 20 (1996): 1559–1582.

# Case Study

# Vivendi

Vivendi Universal SA (Vivendi) is a colorful case study involving a stodgy French water utility run by a CEO who wanted to be a high-flying leader of an international media company. He eventually transformed this water utility into a media giant. The only problem was that he sacrificed shareholders' interests to do so. Shareholders picked up the tab for his grandiose dreams, and when these dreams failed, he walked away with too much of their money in his pockets and in the pockets of others he brought in to assist with his schemes. This is not the story of a crook who willfully robbed the company. There were plenty of those in the 1990s and early 2000s. Although we know of investigations of accounting irregularities at Vivendi, as of this writing we are not aware of any finding of criminal wrongdoing. However, Vivendi's CEO, Jean-Marie Messier, nonetheless did the company and its shareholders a disservice, and he and the board that allowed him to do this were wrong.

Vivendi's roots come from being a 100-year-old water utility that was housed in an entity that they eventually called Vivendi Environment SA. When the division was eventually sold off as part of the bust-up of the company, it raised 2.5 billion euros. This was to be a relatively small amount compared to the losses that Messier's media empire would generate.

## VIVENDI'S DISMAL FINANCIAL PERFORMANCE

If Vivendi's financial performance was good, no one would question that apparent lack of synergy between Vivendi's water and entertainment industry assets. Unfortunately, the combination of the two produced very poor results. The company lost 23 billion euros in 2002, which followed a 13.6 billion euro loss in 2001 (see Exhibit A). This was the largest corporate loss in French history. Vivendi cannot be proud that its 2002 23.6 billion euro loss narrowly passed the prior record of 23 billion euros that was held by French Telecom. As the situation worsened in 2002, major shareholders called for action, but they were just a few years too late.

Vivendi's troubles can be traced to its failed acquisition strategy and the manner in which it financed these acquisitions. As the value of the company's assets—including its expensive acquisitions—fell, it announced in August 2002 that it would take charge of 10 billion euros against the company's second-quarter earnings to account for

**Exhibit A**
Vivendi's Net Income Loss

*Source:* John Tagliabue, "Vivendi Posts $25 Billion Loss; Will Explore Selling Assets," *New York Times* (March 7, 2003).

**Exhibit B**
Bonds and When They Are Due

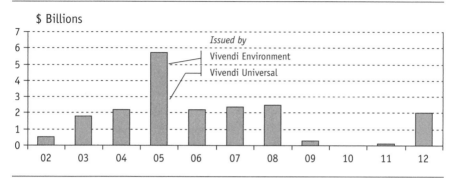

*Source:* John Tagliabue, "Vivendi Posts $25 Billion Loss; Will Explore Selling Assets," *New York Times* (March 7, 2003).

depreciation of its assets and impairment of goodwill.[1] The total charge for the year was 12.6 billion euros, of which about half was against the value of Canal Plus.[2] The poor financial performance of the company caused its bonds to fall to junk status (see Exhibit B).

## VIVENDI AND MESSIER'S ACQUISITION STRATEGY

Messier was apparently not satisfied to be the CEO of a water utility. Water utilities are not exciting or sexy. However, being the CEO of a water utility was the position that he was offered and accepted. If he thought he would have done better as CEO of a major entertainment company, he could have had headhunters pursue such a position for him. Apparently, there were no acceptable offers. His solution? Take a boring water utility and use its assets and cash flows to create that dream job that he wanted.

Messier had a deal maker's background. He was formerly an investment banker at Lazard LLC, where he spent six years of his business career. If you put an investment banker at the helm of a water utility, odds are that he is going to do investment banker–like

---

1. John Carreyrou, "Vivendi Universal Sets Charge up to $9.78 Billion," *The Wall Street Journal* (August 13, 2002): A3.

2. "Messier Mess," Economist (June 6, 2002), *www.economist.com.*

work. At least if he does that, you can't say you are surprised because this was his background and you, the company that put him in that position, knew what his background was. Messier pursued his dream of being an entertainment CEO by engaging in major acquisition of entertainment companies.

One of Messier's big deals was to buy Seagram Universal in 2000. This sale gave the Bronfmans, major shareholders in Seagram, 88.9 million shares in Vivendi, which constituted 8.9% of the company.[3] This acquisition marked Vivendi's major foray into the media industry by buying a business that was a combination between the liquor and soft drinks company, Seagram, and the Universal movie studio. It is ironic that Messier would buy Seagram Universal because this company was formed by the acquisition engineered by young Edgar Bronfman when he took a leadership position at Seagram. We can suspect that he always wanted to be in the exciting movie and record production business, and the beverage business was not enough for him. He used the assets and cash flows of the Seagram family business to finance a venture into the entertainment sector. This deal went through its own rocky period as the movie business proved to not be as exciting to Seagram shareholders as Mr. Bronfman may have thought it was. We will discuss Seagram's own troubles further later.

Messier's acquisition plans did not stop with Seagram Universal. He then bought Canal Plus, a pay-cable French TV network. It also owned shares in British Sky Broadcasting. He then purchased Barry Diller's USA Networks in December 2001 for $10.3 billion, only to see its value drop like many other Messier purchases. The deal brought together the Universal Studios Group with the entertainment assets of the USA Networks to form what they called Vivendi Universal Entertainment. Like with so many other acquisitions, Vivendi stated that it hoped to realize significant synergies that would "improve content, ratings and subscriber fees."[4]

Messier paid 12.5 billion euros for Canal Plus, even though any buyer was significantly limited in its ability to change the European

---

3. "The Bronfman Family Feels Messier's Pain," *The New York Times* (April 25, 2002).
4. Vivendi Universal Press Release, December 17, 2001.

cable company to make programming more profitable. In fact, Canal Plus was not profitable and had approximately 2.8 billion euros in debt.[5] Messier also bought a 44% stake in Cegetal, a French phone company that owned 80% of SFR, France's second biggest mobile phone operator. Vivendi also purchased book publisher Houghton Mifflin for $2.2 billion, which included $500 million in debt. The company also owns an equipment division, which holds U.S. Filter Corporation. At least this company has some connection to the water business in that filters can be used to purify water, but even that is a stretch.

It is hard to see the synergies that Messier saw. Perhaps you had to be inside his mind to understand it. The market certainly did not see it, because the strategy was a dismal failure. "Messier's dream of French cellular phone users dialing up Vivendi Universal-owned songs, movies, and other entertainment content while heading from the Metro succumbed to an increasingly competitive mobile phone market, expensive UMTS third-generation phone licenses and other draining factors."[6]

Exhibit C shows the breadth of Vivendi's business units at the "peak" of its acquisition strategy. Exhibit D shows the market's reaction to Messier's folly.

## SEAGRAM'S OWN HISTORY OF FAILURE IN THE ENTERTAINMENT BUSINESS

As mentioned earlier, the Seagrams and the Bronfmans encountered problems in their own failed acquisition strategy. Ironically, some of their problems came from forays into the media business—something they would be involved in years later. Edgar Bronfman, Jr. was named CEO of the Seagram family company on June 1, 1994. The company had made an impressive name for itself through major positions in the soft drink and liquor businesses. At that time, the

---

5. See note b.
6. Alan Tiller, "Horror Movie: Vivendi's Deal for Seagram Transformed a Water Company into a Film and Music Giant," *The Daily Deal* (June 12, 2002): 24.

## Exhibit C
### Vivendi Universal's Media and Entertainment Properties

| MUSIC | | AMUSEMENT PARKS | |
|---|---|---|---|
| | 1/02–5/02 | | 2001 |
| Albums Sold in U.S. | 73.4 million | Worldwide Visitors | 31.2 million |
| Share of Sales | 27.90% | Amusement Park Chain | |
| Worldwide Sales 2001 | $5.8 billion | Rank | 3rd |

| MOVIES | | COMPUTER SOFTWARE | |
|---|---|---|---|
| Universal Pictures | 1/02–6/02 | PC Games | 1/02–5/02 |
| Box Office Sales | $532.2 million | U.S. Retail Unit Share | 12.7% |
| Box Office Share | 12.0% | | |
| U.S. Studio Rank | 3rd | | |
| Focus | | Educational Software | |
| Box Office Sales | $54.0 million | U.S. Retail Unit Share | 16.8% |
| Box Office Share | 1.2% | | |
| U.S. Studio Rank | 11th | | |

| EDUCATIONAL PUBLISHING | | CABLE TV | |
|---|---|---|---|
| School Books | 2001 | USA Networks | 4/02–6/02 |
| Estimated U.S. Sales | $820 million | Avg. Daily Viewers | 943,000 |
| Share of U.S. Sales | 16.4% | Cable Network Rank | 7th |
| College Books | | Sci-Fi Networks | |
| Estimated U.S. Sales | $188 million | Avg. Daily Viewers | 402,000 |
| Share of U.S. Sales | 7.0% | Cable Network Rank | 20th |

*Source:* Steve Lohr, "Shake Up at Vivendi: The Industry," *New York Times* (July 3, 2002): 1.

family's holdings were valued at $4.1 billion. With young Bronfman at the helm, Seagram sold its stake in DuPont for $8.8 billion. The company then bought 80% of MCA from Matsushita on April 6, 1995. As of this time, the value of the family's holdings were reported to equal $3.8 billion. Edgar was moving from boring to more exciting businesses, while the family was picking up the tab and losing money as a result. In his defense, Edgar appeared to be seeking growth, and the media business seemed to provide higher growth than the

### Exhibit D
### Vivendi's Stock Price Decline

*Source:* finance.yahoo.com.

chemical business. He also liked music, and Universal Music must have had a special appeal to him. He was reported to have written some of his own songs, of which some had been published. It would have been cheaper for his family, however, to buy him a few CDs than to buy the whole company.

The next major move for Bronfman was to sell Seagram's cable channels and a stake in Universal Studios to Barry Diller's HSN on October 20, 1997 (see Exhibit E). At this time, the market valued the company's holdings at $6.1 billion. This was during the midst of the 1990s market boom, and the family's holdings grew like those of many families—it is just that this family's assets are on a far grander scale. The *New York Times* reported their value to peak in March 2000 at $6.9 billion. Here they started on their downward spiral. Media reports have indicated that Bronfman and Diller did not get along, perhaps because Diller got the best of Bronfman in the sale of Universal's television assets, which Diller was able to sell back to Vivendi at a sizable profit. These reports questioned whether Bronfman should have sold the assets in the first place.[7]

---

7. Laura Holson and Geraldine Fabrikant, "Bronfman's Humbled by Their Own Moves," *The New York Times* (July 3, 2002): 1.

### Exhibit E
### Value of Bronfman Family Holdings

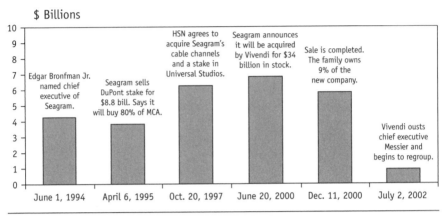

$ Billions

| Edgar Bronfman Jr. named chief executive of Seagram. | Seagram sells DuPont stake for $8.8 bill. Says it will buy 80% of MCA. | HSN agrees to acquire Seagram's cable channels and a stake in Universal Studios. | Seagram announces it will be acquired by Vivendi for $34 billion in stock. | Sale is completed. The family owns 9% of the new company. | Vivendi ousts chief executive Messier and begins to regroup. |

| June 1, 1994 | April 6, 1995 | Oct. 20, 1997 | June 20, 2000 | Dec. 11, 2000 | July 2, 2002 |

*Source:* Laura M. Holson and Geraldine Fabrikant. "Shake-up at Vivendi: The Family; A Wealthy Family Humbled by Its Own Moves," *New York Times* (July 3, 2002).

## MESSIER'S CHANGE IN FOCUS

The change in focus of Jean-Marie Messier was underscored when in the midst of his acquisition binge he, the CEO of this water/world-wide media company, moved to New York on September 4, 2001. To say that Messier was filled with hubris seems to be an understatement. He concedes that this may be a normal characteristic of a CEO. In his book he stated: "Don't ask a CEO to be modest. The costume does not fit him. A strong ego, not to say an outsized one, is more becoming, although each has its way of wearing it."[8] We would have to say that when this ego leads the company down the path of billions in losses, it can be draining on the value of investors' portfolios.

Messier was a colorful fellow who seemed to love the limelight, especially the lights in New York. His focus on U.S. business drew concern from the French, who felt he was forsaking his homeland for

---

8. Bruce Orwall, John Carreyrou, and Martin Peers, "For Vivendi's CEO a High Profile Preceded the Fall," *The Wall Street Journal* (July 2, 2002): A12.

the more exciting United States. Messier appeared on TV shows and in glossy magazines, while his strategy was leading the company down the path to record-setting losses.

## CHANGE IN CONTROL

When Vivendi's major shareholders decided, very late in the game, that they could not take any more foolish acquisition schemes, they decided to replace Messier. This, in part, came from the Bronfmans, who called for an emergency shareholder meeting to replace Messier with someone who French directors would find acceptable (i.e., another Frenchman).[9] They named Jean-René Fourtou, a former chemical and pharmaceutical executive, to replace Messier. Vivendi seemed to tire of the limelight-loving Messier and replaced him with a more conservative executive who was known to sacrifice media attention for the overall benefit of the business. This was the case when Fourtou agreed to take a back seat to German executive, Jurgen Dormann, to make the cross-border merger between Rhone-Poulenc SA and Hoechst AG.[10] The combination of these two companies created the French-German drug giant—Aventis SA. Fourtou had a very different background than that of Messier. Messier was an investment banker, while Fourtou had a management background that involved running companies. One concern that immediately arises is that Fourtou's background is in the pharmaceutical business, having spent 13 years at Rhone-Poulenc, which is a very different business than the water or media business. Fourtou also had worked for 12 years at the French consulting firm of Bossard & Michael, where he left as head of the company.[11]

The call for changes at Vivendi came from not just its investors but also its creditors. The company's three main creditors, Societe Generale, BNP Paribus SA, and Deutsche Bank AG, began to be concerned

---

9. Ibid.
10. John Carreyrou and Vanessa Fuhrmans, "Vivendi Names CEO with Skills Messier Lacked," *The Wall Street Journal* (July 5, 2002): A9.
11. Ibid.

about their capital, which was being put at risk with the acquisition strategy that was not panning out. Their concern was underscored when they initially refused to give the company a standby line of credit when it encountered a liquidity crisis in 2002, unless they could be convinced that a management structure was in place that would lead the company back to profitability.

Vivendi also made changes to the board of directors. It named two French captains of industry, Claude Bebear and Henri Lachmann, to join the board and focus on finance and business strategy.[12] The backlash against Messier in France was quite strong. LeMonde portrayed Messier "as a tearful schoolboy in a Napoleonic hat phoning Hollywood, President Jacques Chirac, Uncle Sam, and his mother for help. This cover article, reporting accusations that Vivendi padded 2001 profits, helped panic the market, on a day Moody's lowered its rating on Vivendi's bonds to junk status."[13]

Messier did not leave Vivendi with empty pockets. He received a severance package valued at about 18 million euros in addition to the $17.5 million that the company paid for a New York apartment for him.[14] The apartment proved to be a contentious issue after he was ousted, because his lucrative compensation package, which was coming after such a dismal corporate performance, drew the ire of investors and the market. The fact that he so eagerly accepted this severance package is somewhat ironic in light of the fact that he had been critical of such packages and golden parachute agreements in his own book: *J6M.com*. In that book he criticized the large severance package given to Philippe Jaffre, who was former CEO of Elf-Aquitaine SA. The wording of Messier's own criticism, as cited in the *Wall Street Journal*, is pretty humorous when you apply it to the package he received a few years after the book was published:

---

12. Mark Landler and Suzanne Kapner, "Industrial Elite of France Reclaims Helm at Vivendi," *The New York Times* (July 5, 2002): C1.

13. Donald G. McNeil Jr., "Little Sympathy for Vivendi's Ousted Chief: A Glutton and Overpaid," *The Wall Street Journal:* C4.

14. John Carreyrou and Martin Peers, "Messier Bids Adieu for $17.8 Million," *The Wall Street Journal* (July 3, 2002): A3.

The possibility of being fired . . . is part of the normal risk inherent to the job of CEO. My contract has no such clause. And I pledge never to negotiate one with my board.

Now that we know what he actually received, this passage is pretty funny. When it came to his own money, human nature kicked in as it so often does. This is something to keep in mind when we read other books by business leaders who feel a need to paint themselves in such glowing terms.

It was very nice that the board finally made management changes well after the acquisition binge that the company went on over a period of years generated many billions in losses. Where were they when these absurd schemes were concocted? Letting a CEO come in and invest many billions of dollars in acquisitions that clearly have little synergy with the core business and that are in risky sectors that the company's management knows little about is not what the directors are paid for. They are there to look after shareholders' investments and to challenge such ill conceived uses of shareholder's capital. The board and the large shareholders who allowed these investments also have to share the blame. The replacement of Messier was a good idea—it just came years too late. When he started to propose such grandiose schemes, the board should have asked him to leave and get someone else in there who could run the business. However, when they got such a flashy investment banker to run the company, what did they expect? Once again, there is plenty of blame to go around.

## POST-FAILURE RESTRUCTURING

Like many acquisition failures, Vivendi began a process of reversing the errors by selling off assets. For example, in April 2002, it sold off its health and business publishing units for 1 billion euros.[15] In 2004 Vivendi sold its Universal Entertainment business to GE's NBC unit for $14 billion. It would have been interesting to know if Jack Welsh

---

15. "Vivendi Agrees to Sell Publishing Unit to Cut Debt," *The New York Times* (April 19, 2002): 1.

would have approved the further expansion of GE into the more risky media and entertainment business. The assets' sales were used to pay down the company's debt and relieve its liquidity crisis. A much slimmed-down Vivendi was left to move into the future.

## LESSONS OF THE VIVENDI FAILURE

The troubles of Vivendi and its poorly conceived acquisition binge provide some valuable lessons for would-be acquirers. Some of these are as follows:

- *Stick to what you know.* Companies should do this unless there are compelling reasons, such as a great business opportunity that will have a high likelihood of success.

- *Make sure you do not make the same mistakes that others did.* This is especially true for Vivendi because it should have learned from the failures of the Bronfman family with its forays into the media business.

- *Beware of the hubris-driven CEO.* Messier was but one of many CEOs who have led companies down the wrong acquisition path —driven by their own egos and blinded to any semblance of good business sense.

# 3

# Merger Success Research

One can try to evaluate the success of M&As by anecdotally considering some of the many deals that are clear failures and comparing them to the various transactions that most would agree are successes. We can then seek to informally extract from these good and bad deals what they did right and what were the possible causes of the failures and the successes. There is nothing intrinsically wrong with such a process, although it has major limitations. It may be easier to do this for a single industry where more common factors may be at play and there are a limited number of deals. However, if one wants to try to arrive at general conclusions that may be applied to prospective deals, then a more scientific process covering a larger number of deals and a longer time period would need to be used. For this reason, we review the various academic research studies that have analyzed merger failures and successes. We will seek to derive some pragmatic information from such studies. Our focus will not be just on studies, which try to determine if deals were failures or successes. Rather, we will more broadly examine research that focuses on different aspects of mergers. For example, we will examine studies that analyze merger premiums to try to discern what causes premiums, and possibly overpayment, to be greater. Some of this research tries to determine under what instances merger premiums were excessive.

Following our examination of selected research drawn from a wide range of studies, we will try to extrapolate various conclusions, which may be of use to merger planners. Although there never will be 100% assurance that the dynamics of prospective deals will correspond to statistics drawn from a wide range of historical studies, managers contemplating mergers and boards approving them should be aware of the knowledge drawn from such studies so they might avoid errors that others have committed.

## CRITERIA FOR DEFINING MERGER SUCCESS USING RESEARCH STUDIES

To begin to research what kinds of deals are successes, we need to agree on criteria for defining a success. What do we want such research to show? One can design a simple study that compares the stock price of the acquiring firm before and after a given deal. We could try to see if the stock price is higher after a deal and then use this finding to make a statement about the benefits of the transaction. However, as we think about such a research design, we can quickly see its deficiencies. It could be that other factors, such as the movements of the market, explain the change. For example, the market rose 10% over the year after the deal while the company's stock price rose only 7%. Put in that light, we would take the rising stock price, which did not increase as much as the market, to be a sign of failure, not merger success.

In light of the lack of a common or benchmark factor, we could expand our research model to include a benchmark. One such measure could be the S&P 500, which is a broad market index that is commonly used to reflect general market movements. We then could conduct a statistical analysis that defines success as returns in excess of the benchmark performance over the study period. Returns in excess of the market return then have to be explained by other factors. We then have to determine if other factors are less significant than the merger, leaving us to conclude that the excess returns are attributable to the merger. The longer the window of analysis, the more likely it is that other factors beyond the merger play a role in explaining the excess returns. This is part of the appeal of studies that focus on a short analysis window where other factors do not enter into the analysis.

What we would ideally like to know is what the returns of the firm would have been without the deal and compare them to the actual returns with the deal. Unfortunately, while this is an ideal, researchers do not have access to the hypothetical returns without the deal. This information usually is unknowable, so we have to resort to our next best alternative, which are our benchmark studies.

## TAKEOVER PREMIUMS AND CONTROL

When an investor buys shares in a company, he or she is seeking to acquire the investment attributes that normally go along with share ownership—the right to a proportionate share of dividends paid and the hope for capital gains if the company does well. Unless the shares purchased are a significant percentage of total shares outstanding, investment purchases of equities usually do not provide the investors with any control of the company, because the shareholding is only a small percentage of the total shares outstanding. This is normally not an issue for investors because they are usually just seeking gains on their investments and are not typically interested in control of the company. However, when a bidder makes an offer for a target, it is seeking to acquire control of that company, and for this it must pay a *control premium*. This is a value in excess of the market price of the shares and varies depending on the degree of control that the purchaser is seeking. Over the period 1982–2003, control premiums have averaged 43.1% (see Exhibit 3.1). The control premium is the source of the gains that target shareholders receive. Having to pay a premium above what the market's valuation of small holdings of the shares puts pressure on the bidder to be able to generate gains from the control transaction in excess of the amount it pays, which includes the premium.

## INITIAL COMMENT ON MERGER RESEARCH STUDIES

There are two groups who do research in this area: academic researchers and private firm researchers. The academic researchers are usually professors of finance, and sometimes accounting or economics, who

Exhibit 3.1 Control Premiums

| Year | Control Premium Offer (%) |
| --- | --- |
| 1982 | 42.5 |
| 1983 | 37.8 |
| 1984 | 39.0 |
| 1985 | 37.3 |
| 1986 | 39.1 |
| 1987 | 38.2 |
| 1988 | 41.9 |
| 1989 | 41.8 |
| 1990 | 42.3 |
| 1991 | 35.4 |
| 1992 | 41.3 |
| 1993 | 38.7 |
| 1994 | 40.7 |
| 1995 | 44.1 |
| 1996 | 37.1 |
| 1997 | 35.9 |
| 1998 | 40.7 |
| 1999 | 43.5 |
| 2000 | 49.1 |
| 2001 | 58.0 |
| 2002 | 59.8 |
| 2003 | 63.0 |
| Average | 43.1 |

*Source: Mergerstat Review, 2004.*

conduct research as part of their academic responsibilities. The typical requirements of most professors are to teach, engage in scholarly activity such as research and the generation of publications, and provide service to their respective academic institutions. The research publication process in finance is similar to that in other scholarly areas. It usually involves one or more researchers doing a study that often gets presented to their colleagues at academic gatherings such as the American Finance Association or the Financial Management Association annual meetings. The work is presented to other academics in a session attended by those interested in the topic. There is usually a discussant who is assigned to comment on the worth of the research.

When researchers are satisfied with the quality of their papers, they would then submit them to a journal, such as the *Journal of Finance, Journal of Financial Economics, Financial Management,* or the various other scholarly journals that exist in the field of finance. The managing editors of these journals then sends the paper out for blind review to peer reviewers, who ideally do not know the names of the authors. The process is not without flaws because often the reviewers may already know who the authors are. In addition, the extent to which reviewers examine the research is variable. However, the review process does add elements of scrutiny that do not exist in other more informal research and publications processes. One drawback of this process is that it tends to be somewhat slow, and it can be years between when a study is started and when it is finally placed in the hands of readers. For example, an article can be sent back for revision by the reviewer, and the authors may have to rework the research to the reviewer's satisfaction. There may be a backlog of articles at the journal, so that it may be as long as a year before an accepted paper is formally published. While this is an annoyance in finance, in other scientific disciplines, such as medicine, where cures and treatments may be waiting the approval of a publication in a quality journal such as the *New England Journal of Medicine,* it may be even more troubling. For our purposes, where we want to extract knowledge not just from studies of recent trends but from an even longer historical time period that covers deals over several merger waves, this may be somewhat less of a problem.

The other avenue of research and publication, the nonacademic route, is where work is done in the private sector, such as the research that is done at investment banks. The research is often done by qualified researchers, who may have similar credentials to what one might find in an academic institution, such as a Ph.D. in finance or economics. The studies may be conducted at the research department of an investment bank, where the researchers are in close contact with those on the front lines of the transactional battles that may be taking place. An example of this are the various research studies done at Morgan Stanley on equity carve-outs and spin-offs. This work does not go through a peer review process, and because of this limitation, academia sometimes places less value on it. This is underscored by the fact that academic researchers often tend to cite only other peer-reviewed research while sometimes totally ignoring private-sector research. This situation is unfortunate, because it results in some potentially worthwhile work being ignored. Moreover, private-sector research tends to be much more timely, sometimes incorporating data that may be as current as the prior quarter. Such studies are often more regularly updated because they are not constrained by journal editors who may be reluctant to publish a similar study as one published a couple of years earlier but just updated to include more recent data while having similar conclusions.

In addition to not going through supposedly blind review, private-sector studies may have more potential for bias. An investment bank may not want to circulate a study that implies that companies should refrain from doing certain types of deals from which the institution derives income. Readers simply have to be aware of this bias potential. One classic example of such a research bias occurred when the investment bank of Kohlberg Kravis and Roberts issued a study heralding the great benefits of 13 leveraged buyouts they conducted.[1] Perhaps the number 13 jinxed them, but not too long after the study was issued, several of the companies featured in the study went bankrupt. This is simply a factor that must be kept in mind when evaluating this research.

## RESEARCH STUDIES

In this chapter we review various research studies with an eye on what they might tell us about potential mergers we may be considering. As part of that review, we will try to provide some details about the various studies so that the reader can better evaluate the extent to which the studies and their results are applicable to various situations they may be evaluating.

We can categorize merger research into two broad categories: short-term and long-term effects studies. The short-term effects studies tend to focus on narrow time windows around events, whereas long-term performance research tries to track the performance of deals over a longer period. The short-term studies are often criticized for being too myopic in that they attempt to evaluate deals based on the response of the stock market in a time window that may be as short

as days. Critics contend that M&A are inherently long-term investments by companies and cannot be evaluated based on the market's
reactions over a period of days. Some of these critics go on to assert
that this is a fundamental flaw in the way business is approached in
markets such as the United States, where we look only at short-term
effects and fail to have the necessary long-term focus that we might
see in other markets. Supporters of such research, however, say that
studies that show the market's initial reaction tend to be a good pre-
dictor of the actual long-term performance of a deal. These asser-
tions will be explored in detail when we review the various studies.
However, let us first review the basic methodology that is often used
in research in this area—the so-called event study methodology.

## Event Studies

Many of the short-term research studies utilize the event study
methodology. Shareholder returns are defined as the change in the
share price over the study period, $t$ and $t + 1$, in equation 3.1, plus
any dividends received during that time period.

$$R_{it} = [(P_{t+1} - P_t) + d_{t+1}]/P_t \qquad (3.1)$$

If researchers were to use unadjusted shareholder returns, they
would have to wonder if the returns they found around the
announcement of a deal were caused by a market-based movement
or were specific to the stock in question. For this reason, researchers
try to measure abnormal returns (AR), which are returns in excess of
the market movement (see equation 3.2). The change in the market
is usually measured by the variation in some benchmark such as the
S&P 500. These excess returns are usually summed over a period of
time with the result being referred to as cumulative abnormal or excess
returns (CAR).

$$AR = R - R_m \qquad (3.2)$$

## Short-Term Research: Bidders and Targets

The short-term research shows different effects for bidders than for
targets. These differences have tended to persist over many years
of research, where studies were done of samples drawn from different

time periods. We will start our discussions by considering some of the earlier research that continues to be cited today and then see how the conclusions put forward in that research have changed in light of more recent studies. It will become apparent that many of the conclusions that were reached in earlier research remain true when compared with later research.

One particularly noteworthy early paper was the survey of prior research done by Michael Jensen and Richard Ruback.[2] This survey showed that mergers created value for target company shareholders but left acquiring firm stockholders in a similar position to what they were in before the deal. Jensen and Ruback found that target firm shareholders in tender offers experienced 30% gains following the deal announcement, while mergers brought about 20% gains. They found that the bidder's stock had a 4% gain, while in a merger there were no changes in shareholder value. The 4% gain in tender offers is somewhat counterintuitive and should be taken with a grain of salt. The fact that they found gains in tender offers were higher than mergers and that both were significantly positive is an intuitive result.

Some look at this research and conclude that in general, mergers create value. However, that really depends on one's perspective. It also sheds light on the difference between an academic researcher's perspective and that of a practitioner. The difference between these two perspectives may help explain why academics looking at this study may conclude that mergers create value while practitioners conclude that mergers may result in losses. Engaging in such transactions is often a major endeavor for acquirers. Just how significant this is depends on the size of the deal. Doing a deal of a significant size— say, acquiring a company that is at least 10% or perhaps 20% of the size of the bidder—and being left in a similar position as before the deal usually would not be considered a success. Even worse would be to acquire such a company and incur losses for the bidder's own shareholders. It is of little benefit to the acquirer's shareholders to note that from a societal perspective, where we may choose to combine the losses of the bidder's shareholders with the gains of the target company's shareholders, the net effect was positive. All this means is that the bidder's shareholders helped finance the short-term gains of the target company's shareholders, who left the scene with the bidder's money in their pockets. To simply conclude that the net effects are positive because most, if not all, of the gains went to target equityholders is of little comfort to bidder shareholders. Because the bidder most likely is the one initiating the deal, we have to conclude that such deals are at best a disappointment from the bidder's perspective.

We should not draw too strong conclusions from studies such as those early ones reviewed in the Jensen and Ruback survey, because several important factors need to be considered. One factor is the size of the deal compared to the size of the bidder. The smaller the target is relative to the bidder, the less of an effect it should have on the stock price of the bidder. However, later studies have attempted to address the size effect and have come to somewhat similar conclusions as did Jensen and Ruback. Another factor to consider is that these early studies came from a period prior to the fourth and fifth merger waves where we witnessed an unprecedented volume of deals —including many deals that were very different from earlier periods. Considering early research is helpful but we may want to place more weight on more recent studies while still being mindful of the findings drawn from earlier periods. We will now review some of the later research.

## More Recent Research

Pursuing an area of focus derived from the Jensen and Ruback study, Bradley, Desai, and Kim analyzed a sample of 236 tender offers over the period 1963–1984.[3] This period covered the third merger wave through the start of the fourth wave. The time period of examination was a 10-day window—five days before and after the announcement of the bid. Their results were somewhat similar to the original Jensen and Ruback findings. Target shareholders gained 31.77%, while bidding shareholders received a gain that was less than 1% (0.97%). From the bidder's perspective, this is hardly a windfall. However, we must be cautious in interpreting the results, because targets are generally smaller than acquirers, so the impact on the buyer will usually be smaller. Nonetheless, the gains are less than spectacular. For target shareholders, it is a windfall. However, the results raise questions about the advisability of the bidder doing the deal in the first place.

Subsequent research has come up with similar findings to that of Bradley, Desai, and Kim. For example, Kaplan and Weisbach looked at 271 large acquisitions over the period 1971–1982.[4] They found that median bidder returns over a five-day window on either side of the announcement date were approximately −1.75%. Once again, the market was voicing its concern about acquisitions. As expected, median target returns were a positive 24.76%—not surprising with target shareholders being able to walk away with a significant premium. We will discuss the Kaplan and Weisbach study later in Chapter 6, when we discuss using divestitures and other forms of sell-offs to reverse bad deals. However, the Kaplan and Weisbach study segregated acquisitions that were subsequently divested and further separates those that can be considered failures from nonfailures in the divested group. One interesting result is the difference in the negative acquirer returns for those divested that were successful versus those that were not. Unsuccessful acquisitions that were divested had a −4.42% return, while those that were divested but judged to be successful (i.e., sold off at a price that would categorize it as a success from the bidder's perspective) had a −0.64 return. This implies that the market is fairly good at detecting the difference between successful deals and those that will not fare as well. It also further confirms that the market is somewhat negative on acquisitions in general. The fact that the market demonstrates the ability shown in the Kaplan and Weisbach study causes us to place even more weight on the consistently negative reaction to acquisition announcements by bidders.

### Are Certain Types of Bidders and Targets More Likely to Realize Certain Returns?

Two studies focused on financial characteristics of bidders and targets, as measured by their Tobin's q ratio. Tobin's q is a ratio developed by the late Nobel prize–winning economist and professor at Yale University, James Tobin.[5] It is defined in equation 3.3.

$$\text{Tobin's q} = \frac{\text{market value of debt} + \text{equity}}{\text{estimated replacement cost of assets}} \qquad (3.3)$$

The ratio is somewhat similar to a more often cited financial measure, the market-to-book ratio, which is the ratio of the stock price to the book value per share. In Tobin's q, we include the market value of the company's equity but also its debt securities, thus more broadly reflecting the company's capitalization. In the denominator, we include all assets, not just equity. We also try to include replacement costs of assets as opposed to a book value, such as in the market-to-book ratio, which would reflect historical costs. From a research perspective, we have to use the values on a company's books, which are recorded at original costs less accumulated depreciation, and adjust to reflect the inflationary increases in asset values that may have occurred.

Lang, Stulz, and Walking analyzed bidder and target abnormal returns in 87 successful tender offers over the period 1968–1986.[6] They found that total returns for bidders and targets were higher when targets have higher q ratios and bidders have lower q ratios. Bidders with higher q ratios tended to experience positive abnormal returns, whereas bidders with low q ratios tended to experience negative abnormal returns. They defined the best takeovers as those in which a company with a high q ratio took over a company with a low q value. They concluded that the worst combinations were those in which the bidder had a low q ratio and acquired companies with high q ratios. One way to interpret the meaning of a q ratio is that a higher q implies better management who are realizing higher firm values for the assets they are managing. A low q ratio may be interpreted as poor management. Applying this meaning implies that the greatest values to be achieved through tender offers are where better-managed companies take over more poorly managed targets. Their results imply that the market rewards deals where better-managed companies acquire less-well-managed firms because such combinations allow the acquirer's management to possibly realize more value from the less-well-managed target companies.

From the target's perspective, well managed targets, those with higher q ratios, benefit less from takeovers than less well managed companies which have lower q ratios. This makes sense from a managerial skills perspective as such well managed companies are not going to be improved by, and may even be hinder by, poorly managed bidders.

## SUNTRUST AND NCF: FALLING ACQUIRING
## AND RISING TARGET STOCK PRICES

An example of a negative market reaction to an acquirer's intentions to buy a target while responding favorably to the target's prospects is the May 2004 offer by SunTrust Banks, Inc. to buy National Commerce Financial Corp. (NCF). (See Exhibit A.) SunTrust made a $6.98 million offer for Memphis-based NCF. Several aspects of this bid caused the market to be less than enthused about its benefits to SunTrust. SunTrust became embroiled in a bidding contest with Cincinnati's Fifth Third Bancorp. Both companies made partially stock-financed offers, and NCF's board eventually determined that it preferred the SunTrust bid to the very similar Fifth Third Bancorp's bid, with both offers coming in around $33.46 per share. Under SunTrust's offer, it would pay NCF shareholders $1.8 billion in cash and 77.5 million shares. However, while SunTrust believed that the deal, which would make SunTrust the seventh largest bank in the United States, improved the long-term outlook for the bank, as with many acquisitions, the market did not agree.

The market sensed that SunTrust had many of the characteristics that research studies have shown are not favorable to bidders. First, it was a bidding contest in which SunTrust had to outbid a rival. This usually implies a higher cost. The second issue the market was concerned about was the fact that being a stock-financed offer, it brought with it the potential for equity dilution. The long-term benefits of NCF would have to be sufficient to offset these dilutive effects, and the market, by bidding down SunTrust's stock values, implied that it did not see such offsetting gains. The market also had a problem with the premium that SunTrust was paying, which was about 18 times estimated 2004 earnings. This was higher than other recent offer premiums for banks, such as the 15 times earnings premium paid by Royal Bank of Scotland PLC for Charter One Financial Corp/Citizens Financial Group, Inc. $10.5 billion deal.[a]

When we examine the market's reaction to the Royal Bank of Scotland's bid for Charter One, we see that the market does not discount all bidder's stock prices but focuses on those that have negative attributes such as overpricing (see Exhibit B). While the bid was substantial, the market believed that Royal Bank of Scotland did not overpay and that the deal had many strategic advantages, such as increasing Royal Bank's presence in the lucrative U.S. banking market. This is not to imply that

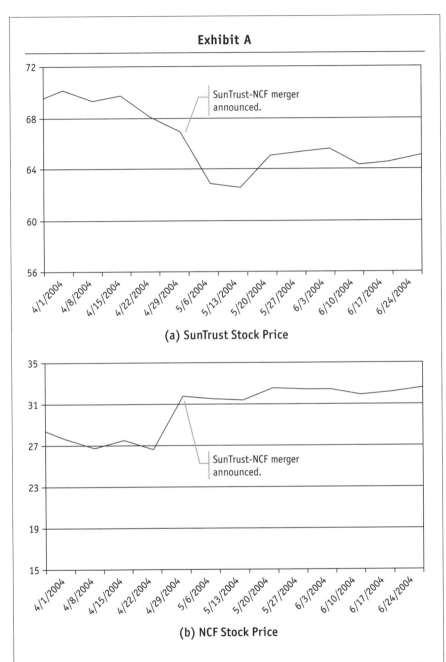

Exhibit A

(a) SunTrust Stock Price

(b) NCF Stock Price

Charter One's bid was cheap because the offer valued the Cleveland-based Charter One at 3.1 times its net asset value, which itself was higher than the recent average of many recent banking deals, which had been

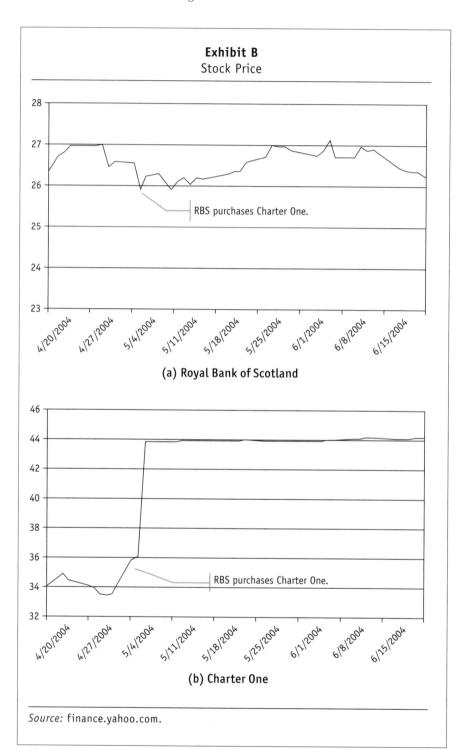

**Exhibit B**
Stock Price

(a) Royal Bank of Scotland

RBS purchases Charter One.

(b) Charter One

RBS purchases Charter One.

*Source:* finance.yahoo.com.

around 2.5 times net asset value.[b] The market, however, may have been impressed with the Royal Bank of Scotland's acquisition track record, and such a bidder might fall into the category of a better-managed acquirer.

The market for banks kept rising as 2004 progressed, as reflected by the $14.3 billion bid by Wachovia for SouthTrust. That stock-for-stock swap was a 20% premium above the preannouncement SouthTrust closing stock price of $41.83, which amounted to an offer that was 3.2 times the 2003 year-end book value of SouthTrust.[c]

---

a. Vipal Monga and Peter Moreira, "Sun Trust Stock Pounded Over NCF Deal," *Daily Deal* 12, no. 39 (May 11, 2004): 1.
b. Richard Thampson, "Royal Bank of Scotland Joins Top Tier of U.S. Bank with Charter One Bid," *Knight Ridder/Tribune Business News* (May 5, 2004).
c. Peter Moreira and Vipal Monga, "Wachovia Bids for Regional Heft with $14.3B SouthTrust Merger," *Daily Deal* 12, no. 68 (June 22, 2004): 1.

The Lang, Stulz, and Walking findings focused solely on tender offers, which are often hostile deals. Their findings are interesting, but they raise questions about whether they are applicable only to tenders offers or more generally to all kinds of deals. Henri Servaes of the University of Chicago analyzed takeover gains and the related q ratios for a large sample of both 704 mergers and tender offers over the period 1972–1987.[7] Servaes's findings confirmed the Lang, Stulz, and Walking findings and also determined that they apply both for mergers and for tender offers. Basically, he found that bidder, target, and total returns are higher when the target has a lower q ratio that is performing poorly and when the bidder is performing well as reflected by a higher q ratio. His findings were true after controlling for the characteristics of the offer—namely, whether it was a tender offer or a merger. This result is intuitive because if it were true for tender offers, there would be little reason why it would not also apply to mergers, as Servaes's research found it did.

The Lang, Stulz, and Walking and Servaes studies imply that if better-managed companies can find less-well-managed targets, there is an opportunity for both the bidder and the target to realize gains. Remember, target shareholders will gain, because the target will receive a premium. However, unless there is a real opportunity for the bidder to gain from the deal, the market may not reward such a takeover plan. However, when the acquirer is better managed and the target is not, the market senses an opportunity and reacts positively. The results of the study also imply that the market frowns on poorly managed bidders pursuing mergers and takeovers. This should be obvious because if a potential bidder is not managing its current assets well, why would the market believe that it could gain from expanding the assets under its control? Conversely, if a target is well managed, then it is going to be difficult for a bidder to come in and generate even better returns from the target's own assets. Moreover, if the target is realizing good values from its assets, then the bidder is going to have to pay a premium that reflects that. This puts great pressure on the bidder to do even better than the target's good managers. Occasionally, this will be possible, but the market, through its announcement reactions, is generally skeptical. Finally, these studies supported the improved management motive for M&As under the specific circumstances we have described.

## MERGERS OF EQUALS: ACQUIRERS VERSUS TARGET GAINS

We have reviewed various research studies, which showed that shareholder returns for bidders were either negative or zero, while target returns were positive. One exception to the dismal acquirer performance in mergers is a "mergers of equals." These are friendly combinations of companies usually of similar sizes. The deals are often characterized by extensive negotiations between the management of both companies. Julie Wulf of the University of Pennsylvania analyzed a large sample of 17,730 mergers, of which $1,457 were stock swaps and 273 were tender offers over the period 1991–1999.[8] The results of her analysis of this sample proved to be very different from those of more typical acquisitions. First, she found that the combined bidder and target returns for her sample were not that different from non–merger-of-equals deals. However, her results showed that bidders captured more of the gains, while target shareholders received lower returns. Bidders gained at the expense of target shareholders. It seems that the extensive negotiation process enabled bidders to extract for gains from target shareholders more than what would occur in a more traditional combination of firms where a larger company buys a target.

As discussed in Chapter 5, target management and directors seem to trade off higher returns for their shareholders to receive positions in the new company. This raises significant corporate governance concerns, as we would assume that managers and directors are fiduciaries for shareholders and should only be concerned about target shareholder gains and not their employment status. In addition, it seems that when the bidder can offer target management and directors opportunities in the combined entity, they may be able to get away with lower premiums and save their shareholders' money. Given that these target directors and managers can often be removed at a lower date, these gains may be coming at a modest price.[9]

## FIRM SIZE AND ACQUISITION GAINS

One issue of interest is how relatively larger acquirers do relative to some bidders. Moeller, Schlingemann and Stulz analyzed a large sample of 12,023 acquisitions and their announcement returns over the period of 1980 to 2001.[10] Not surprisingly, they found that the average dollar change in wealth of acquiring-firm shareholders was negative around the time of the announcement. After observing the overall returns, they then examined the acquisition performance of smaller firms that they defined as those that have market capitalizations below the twenty-fifth percentile of the New York Stock Exchange. They found that smaller firms do more profitable acquisitions while larger companies do deals that cause their shareholders to lose money. During their sample period small firms earned $9 billion from acquisitions. Remember, smaller firms tend to make smaller deals. Large companies, on the other hand, caused their shareholders to lose $312 billion!

Moeller, Schlingemann and Stulz explained these results by remarking that in small firms the incentives for managers are more in line with those of shareholders, whereas this is not the case for larger companies. Thus, managers in small companies have more incentives to do deals that will increase shareholder wealth. In addition, they pointed out that large companies tend to have managers who may be afflicted with hubris that may cause them to do deals that are in their interest as opposed to shareholders' interest. They also noticed that large acquirers tended to pay more for their targets than smaller companies, and large companies were more likely to complete an offer.

## LONG-TERM RESEARCH STUDIES

While many of the short-term studies focus on the shareholder wealth effects around a relatively short-term window, such as the announcement of the deal, longer-term studies try to follow the performance of the merged companies for an extended period after the deal. One such study was conducted by Healy, Palepu, and Ruback.[11] They looked at the 50 largest deals over the period 1979 to 1984. They focused on large deals because those involving larger targets would reasonably have the greatest impact on the acquirer—whether that impact is positive or negative. On average, targets represented 42% of the size of acquirers based on total assets.

They grouped their merged companies into three subcategories that vary in terms of the degree of overlap of their businesses: high, medium, and low. The sample of the companies they analyzed included several oil industry companies (e.g., DuPont and Conoco, and Diamond Shamrock and Natomas, or Occidental Petroleum and Cities Service). The oil industry featured a significant number of large deals during this time period. The sample also included some large diversification deals, such as the U.S. Steel merger with Marathon Oil, as well as the Coca-Cola merger with Columbia Pictures. However, other transactions in the sample included companies within the same industry, such as LTV Group and Republic Steel.

Healy, Palepu, and Ruback mainly focused on changes in accounting variables such as operating cash flows. Using such variables, they compared the performance in a five-year period after the deal. They found significant improvement in operating cash flows following the deals. Cash flow changes were traced to variation in sales and asset turnover. They also related the changes in the accounting variables they studied to the abnormal returns of the merged companies' stock. They found a positive relationship between the accounting variable performance and the announcement stock returns. This result is interesting because it implies that the market accurately forecasted the performance of the postmerger entity. It implies that we *may* be able to use the market reaction to provide us with some indication of the future success of an announced deal.

The cash flow gains found by these researchers *were greater when the businesses were overlapping*. However, this result was not consistent in all cases of related transactions. For example, while LTV and Republic's businesses were highly overlapping, the deals did not feature strong positive performance. Presumably this can be explained by the overall troubled nature of the U.S. steel industry at that time. Nonetheless, this inconsistent result was the exception, not the norm. One of the lessons we can take away from this study is that the likelihood of realizing gains will be greater when the businesses are related, although if the companies are troubled and in a troubled industry, such as the U.S. steel industry, merging with a similar company, one that may have some of the same problems, may not be a solution. This conclusion has been supported by a variety of other research studies supporting combinations of companies in the same or a related industry and while raising questions about deals outside a company's own industry.

Another long-term study was conducted by Andrade, Mitchell, and Stafford.[12] Their research featured a large sample of approximately 2,000 mergers over the period 1973–1998. Such a sample has many advantages over the Healy, Palepu, and Ruback sample because it considered deals from both the fourth and fifth merger waves, whereas the Healy, Palepu, and Ruback sample only took us up to the start of the fourth merger wave. The other major advantage of the Andrade, Mitchell, and Stafford sample is its sheer size: 2,000 mergers versus 50 from Healy, Palepu, and Ruback. Using a larger sample covering a more recent time period, we may have greater confidence that the results would be applicable to the current time period. Although the sample was larger, the period longer and more recent, the results of the Andrade, Mitchell, and Stafford study are similar to the Healy, Palepu, and Ruback findings. They found that improved postmerger performance in terms of cash flows was mirrored in positive stock returns of the two merger partners around the time of the announcement. Once again, this implies that the market seems capable of determining if a deal is going to improve the merged entities.

## LONG- VERSUS SHORT-TERM PERFORMANCE AND METHOD OF PAYMENT

A review of the research literature shows that the long-term valuation effects vary by the means of payments. That is, the effects on bidders and target are different depending on whether the bidder uses cash or stock. Also, more hostile deals tend to be cash offers because cash is often more attractive to target shareholders than stock, although this may not always be the case, depending on who the bidder is. Stock of such successful companies as Microsoft is more attractive than the equity in a company with a less stellar track record. Although the value of cash is obviously fixed, stock values can vary with the passage of time. Given the amount of time that it may take for a deal to close, many equity-based deals feature *collars*, which are agreements that merger parties enter into that allow the exchange ratio to be adjusted in some predetermined manner to offset the ups and downs of the market. A collar may provide that if the value of the bidder's shares declined before the completion of the transaction, the value being offered by the bidder may continue to equal its initial value through an automatic increase in the number of shares to offset the decrease in the per-share market value.

### Target Companies: Short-Term Effects of Method of Payment

Research studies have shown that the positive shareholder wealth effects that targets typically enjoy are greater when the offers are financed with cash than when they use equity for their consideration. One study of 204 acquisitions by Huang and Walking found that cash offers featured substantially higher returns before and after controlling for the type of acquisition and the amount of resistance.[13] Other studies have also shown higher premium for cash offers.[14] By controlling for the intensity of resistance, Huang and Walking attempted to filter out the influence that hostility may have played in determining premiums. Having eliminated hostility, they then attributed the higher premiums of cash offers to tax effects. The reasoning is that when shareholders receive stock, as opposed to cash, they may possibly avoid taxes on the gains they receive from the sale of their stock. They concluded that bidders had to offset the adverse tax effects on target shareholders by offering a higher premium.

Hostile deals are known to bring about bidding contests in which various rivals increase their premiums to prevail in the takeover battle. However, using a sample of 84 target firms and 123 bidding firms between 1980 and 1988, Sullivan, Jensen, and Hudson found that the higher returns associated with cash offers persisted even after offers were terminated and the targets, at least initially, remained independent.[15] These researchers interpreted these results as an indication that the market had changed its evaluation of these targets of cash offers. Presumably, the market has also raised its assessment of the probability that another high-premium cash offer will occur. From a management perspective, this research suggests that being the recipient of cash offers is good for target shareholders, even if the target fights off the bidder and remains independent. Obviously each situation is unique, and one might suspect that if the target's resistance is so strong, then the market might conclude that even if another bidder surfaces, the target will still be able to remain independent, so there is no reason to change its assessments of the probability that it will eventually be taken over in a high-premium all-cash offer.

## Bidders: Short-Term Effects of Method of Payment

The prior research we have surveyed often showed that the shareholder wealth effects for bidders were either negative or neutral. Bidder shareholders either experienced short-term losses or were left unaffected by the deal. One study by Saeyoung Chang analyzed the short-term market responses of bidder shares when they made takeover offers.[16] He looked to see how these bidder shareholder wealth effects were different depending on whether the bids were stock or cash offers. His study analyzed a sample of 281 transactions over the period 1981–1992, and he found that bidder's short-term returns were basically zero and not statistically significant for cash offers but were a negative –2.46% for stock offers. Once again, we find that the shareholder wealth effects for bidders are negative, providing us with additional reason for potential bidders to be extra cautious when contemplating mergers and acquisitions.

## BIDDER LONG-TERM EFFECTS: METHODS OF PAYMENT

One of the leading studies on this issue was conducted by Loughran and Vijh. They followed acquirers for a five-year period after acquisitions.[17] They found that in stock deals, bidders averaged negative excess returns equal to $-25\%$, whereas for cash tender offers the returns were a positive 61.7%. The positive returns for cash deals does provide support for such transactions, but the negative returns for stock deals implies that if target shareholders receive stock in exchange for their shares, they are advised to sell the stock as opposed to holding shares in the bidder for an extended period. These findings are somewhat supported by Aloke Ghosh, who analyzed total asset turnover following acquisitions. He found that total asset turnover improved for those companies that used cash to finance deals, whereas other performance measures, such as cash flows, declined for those companies that used their stock to pay for their acquisitions.[18] In trying to discern a reason for the different effects Ghosh found with respect to payment, he noticed that companies that used cash tended to be larger. This provides some mild support to larger bidders doing all-cash offers.

## BIDDER'S PERFORMANCE OVER THE FIFTH MERGER WAVE

Using their large database of 12,023 acquisitions over the period of 1980 to 2001, Moeller, Schlingemann, and Stulz analyzed the performance of acquiring firms through the two major merger waves we had during that time period.[19] Their results are quite interesting. They found that over the period 1998 through 2001 shareholders in bidders lost $240 billion! This dwarfs the $8 billion they found that acquiring firm shareholders lost in all of the 1980s. While some prior studies showed that the net effect on shareholders' returns may have been positive when we consider target shareholder gains, Moeller, Schlingemann, and Stulz found that even when these target shareholder benefits were taken into account, the net effects were still a negative $134 billion (all amounts in 2001 $). We already know that from the perspective of acquiring firm shareholders, these net effects are irrelevant because, if anything, they merely show how target shareholders gain at acquiring firm shareholder's expense.

When we look at Exhibit 3.2 we see that over the 1990s the returns to acquiring firms shareholders were generally positive. This is consistent with what we know about merger strategy of many corporate managers who started off the 1990s stating that they would not engage in short-term-oriented deals, but would only pursue more strategic and better thought out deals. This seemed to hold true until we got to the latter part of the fifth merger wave when things seemed to get out of control. Moeller, Schlingemann, and Stulz investigated the source of the negative returns and found that much of it could be attributed to larger deals that often were big losers. They found 87 acquisitions over the period 1998 to 2001 in which acquiring firm shareholders lost at least $1 billion. In their sample they found that almost all of the large-loss deals—those with losses of at least $1 billion—occurred in this four-year period. They also noticed that a disproportionate amount of the large-loss deals were done by serial acquirers.

**Exhibit 3.2**    Yearly Aggregate Dollar Return of Acquiring-Firm Shareholders, 1980–2001

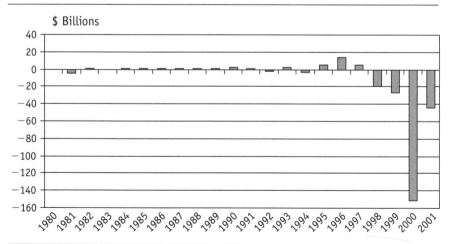

*Source:* Sara B. Moeller, Frederik P. Schlingemann, and René M. Stulz, "Wealth Destruction on a Massive Scale? A Study of Acquiring-Firm Returns in the Recent Merger Wave," *Journal of Finance* 60, no. 2 (April 2005).

When we try to explain the reason for the large losses for acquiring firm shareholders at the end of the fifth merger wave, it is not hard to believe that hubris played a role. At the start of the fifth merger wave, managers seemed to be pursuing more sound merger strategies. They initiated a large number of deals, and many of them seemed to be working out well. The market rose significantly, and when this occurs there is a tendency for managers to believe that they are doing a great job and can do no wrong. It is hard for boards and shareholders to disagree when faced with such performance. The more this occurs, the more unchecked managers become. However, as the fifth merger wave continued, many of the desirable targets were snatched up. What we were left with was a pool of somewhat less desirable companies being pursued by hubris-filled managers running companies with high valuations and valuable stock to offer targets. This is a bad combination. While managers who pursued the large-loss deals are at fault, blame must be shared by the boards that left them unchecked. Boards should have been aware that the high valuations were caused by irrational overvaluation that affected the market in general and were not the product of specific managerial efforts. The fact that boards should have been more diligent is underscored by those large offers that were withdrawn. Here the market response was clearly positive. Unfortunately, Moeller, Schlingemann, and Stulz only found six instances in large loss deals that ended up being withdrawn.

## CONCLUSION

A larger number of research studies have been conducted on the valuation effects of mergers and acquisitions. These studies show that the gains in such transactions vary greatly, depending on whether you look at the deals from a bidder or a target's perspective. Targets tend to do well in takeovers because in order to take over a company, a bidder usually has to pay a premium for control of the company. Bidders, however, may not fare as well.

We have reviewed an extensive body of research of the shareholders' wealth. The studies can be categorized in a few different ways. One way is to group them into short-term versus long-term studies.

Many of the short-term studies are event studies that consider the market's reaction to announcements of mergers and acquisitions. Generally, the shareholder wealth effects around announcements for bidders are poor, while for targets they are good because target shareholders are able to receive the premium. Long-term studies focus on certain performance measures and try to determine some of the same effects as the short-term studies. The bottom line of this body of research is that when we consider many of the available short- and long-term studies, we see that while combined net returns for bidders and targets are often positive, implying that from a societal perspective mergers and acquisitions generate value, the benefits to the bidders and targets can be very different. One exception to this was the performance of bidders toward the end of the fifth merger wave where bidders' performance was so poor that the net effects of the deals were clearly negative.

Target shareholders usually do well, while bidder shareholders often have neutral and sometimes negative effects. From a bidder's perspective, research results on mergers and acquisitions are not impressive, and sometimes this is an understatement. From a managerial perspective, this means we have to be careful in evaluating a deal. It does not mean that acquirers should avoid mergers and acquisitions—definitely not. It just means that too often these deals are not done for the right reasons, and the results are not consistently positive. When we review the results of the various research studies, it leads us to believe that we could do a better job in selecting targets, determining a price, and evaluating our merger strategy. If more companies did a better job in these areas, we believe the results for bidders would be better than they are.

## ENDNOTES

1. Presentation on leveraged buyouts, Kohlberg, Kravis, and Roberts, January 1989.
2. Michael C. Jensen and Richard S. Ruback, "The Market for Corporate Control," *Journal of Financial Economics* 11 (1983): 5–50.
3. Michael Bradley, Anand Desai, and E. Han Kim, "Acquisitions and Their Division Between Stockholders of Target and Acquiring Firms," *Journal of Financial Economics* 21 (1988): 3–40.

4. Steven N. Kaplan and Michael S. Weisbach, "The Success of Acquisitions: Evidence from Divestitures, *Journal of Finance* 47, no. 1 (March 1992): 107–138.

5. James Tobin, "A General Equilibrium Approach to Monetary Theory," *Journal of Money Credit and Banking* 1 (February 1969): 15–29.

6. Larry Lang, Rene M. Stulz, and Ralph A. Walking, "Managerial Performance, Tobins q and the Gains from Unsuccessful Takeovers," *Journal of Financial Economics* 24 (1989): 137–154.

7. Henri Servaes, "Tobins q and the Gains from Takeovers," *Journal of Finance* 46, no. 1 (March 1991): 409–419.

8. Julie Wulf, "Do CEOs in Mergers Trade Power for Premium: Evidence from Mergers of Equals," University of Pennsylvania Working Paper, June 2001.

9. It should be noted that these comments do not address any severance provisions or other compensation that may go to target managers if they leave these positions.

10. Sara B. Moeller, Frederik P. Schlingemann, and Rene M. Stulz, "Firm Size and the Gains from Acquisitions," *Journal of Financial Economics* 73 (2004): 201–228.

11. P. Healy, K. Palepu, and Richard Ruback, "Does Corporate Performance Improve After Mergers?" *Journal of Financial Economics* 31, no. 2 (April 1992): 135–175.

12. Gregor Andrade, Mark Mitchell, and Erik Stafford, "New Evidence and Perspectives on Mergers," *Journal of Economics Perspectives* 15 (Spring 2001): 103–120.

13. Yen-Sheng Huang and Ralph A. Walking, "Target Abnormal Returns Associated with Acquisition Announcements," *Journal of Financial Economics* 19 (1987): 329–349.

14. Alfred Rappaport and Mark Sirower, "Stock or Cash? The Trade-Offs for Buyers and Sellers in Mergers and Acquisitions," *Harvard Business Review* (November/December 1999): 33–44.

15. Michael J. Sullivan, Michael Jensen, and Cad D. Hudson, "The Role of Medium of Exchange in Merger Offers: Examination of Terminated Merger Proposals," *Financial Management* 23, no. 3 (Autumn 1994): 51–62.

16. Saeyoung Chang, "Takeovers of Privately Held Targets, Methods of Payment, and Bidder Returns," *Journal of Finance* 53, no. 2 (April 1998): 773–784.

17. Tim Loughran and Anand M. Vijh, "Do Long-Term Shareholders Benefits from Corporate Acquisitions?" *Journal of Finance* 52 (December 1997): 1765–1790.

18. Aloke Ghosh, "Does Operating Performance Really Improve Following Corporate Acquisitions?" *Journal of Corporate Finance* 7, no. 2 (June 2001): 151–178.

19. Sara B. Moeller, Frederick P. Schlingemann, and Rene Stulz, "Wealth Destruction on a Massive Scale? A Study of Acquiring-Firm Returns in the Recent Merger Wave" *Journal of Finance* 60, no. 2 (April 2005).

# Case Study

## Montana Power—Moving into Unfamiliar Areas

So often it is a prescription for disaster—moving into business areas that you really do not know well. So also is moving from a stable, albeit low-growth business, that you have enjoyed a long history of profits in, and moving into a high-growth but rapidly changing business. The risk of such ventures seems to be so obvious that it is a wonder that they are even suggested by management and approved by a board of directors. It is also a wonder that experienced investment bankers and advisors would support such deals. However, this is what happened in the utility industry in the 1980s and 1990s. Spurred on by deregulation, many power utilities decided to try to spice up their corporate lives by taking the capital generated by the supposedly boring and low-growth utility business and investing in more exciting areas. Such was the case in the fifth merger wave when Montana Power decided to enter the high-flying telecommunications business.

On the surface, the decision might have displayed some merits. The fact that the power utility business was slow growth and generally dull is well known. In February 2001, Montana Power announced that it was spinning off its utility entity, Montana Power, to concentrate on its telecommunications business — Touch America.[1] Montana Power was not a newcomer to the utility business. The company was founded in 1912. It moved into oil and gas in the 1930s and then expanded into coal in the 1950s. Its first move into telecommunications began in the 1980s, when it took advantage of the breakup of AT&T. It slowly began to expand its position in the telecommunications business by laying more fiber-optic cables and building more of its own network. The combined company eventually sold off its boring power utility for $1.3 billion and invested the proceeds into the high-flying telecommunications business.

The energy distribution business was sold to NorthWestern Corporation for $612 million in cash plus the assumption of $488 million in debt.[2] The monies from the sale were invested in Touch America's telecommunications business. In August 2000, PanCanadian Petroleum Ltd. agreed to purchase Montana Power's oil and gas business for $475 million.[3] This acquisition increased PanCanadian's oil field capacity by providing it with properties in Alberta, Montana, and Colorado. It was indicated by PanCanadian that the acquired fields had reserves of 550 billion cubic feet of gas and 20 million barrels of crude oil.

## MOVEMENT OF UTILITIES INTO NONUTILITY BUSINESSES

The movement of Montana Power into other nonutility business areas was not unique to this company. When the power utility business was deregulated, it allowed these once very conservative companies to engage in other business ventures, and mergers and acquisitions were the fastest way for them to do so. One leading example is Duke

---

1. Bruce Christian, "Montana Power Decides Future Lies in Telecom," Wholesale Channel (June 2001), *www.phoneplusmag.com*.
2. "Montana Power and Northwestern in $612 Million Deal," *The New York Times* (October 3, 2000).
3. PanCanadian Will Acquire Oil and Gas Assets," *The New York Times* (August 29, 2000).

Power, a venerable power company. After a series of deals outside the power generation business by the end of the 1990s, about 40% of Duke's earnings came from unregulated businesses. The market, however, was not that keen on many of the moves of these power company executives. When the S&P 500 was trading at 25 times earnings in late 1999, at the peak of the stock market boom of the 1990s, Duke was only trading at 15 times earnings. Utilities executives were frustrated that the company did not reward them for their various forays outside of the power utility business, but the market had a more objective view of their deals than the utility executives, which were naturally more excited about these business ventures than the market.[4]

## SELLING UTILITY ASSETS AND
## BUYING TELECOM ASSETS

By the time Montana Power had completed its auction for its power utility business, it had sold off such hard assets as power plants, transmission lines, gas, coal and oil fields, as well as dams. These combined power utility assets allowed the company to show steadily growing revenues but also stable profitability (see Exhibit A).

The sale of the bulk of the utility assets was done over roughly a two-year period. In exchange the proceeds were used to enable the company to become one of the larger broadband companies in the United States (at least until the company went under).

Touch America was a rapidly growing telecommunications company. In the summer of 2000, it entered a deal with Quest to buy its in-region long-distance network. Because of regulatory constraints, Quest had to divest this part of its business pursuant to an agreement related to its acquisition of U.S. West, which was one of the seven super-regionals that were formed in the breakup of AT&T. In the sale, Quest gave Touch America its long-distance operations in a 14-state area for $200 million.[5] This acquisition gave Touch America a

4. Suzanne McGee and Rebecca Smith, "Deals and Dealmakers for Utilities," *The Wall Street Journal* (November 26, 1999): C1.

5. "Unit of Montana Power Is Buying Quest Phone Business," *The New York Times* (March 17, 2000).

**Exhibit A**
Montana Power Company Revenues and Net Income

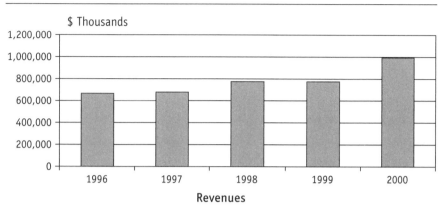

Revenues

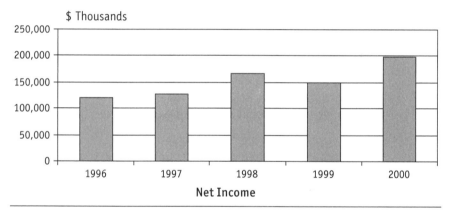

Net Income

*Source:* Montana Power Company 10K.

business with sales of approximately $300 million in revenues and 250,000 customers.

After the sell-off of the power utility, Montana Power changed its name to Touch America Holdings, Inc. in February 2002. The company was traded on the New York Stock Exchange. For a while the company was highly touted by the market and the industry.[6] Touch America started off as a growing company in a growing business while being largely debt-free. Initially it seemed that the combination of rapid growth without debt pressures made Touch America seem highly desirable. An examination of the comparative growth of Montana

---

6. Steve Skobel, "Rising Starts," *Telecom Business* (July 1, 2001).

Power's telecommunications and utility revenues over the period 1998–2000 provides an indication for why its CEO, Bob Gannon, was so interested in leaving the utility business and moving full speed into the telecom business (see Exhibit B).

However, all was not well in the telecom industry, and Touch America's fate went down with the industry. In just one year after its impressive 2001 performance, by the second and third quarters of 2002, the company lost $32.3 million and $20.9 million, respectively. This occurred even though revenues increased from $73.6 million to $76.6 million. Part of Touch America's problems stemmed from a billing dispute it had with Quest where Touch America claimed that Quest owed it $46 million.[7] However, on March 27, 2003, an arbitrator ruled that Touch America owed Quest $59.6 million plus interest. The FCC fined Quest for its violations of telecom rules.[8] The stock collapsed to $0.53 per share and was then delisted by the New York Stock Exchange.[9] At the time that Montana Power had sold off its nontelecommunications assets, the stock traded at $65 per share.

**Exhibit B**
Montana Power Company Revenues by Sector

Source: Montana Power Company 10K.

---

7. "Touch America Says Quest Owes It $46 Million," *Reuters Limited* (January 23, 2003).
8. David Shabelman, "Touch America Loses Touch with Liquidity," *The Daily Deal* (June 23, 2003): 9.
9. Matt Gouras, "Touch America Trading Suspended; Company Made Disastrous Move into Telecommunications," Associated Press Newswires.

## MONTANA POWER LEADERSHIP
## IN ITS MERGER STRATEGY

The chairman and CEO of Montana Power, Bob Gannon, led the company into its transformation from a power utility to growing telecom business. The following passage is part of his pitch to the market and shareholders:

> We remain on track to transform Montana Power into Touch America, our growing broadband information transport company, says Bob Gannon Montana Power's chairman, president and chief executive, as well as chairman and CEO of Touch America. We are meeting the company's goals of receiving good, solid values for our energy businesses and a promising future for their employees.[10]

Gannon did not transform the company on his own. He was aided by deal makers at the investment bank of Goldman Sachs. The Butte, Montana, native used his background as a CEO of a stodgy power utility to try to compete in the swirling telecom sector and its mounting supply versus weakening demand economics. Although competition has increased in the power utility business after deregulation, the telecom sector featured even more intense competition combined with rapid technological changes that even seasoned veterans of the business could not keep up with.

It seems that Bob Gannon did not encounter great dissent while he was promoting his plans. He was reported to have been cheered at the company's annual meeting.[11] Some Wall Street analysts and media pundits praised Gannon's makeover plan when he first presented it, as, for example, in the following quote:

> In addition to its capital position, Touch America looks strong in terms of operating performance. From first quarter 2000 to first quarter 2001, Touch America's revenues increased from $25

---

10. Bruce Christian, *Wholesale Channel* (June 2001), www.phoneplusmag. com.

11. Bill Richards, "Power Outage for Montana Utility, a Gamble on Telecom Looks Like a Bad Call," *The Wall Street Journal* (August 22, 2001): A1.

million to \$144 million with operating income up 95 percent. This solid balance sheet has attracted Wall Street's attention and earned a buy rating from Kaufman Brothers.[12]

Gannon was able to convince many that Montana Power had a rosier future in the telecom business than in the power utility sector.

By the end of 2002, Touch America was quickly losing large sums of money. In November 2002, the company reported a third-quarter loss of \$18.5 million. This loss, however, was better than the second-quarter loss of \$37.3 million. Here again is another lesson we can derive from this case study. If you see a business that is rapidly growing, it is often also rapidly changing, and rapidly changing businesses tend to be unpredictable. So when you leave a stable business, such as that which Montana Power had, and you enter a rapidly growing but rapidly changing business, you have to be prepared to take on the risk associated with such a change. Any future profits and cash flows have to be discounted using a significant risk premium, and the risk-adjusted cash flows should then be compared before making the change. One wonders to what extent this was ever done by Touch America and its investment bankers as they rushed to get rid of a century-old business and fly into the booming (and busting) telecom sector.

## ROLE OF SHAREHOLDERS IN THE TRANSFORMATION OF THE COMPANY

What is amazing about the dramatic transformation of the company is that it never sought or received its shareholders' approval for the dramatic change in its business! The stock was held by many investors, including local pension funds that did not support the changeover. More than one-third of the company's shareholders lived in the state of Montana. When the stock collapsed, investors filed suit, commencing a long legal battle for shareholders' rights.

---

12.  Primedia Business Magazines and Media.

## TELECOM FIELD OF DREAMS

Parts of the woes of Touch America were felt by many other players in the ill-fated American telecommunications industry. In a capital investment strategy that came right out of Kevin Costner's Field of Dreams—Build It and They Will Come—telecom managers invested heavily in network expansion and fiber-optic cable laying throughout the 1990s and early 2000s. Billions of dollars were spent on laying fiber-optic cable as telecom and nontelecom companies expanded. For example, 360 Networks held over 87,000 miles of fiber-optic cable linking urban areas in North America, Asia, and South America.[13] Touch America was one such company: "Renamed Touch America, the company's fiber network will span 26,000 route miles by year end, making it one of the largest and highest capacity long haul networks in the U.S."[14]

Montana Power was not the only utility company that invested in the telecom sector. For example, Carolina Power and Light began a telecom business called InterPath Communications, which was valued at one point at $1 billion. AFN was a telecom wholesale service provider that assembled a network that was consolidated from the telecom assets of four utility companies: Allegheny Energy, American Electric Power, First Energy, and GPU.

The timing of Gannon and Montana Power's move was highly suspect. Montana Power sold off its power utility assets to enter the telecom sector in pursuit of the high growth that had been going on in that area for a while. However, they were a late arriver on the telecom scene. As such, they bought at the peak of this market. They overpaid for their telecom assets and their values were about to collapse. Those that sold to them gained at the expense of these power utility executives, who did not know what they were doing.

## BANKRUPTCY FILING

Touch America finally filed for Chapter 11 bankruptcy protection on June 19, 2003, in Wilmington, Delaware. The bankruptcy filing revealed

---

13.  Lucy I. Vento, "Who Will Profit from the U.S. Fiber Network Glut," *Business Communications Review* (September 1, 2001).

14.  Ibid.

that the company listed $631.5 million in assets with $554.2 in liabilities, but this did not show the liquidity problems of the company. In its heyday the telecom business of Montana Power was valued at $2.9 billion.[15]

The bankruptcy filing led to a process of trying to sell the assets in the face of objections from various creditors. The company sold off assets to generate cash, but these sales came into a depressed market and could not fetch the cash needed to stave off the collapse of the company. For example, it sold its private line and Internet business for $26 million to 360 Networks, Inc., a Canadian-based broadband/telecom company.

## LESSONS FROM THE MONTANA POWER CASE

The Montana Power case is an extreme one in that it is unusual to have management recommend and a board endorse a strategy of selling off a long-established, stable, and profitable business to enter an uncertain industry in which management had little expertise. Nonetheless, the lessons of this extreme failure are instructive:

- *Stick to what you know.* You need to be extremely careful about moves into business areas in which you have not established expertise.

- *Beware of rapid-growth/rapidly changing businesses.* These are often high-risk areas, and projected earnings and cash flows need to be discounted using a fully risk-adjusted discount rate. If it is so uncertain that you can't come up with a reliable risk premium, then that may tell you something in and of itself.

- *Beware of dramatic corporate transformations.* These huge changes are not doing shareholders a service. If shareholders want to be in that other business, they can much more easily sell their stock in your company and buy shares in the other sector.

---

15. See note d.

# 4

## Valuation and Overpaying

Some deals that may have been described as merger failures after the fact may be nothing more than instances of overpaying. Many companies are good acquisition targets at one price but failures at another. As sensible as this proposition seems, it does not apply to all deals. Some companies would not be good acquisitions at virtually any price. Targets that would attract away important company resources, including management time, may not be worth the total resources required—especially after the full cost of the acquisition has been considered over the course of time.

Determining the correct price is a key factor in making a deal profitable. This is a simple and true proposition for the purchase of any asset in a company that may be acquired; it is merely a more complicated transaction, but the basic truism applies—make sure the price is correct. How do we determine what the correct price is? In order to know this, we have to know how to properly value companies. Once we fully understand the proper valuation methodologies, we can identify the main assumptions that are driving the valuation model that results in the price for the target. At that point we can critically analyze the reasonableness of those assumptions. If some are deemed to be unreasonable or overly optimistic, then we can readily recompute the value using more realistic assumptions. In order to do this, we need to understand the fundamentals of business valuation. This is the focus of this chapter.

## VALUATION: PART SCIENCE AND PART ART

When we review the main valuation methods, they appear scientific and exact. There are accepted methodologies and exact methods of determining a company's value. However, with each method, important and key assumptions enter into the valuation model. These assumptions are often derived based on subjective determinations made by the evaluators. They make these subjective judgments based on their experience and any other knowledge they may draw on.

When one considers the subjectivity of the valuation process, it may be easy to conclude the opposite. That is, that the process is so subjective that there is no objective basis for the values that are derived and that they are not to be relied on. However, we have a market that regularly evaluates prices and values at which assets, and in this companies, are offered and sold for. Bidders typically pay a premium above the market price of stock, for reasons that we will explain later in this chapter, and the market registers its approval or disapproval of offer prices for targets. This, in part, is the reason for some of the adverse reactions we saw in Chapter 3 to many bids by acquirers. Part of these negative stock price reactions is the market registering its concern that the offer price is too high relative to its own evaluation. So the market is an objective evaluator that regularly scrutinizes bids and determines if they are appropriately valued. This does not mean that a bidder is not correct in paying a price that the market questions. It is certainly possible that the market—that conglomeration of many investors each coming to a more or less independent assessment of the value of a target—is wrong and a bidder is right in seeing more value in a target than what the market is recognizing. However, when the market says the bidder is wrong, then the bidder better have a very good basis for justifying this value. We have seen in Chapter 3 that the initial stock market response to deals is often prescient. Directors should bear this in mind prior to approving an acquisition and require that management provide extra justification for the anticipated gains from the deal.

## Bidder Valuation, Corporate Governance, and Value Management

The bulk of this chapter is devoted to valuation of target companies that a bidder may want to acquire. We will be discussing the various methods that bidders may use to value targets. However, we should also point out that the same methods that are used to value targets can be applied to value the bidder—separate and independent of acquisitions and mergers. When we are able to identify the key drivers that are used to determine corporate value, we can focus on the bidder and the value of those drivers for the company. The company should be managed in a way that maximizes its own value to achieve the greater gains for shareholders. The key drivers must be kept at levels that result in the greatest value of the company. Instead of using antitakeover defenses to prevent takeovers, directors and managers should bear in mind that one of the strongest antitakeover defenses is to increase the value, and resulting price, of the company. Value maximization can be one of the more potent antitakeover defenses. When the company is not managed in a way that increases the value of the company, it can become vulnerable to a takeover. However, when management is doing a good job and the value of the company rises in the market, it becomes a more expensive target. If such better-managed companies receive unwanted bids, they may be able to make a compelling argument that their management is in the best long-term interests of shareholders.

Such better managers can also make more effective arguments for deploying antitakeover defenses because they can assert that it is in shareholder's interests to continue to run the company under their control. Shareholders will have to project what such a continuation of current management's reign would bring them and compare this to the premium being offered by the bidder.

## VALUATION: BUYER VERSUS SELLER'S PERSPECTIVE

It is important to recognize that the value of a target company to itself may be different from the value of that same company to a buyer. The buyer may put the target's assets to different uses and be able to leverage these assets in a different manner that may pay higher returns than what the target was able to realize. The source of these gains may be synergistic benefits. The ability to possibly realize synergistic gains may allow the buyer to pay the target a premium above the value that the target could realize if it were to remain independent. Nonetheless, we need to recognize that an acquisition value is different than the value that one would place on a company independent of the deal. The acquisition valuation process is different because we may incorporate cost savings or revenue enhancements into the projected cash flows. We can value the same company, but for different purposes, and get a very different value. One is not right and the other wrong. Ironically, both can be correct.

## Most Commonly Used Valuation Methods

There are several different methods of valuing businesses. Some are used more for certain valuation exercises, while in other circumstances other methods are used. For the sake of completeness, we will review each method but point out those that are most relevant to valuing public companies for acquisitions:

- *Discounted future earnings and cash flows.* This method involves projecting earnings and cash flows and then discounting them back to present value terms using a risk-adjusted discounted rate. There are several key determinants of value in this method. One is the earnings or cash flow base that is being used, another is the growth rate utilized to forecast the future values, and the last is the discount rate used to convert the future projected value to present value terms.

- *Comparable multiples.* This simple method is used to value large public companies but can also be applied to smaller, closely held businesses. Various different multiples are applicable to specific industries. These multiples are averages and have to be adjusted to be applicable to the particular company being valued.

- *Capitalization of earnings.* This valuation technique is similar to the discounted future earnings approach. The process of capitalization computes the present value of an income stream that is treated as a perpetuity. A capitalization rate that is adjusted for both growth and risk is used to capitalize an earnings base, thereby converting it to present value.

- *Asset-oriented approaches.* Several different alternative asset-oriented methods are used to value companies. Some of these approaches are net asset value or fair value, book value, and liquidation value. Asset-oriented methods are more appropriate for certain businesses such as real estate entities, which derive their value directly from the assets they own.

- *Industry-specific approaches.* Certain industries utilize valuation methods that are specific to the nature of the business being valued. One example is the cable industry, which relies on methods that are tied to demand indicators such as the number of subscribers. One should be careful utilizing such methods because if they do not translate into other more straightforward variables such as cash flows, then their value becomes questionable. We have only to look back at the recent past and see how such unique methods of valuing companies based on factors such as hits on websites were used to create high valuations for unprofitable businesses during the internet boom of the 1990s.

Having introduced each of these methods, let us discuss two of the more commonly used ones in greater detail: discounted future cash flows and comparable multiples.

The discounted cash flow (DCF) valuation method can be broken into three main analytical steps:

1. Projecting future cash flows
2. Measuring the length of the projection period
3. Selecting the appropriate discount rate

## Projecting Free Cash Flows

When we project out cash flows for valuing a business, we usually project free cash flows (FCF). These are the cash flows after an allowance has been made for expected capital expenditures. These are the capital expenditures that will be needed to maintain the business at the same or greater level in the future. The importance of capital expenditures in the valuation process was underscored in the 1988 takeover of the Resorts Casino by Merv Griffin for $302 million. This takeover was a hostile one, and in hostile bids the bidder often does not have access to some of the information that a bidder can normally ask for in a more friendly deal. In a hostile offer, targets usually provide only what they are compelled to, and a bidder often has to rely mainly on public information. Sometimes this is not as detailed as what one would get if there were a more free give-and-take, such as what we get in a normal negotiation process where the bidder can ask the target to provide certain information to justify the price it is asking for the company. In this takeover, Griffin underestimated the amount of capital expenditures that would be needed after the takeover to bring the older Resorts Casino up to the level of some of the other, more modern casinos in Atlantic City. Donald Trump, the seller, was able to get a good price because he resisted the takeover and Griffin had to increase his offer. In this case, Griffin was the victim of the winner's curse. He overpaid for the casino and discovered only after he acquired the business that he would have to invest significant sums to upgrade the property to make it competitive. So we see that correctly estimating the capital expenditures can be an important factor in determining the proper value of the target and not overpaying. It is also one of many reasons why bidders *may* be able to do more accurate valuations for companies within their own industry, presumably companies they are more familiar with, than those outside their industry boundaries.

The DCF valuation process can be expressed as follows:

$$\text{Value} = \sum_{i=1}^{n} CF_i / (1 + r)^t$$

where

$CF_i$ = the $i$th period's cash flows
$n$ = the number of periods
$r$ = the risk-adjusted discount rate                    (4.1)

One of the first steps in the valuation process is to determine the length of the projection period. Often this is selected to be five years, but other times longer periods, such as seven years, can be used. The next step is to select the free cash flow base that is the starting point on which the cash flows are based. This base is usually drawn from the company's historical cash flows. A growth rate, $g$, is applied to the base to project the future cash flows. This growth rate is a judgment call based on the evaluator's opinion about the ability of these cash flows to grow in the future. Among the factors that are considered is the historical growth rate, but just extrapolating out the historical growth rate is insufficient. We also need to consider a whole host of factors, such as the future of the industry and the ability of the company to grow over the projection period.

$$\text{Value} = \sum_{i=1}^{5} CF_t/(1+r)^t + V_5/(1+r)^5 \qquad (4.2)$$

While many valuations that use discounted cash flows employ a five-year period for the first part of Equation 4.2, this is not a hard-and-fast rule. Other lengths, such as seven years, are also acceptable. One of the factors that determines the length of the future projection period is the length of time that the expert feels confident that he or she can accurately forecast.

The value in year five, $V_5$, includes the cash flows for that year but also the capitalized value of the cash flows that the business would derive after the fifth year. These cash flows are treated as a perpetuity and are capitalized by dividing the cash flow value for the sixth year by the growth-adjusted discount rate $(r - g)$. That is, the sixth year's cash flows are computed by multiplying the fifth year's cash flows, $FCF_5$, by $(1 + g)$. This value is then divided by the capitalization rate, which is the difference between the discount rate, $r$, and the long-term growth rate, $g$. The value $V_5$ is a fifth-year value, and it must be brought to year zero terms by dividing it by $(1 + r)^5$. This discounted value of the cash flows after year five is sometimes referred to as the *residual*. In many valuations it is a significant part of the entire firm value.

At this point we can see that two of the major factors or assumptions that enter into the DCF valuation method are the growth rate used to project the future cash flows as well as the discount rate that is used to convert them back to present value terms. We will discuss each now.

## Growth Rate Used

The growth rate is a key assumption. Higher growth rates mean higher values and lower rates bring about a lower price for a business. Determining a relevant growth rate implicitly means that the evaluator is making an assumption about the expansion of the firm, the growth of the industry, and the ups and downs of the economy. Clearly, a host of factors determine how a company will grow. Other relevant factors include the actions of competitors and the degree of competition in the industry. Still other factors can be the costs of materials, labor, and other inputs. This says nothing about unpredictable events such as labor strikes or natural disasters, let alone man-made disasters such as the attack on September 11, 2001.

If one is optimistic about the outlook for a particular business, this may be translated into higher growth rates and higher values for the business. When someone such as a member of a board of directors is evaluating a particular price that has been set for a business, it would be reasonable to make some basic inquiries into the valuation model. If a DCF model was used for that valuation, we need to know what growth rate was used and for what time period. Sometimes for new businesses, higher initial growth rates are used for an initial high-growth period, and then after some period of time the company is expected to mature at some lower growth rate, such as the rate of growth for the industry. Once one is able to dissect how the value was arrived at and what the fundamental assumptions are, then one can assess the reasonableness of each assumption. If we find that a $3 billion value is based on a 15% growth rate for the first five years, then we can critically examine that assumption. If it is reasonable, and if the other assumptions in the model are also reasonable, then perhaps the value is also appropriate. If the growth rate assumption is overly optimistic, then perhaps new values, using other lower growth rates, should be utilized.

### Synergy and Growth

In Chapter 2 we discussed synergy and how combinations of companies could possibly bring about more increased profitability than what could be achieved by keeping the companies separate. We discussed two forms of synergy: revenue-enhancing synergy and cost-based synergy. Of the two, revenue-enhancing synergy is the most difficult to achieve. It is far easier to hypothesize about than to actually achieve. One way to enhance revenues that is often proposed in mergers is that the two companies could cross-sell each other's products or services. Another is that the combined companies could offer a broader product line of range or services to sell, and the buyers would want to expand the relationship and buy more services or products from the same seller. Often this does not work. If exaggerated revenue-based synergies have been built into a valuation model through an unrealistic revenue base or profit growth rate, then an adjustment may be warranted. Again, knowledge of how the model works and being able to know the key driving assumptions can be invaluable in reviewing a business valuation.

We have already discussed cost-based synergies. This is where companies are combined and redundant costs are eliminated. The combined companies leverage their assets to try to extract more revenues from a lower aggregate cost base. Although this is sometimes difficult to do, the instances of companies being able to successfully accomplish it are far more common than realizing revenue-based synergies. In certain industries, such as the petroleum industry, it seems to be much easier to do, and there are impressive examples such as Exxon Mobil, which was an even greater success at achieving cost-based synergies than even they thought they would be. If one is in an industry where other companies have combined and have been able to achieve such successes, then there may be a better basis for believing that another proposed merger will also achieve such success. However, if one is in an industry in which this has been unsuccessfully attempted by others, then the proponents of such a deal need to have a strong explanation for why they will be able to achieve what others could not. This is definitely not to say that just because others have failed, all will follow in their path; however, we have to be able to demonstrate that we have a solution to the problems that others encountered.

## Discount Rate Used

The discount rate is used to convert future projected amounts to present value terms. It can be broken down into two broad components as follows:

Discount Rate = Time Value of Money Component + Risk Component

The time value of money component compensates investors for the use of their funds in an investment, in this case the purchase of a company—usually a long-term investment. When the return on the invested capital is "guaranteed," a risk-free rate is assigned. An example would be a U.S. Treasury security, for which we assign the rate offered on those investments. The rate on those investments varies depending on the supply and demand for Treasuries. However, because all investments in companies carry with them some level of risk, we need to add a premium to that risk-free rate to compensate investors for the likelihood that the monies will be forthcoming in the future that is less than what Treasuries offer. In finance we measure this anticipated likelihood by the expected variability of those cash flows. When those cash flows are more variable than Treasuries, we add a specific risk premium. Our guide to the right risk premium comes from our examination of cash flows of other securities that are traded in the marketplace, which pay cash flows that have a similar variability to those from the investment in question. This is often tough to do, so we move up the risk ladder (see Exhibit 4.1) and then decide where our investment in a particular company fits in this upward-sloping trade-off.

When we evaluate prices that have been put on companies using a DCF model, we need to ask what discount rate was used for the analysis and what rationale was used in arriving at that discount rate. If, for example, a large company is acquiring a smaller company that is in a riskier line of business, and the evaluator has used a discount

Exhibit 4.1    Risk-Return Tradeoff

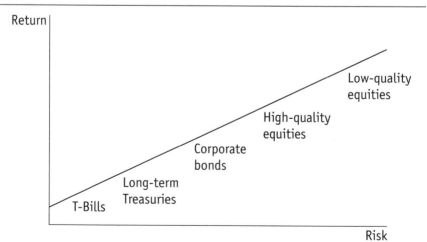

rate that reflects the acquirer's cost of capital, then this rate may not fully reflect the risk of the venture that the company would be entering into with the acquisition of the smaller, more risky company. If this is the case, then a higher discount rate, one that better reflects the risk of this specific business, needs to be employed. When such a rate is used, we will get a lower value for the business. However, if the acquirer believes that a combination between the two companies would lower some of the risk characteristics of the target, then a lower discount rate than the one that would be uses to value the target as a stand alone company may be in order. This would be one reason why the target could be more valuable as part of the bidder than on its own. The bidder just has to make sure this assumption is realistic.

## SYNERGY, VALUATION, AND THE DISCOUNT RATE

When one values a company, we choose a discount rate that reflects the risk of the business being acquired. However, when a company pursues an acquisition based on the anticipation of enjoying synergistic benefits and where the value of the benefits are reflected in the projected free cash flows in the DCF model, we have to also select a discount rate that reflects the anticipated variability of those synergy-based cash flows. In effect, when we value a business using synergistic cash flows, the risk of the deal is partially a function of the likelihood that the synergies will be realized. If this is a riskier proposition, then this risk must be built into the risk premium that is added to the discount rate. We cannot include the anticipated synergy in the cash flow projection and ignore these risks when deriving the discount rate. Anticipated synergies have their own risks that need to be assessed and incorporated directly into the valuation model. Sometimes this may be more difficult to assess than others. If several prior acquisitions in that industry have successfully resulted in such synergies, then measuring an appropriate synergy risk premium may be easier to do. If, however, a bidder is proposing to achieve certain synergistic gains that other companies have unsuccessfully tried to do, then this may warrant a higher risk premium.

When evaluating the price of a company that is being acquired partially for anticipated synergistic benefits, we have to consider the type of deal we are considering and evaluate the likelihood that the synergistic gains will ever materialize to the extent that they have been forecasted in the projected free cash flows. Synergistic benefits are usually more likely to materialize when similar businesses are combined. When the two companies are in the same business, then the buyer is in a better position to project whether specific synergies will ever come to fruition. Deals across industry boundaries, such as conglomerate M&As, may be less likely to produce synergistic benefits as opposed to acquisitions within the buyer's industry. Horizontal deals often are more likely to generate cost-based synergies. Vertical mergers and acquisitions may provide the buyer with better access to markets or supplies but may not provide any real synergies. Within-market deals may be more likely to provide synergies than market-extension deals. When we evaluate these proposed synergies, we should consider any prior M&As that made similar claims. Did they materialize? If prior ones failed, then why is this deal going to produce the sought-after synergies? Perhaps the bidder has a better acquisition strategy than other less successful dealmakers. If there have been other cases of such successfully-realized synergies, then maybe there is a road map for how they will be achieved. In this case we have a greater comfort with the idea that such synergies will be realized. If so, then maybe we do not need to add as much of a risk premium to the discount rate as we would if the synergy track for similar deals is sketchy.

## FINANCIAL SYNERGIES AND THE DISCOUNT RATE

In Chapter 2 we also discussed financial synergies, which were synergistic benefits that were related to a company cost of capital. The example we used was that of McCaw Cellular, which had a higher cost of capital than AT&T, which acquired it. If such synergies are a major factor driving the acquisition, then we may want to use a discount rate that partially reflects the bidder's cost of capital while also using a risk premium that reflects the risk that the cash flows that are projected will be realized. If the bidder is providing better access to capital markets at lower rates than what the target could achieve, then this cost factor would make earnings higher for a combined company

## APPLYING THE DISCOUNTED CASH FLOW
## METHOD OF BUSINESS VALUATION

This case study applies the discounted cash flow method of business valuation to a company that has $2.5 billion in sales in 2002. Sales are expected to grow at declining rates of growth over the next five years from 10% in 2003 to a maturity growth rate of 6% ($g$) after the fifth year. For the purposes of this simple example we define free cash flow is defined as the difference between net operating income after tax (NOPAT) and new net capital expenditures.

NOPAT = Earnings Before Interest & Taxes (EBIT) (1 − tax rate)

FCF = NOPAT − new net capital expenditures

The discount rate is taken to be the weighted average costs of capital for the company that this case study assumes is 12% ($r$). The capitalization rate that is used to compute the terminal value of the company after year five is the difference between this rate and the long-term growth rate:

WACC = $r$ = 12% and $k$ = Capitalization rate =

$r − g$ = 12% − 6% = 6%

The enterprise value of the company is the present value of its future projected cash flows. This value is computed as the sum of the present value of the individually projected cash flows for the first five years and the capitalized terminal value. This value is computed as follows:

Terminal Value = $FCF_6/(r − g)$

It is important to remember that this terminal value is itself a year five value because it is the value of the company's cash flows that are projected to be received after year five. Therefore, it must be brought to present value by multiplying it by the PVIF applicable to year five. Valuation Equation:

$$\frac{FCF_1}{(1 + k)_1} + \frac{FCF_2}{(1 + k)_2} + \ldots + \frac{FCF_5}{(1 + k)_5} + \frac{FCF_6/(r − g)}{(1 + k)_5}$$

Assumptions: Sales Growth: Growth at 10% per year declining by 5% and 6% thereafter.

Shares Outstanding (mil): 40

| Years | 1 | 2 | 3 | 4 | 5 |
|---|---|---|---|---|---|
| Sales growth rate | 10.0% | 9.5% | 9.0% | 8.0% | 7.0% |
| After-tax operating margin | 6.0% | 6.0% | 6.0% | 6.0% | 6.0% |
| Net op. cap. exp. %/sales | 5.0% | 5.0% | 5.0% | 5.0% | 5.0% |
| Weighted average cost capital (WACC) | 12.0% | | | | |
| Long-term growth rate | 6.0% | | | | |
| Sales base level—2002 | 2,500 | | | | |
| Free cash flows (1–5): | | | | | |
| Sales (mil $) | 2,750.0 | 3,011.3 | 3,282.3 | 3,544.8 | 3,793.0 |
| NOPAT | 165.0 | 180.7 | 196.9 | 212.7 | 227.6 |
| Net operating capital expenditures | 137.5 | 150.6 | 164.1 | 177.2 | 189.6 |
| Free cash flows (FCFs) | 27.5 | 30.1 | 32.8 | 35.4 | 37.9 |
| Present value of FCFs | 24.6 | 24.0 | 23.4 | 22.5 | 21.5 |

| Terminal value calculation | | Total enterprise value | |
|---|---|---|---|
| Free cash flow year 6 | 40.2 | Present value of FCFs (years 1–5) | 116.0 |
| Term. value of company in year 5 | 670.1 | Present value company's terminal value | 380.2 |
| Present value of terminal value | 380.2 | Total enterprise value | 496.2 |
| | | Deduct market value of debt and preferred | 100.0 |
| | | Total value common | 396.2 |
| | | Shares outstanding | 40.0 |
| | | Price of share of stock | 9.9 |

*Source:* Patrick A. Gaughan, *Measuring Business Interruption Losses and Other Commercial Damages* (Hoboken, NJ: John Wiley & Sons, Inc., 2004), 281–282.

compared to the target's earnings power. It probably also means that more capital can be acquired, not just a better rate. This may mean that overall cash flows are greater, because with the enhanced capital access the combined company can pursue a higher volume of business than what the target could on its own. Financial synergies such as these may mean that the discount rate used to value the target's business by itself would be higher than the discount rate that would be relevant if the business were bought by the bidder. This is another potential source of synergy that may enable the buyer to find more value if acquiring the target than what the target could achieve on its own.

In addition to providing better access to external capital, a bidder may be able to provide the target with access to its own internal capital market. Bidders who are much larger than the targets may be able to use their cash flows to help fund the target's projects. This may be important to bidders who view the risks of the target's projects differently than external capital providers, who may see greater risk than the bidder does.

## Comparable Multiples

Comparable multiples are regularly used to value business. They are a quick and easy method to come up with a value for a company. Like DCF they can be used to value both public and closely held businesses. There are two basic steps in using comparable multiple analysis: (1) selecting the correct multiple and then (2) applying it to the relevant earnings base. We will see that there are abundant areas for judgment and subjectivity in the selection of these two parameters.

Common multiples that are used are price-earnings multiples, so-called P/E ratios, price-to-book, enterprise value to EBITDA, price to revenues, as well as other combinations. Usually some normalized value of these measures is used, especially when the levels of the values fluctuate greatly. Once the multiple is derived, it is then applied to either the current year or an estimate of the next year's value of the base selected. Perhaps the most commonly cited multiple is the P/E ratio, which is the ratio of a company's stock price (P) divided by its earnings per share (EPS). When we multiply a P/E ratio by a target company's EPS, we get an estimated stock price. For example, let us say that we have analyzed 10 comparable companies and have found that the average P/E ratio is 17. We can then multiply this value by the target company's EPS, which we assume in this example is $3 per share. $17 \times \$3 = \$41$. When the multiple is derived from an analysis of historical earnings, they are referred to as *trailing multiples*. When they are based on forecasts of future earnings, they are called *forward multiples*.

Other commonly used multiples are EBITDA multiples—sometimes called cash flow multiples because EBITDA is used as a proxy for cash flows. We usually obtain EBITDA multiples by dividing enterprise value, including the sum of equity and debt capital, by a given company's EBITDA level. This is done for our group of comparable companies to derive our average value. That value is then applied to the target company's EBITDA value to obtain its enterprise value. We then back out the debt of the target from this value to get the value of its equity.

When we use comparable multiples, one obvious key issue is comparability. Are the companies that were the source of the comparables sufficiently similar? Are they more valuable or less valuable? If, for example, the company being valued is a troubled concern, then it may not be worth the same multiple of other, more healthy companies in the same industry. This would be reflected in both a lower multiple and base that it would be applied to. However, comparable multiples are forward-looking measures. A buyer is paying seven times EBITDA in our prior example, not for access to the past EBITDA level but for future cash flows. When the market establishes different acquisition multiples for companies that have been purchased, it is making a statement about the ability of those companies to generate future cash flows, and that is what establishes the multiple at a given level. So comparability is the key. It is more than just saying that a company being acquired shares the same Standard Industrial Classification (SIC) or North American Industry Classification System (NAICS) code and is in the same industry. Finding multiples for companies in the same business as the target is a first step, not the final step, in the process. Having established a range based on prior acquisitions and the multiples that were paid, the

## USE OF COMPARABLE MULTIPLES TO DETERMINE
## ENTERPRISE VALUE EXAMPLE

Enterprise value is a broad measure of value that reflects the value of the capital, both debt and equity, that has been invested in the company. In this case study, we will measure enterprise value using comparable multiples derived from similar businesses that have been sold before the current valuation. As previously noted, comparable multiples are applied to specific performance measures. Some common performance measurements are as follows:

- *EBITDA.* Earning before interest, taxes, depreciation, and amortization
- *EBIT.* Earning before interest and taxes
- *Net income.* Earnings after interest and taxes
- *Free cash flow.* Operational cash flow less capital expenditures

The example depicted in Exhibit A uses an EBITDA performance measurement. This is used as a base in Exhibit A, which shows how an enterprise value/EBITDA multiple may be computed. Exhibit B, however, shows how such a multiple can be derived from other comparable historical transactions.

### Exhibit A
EBITDA Multiple

| | |
|---|---|
| Net income | $ 2,000,000 |
| Taxes | 700,000 |
| Interest | 250,000 |
| Depreciation and amortization | 150,000 |
| EBITDA | $ 3,100,000 |
| Equity acquisition price | 12,000,000 |
| Interest bearing debt | 2,500,000 |
| Total enterprise value | 14,500,000 |
| Multiple | 4.68 |

Exhibit A illustrated the relationship between total enterprise value ($14,500,000) and EBITDA ($3,100,000). The application of the multiple indicated the EBITDA performance of a target company to be acquired

**Exhibit B**
OCI, Inc., Summary of Acquisitions

|  | Court Company | Rotary Company | Bay Products | Western Manufacturing |
|---|---|---|---|---|
| Net income | 748,125 | 304,000 | 776,000 | 2,374,000 |
| Taxes | 785,625 | 110,000 | 400,000 | 1,411,000 |
| Interest | 48,750 | 45,000 | 182,000 | 1,407,000 |
| Depreciation/ amortization | 458,125 | 233,000 | 392,000 | 3,498,000 |
| EBITDA | 2,040,625 | 692,000 | 175,000 | 8,690,000 |
| Equity acquisition price | 14,052,000 | 4,600,000 | 14,600,000 | 54,300,000 |
| Interest bearing debt | 498,000 | 1,863,000 | 2,616,000 | 15,954,000 |
| Total enterprise value | 14,555,000 | 6,463,000 | 17,216,000 | 70,254,000 |
| Multiple | 7.13 | 9.34 | 9.84 | 8.08 |
| Average EBITDA multiple | 8.60 | | | |
| Weighted average EBITDA multiple | 8.24 | | | |

will result in an estimate of total enterprise value. Equity value can then be determined by deducting interest-bearing debt from total enterprise value.

An example of the application of the comparable multiple theory can be illustrated in the following case. We are attempting to determine the appropriate value of Wilson Company, which is being acquired by OCI, Inc. OCI has made several acquisitions over the past years (see Exhibit B). Historically, OCI has paid between 7 and 10 times EBITDA, averaging 8.6 times on an unweighted basis or 8.24 times on a weighted basis, depending on the size of the transaction.

We can apply this multiple to the financials of Wilson Company, the target, to determine its approximate value (see Exhibit C). It should be pointed out that the results of Wilson's historical financial performance should be adjusted for nonrecurring or unusual items, which are not anticipated in the future.

**Exhibit C**
Valuation of Wilson Company

| | |
|---|---:|
| Net income | $  1,539,000 |
| Taxes | 928,000 |
| Interest | 374,000 |
| Depreciation and amortization | 1,194,000 |
| EBITDA | 4,035,000 |
| Average multiple | 8.24 |
| Total enterprise value | 332,484,000 |
| Interest bearing debt | 8,990,000 |
| Total equity value | $ 24,258,400 |

evaluator needs then to see how the target compares to those companies from which the average multiple was derived. If the target has many features that would enhance its future earning power, then perhaps a higher multiple should apply. It is likely that the target is aware of this and may be asking for such a multiple. If it is not, either the seller is naïve or this assessment of higher than average future earning power may be misguided.

## Takeover Bids and Control Premiums

Takeover bids typically include a premium above the market value of the stock. This premium is paid for several reasons, but one of the most fundamental is that the buyer pays for control of the target, which is more than what would be received from the purchase of a noncontrolling stake in the company.

There is a major difference between the price of a single share quoted on an organized exchange and the per-share price of a controlling stake, such as a 51% block of stock. When a buyer buys a controlling interest in a company, the buyer receives both a proportionate share in the investment attributes of the target as well as the right to control the target. With control the buyer can change the use of the target's assets in a manner that will maximize the value of the acquirer's stock. However, for this additional characteristic, the buyer will have to pay a premium—or what we are calling the *control premium*.

The value of the average control premium paid for companies acquired in the United States over the period 1980 to 2003 is shown in Exhibit 4.2. We see that over this time period, the average value was 43.6%.

## Bidding Contests and Overpaying

Target companies usually benefit when they are the focus of bidding contests, while acquirers usually end up paying more when they are forced to compete with other bidders for a target company. This is a common-sense result. However, it has been supported and documented by Cooter and Zenner, who showed that the final premium in bidding contests is higher than in offers where there is only one bidder.[1] This result is not unique to corporate takeovers but applies generally to many types of auction processes. This is why courts have encouraged target companies to pursue their "Revlon Duties." These

Exhibit 4.2   Control Premium Paid

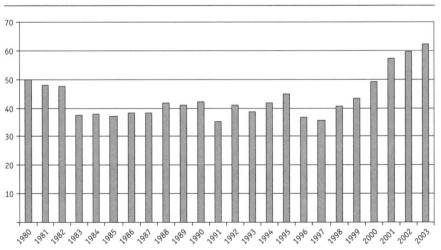

*Source: Mergerstat Review, 2004.*

duties are named after the court decision in the wake of the takeover of Revlon by Ronald Perelman's company, where Revlon sought to give a preferred acquirer, the firm of Forstmann Little, benefits that it would not provide Perelman's group. These benefits, which included lock-up options, in effect would prevent Perelman from going forward with the bidding and would thereby hurt shareholders. Courts have encouraged targets to make sure they get the best price for the company when it is being sold, and such prices often come in a bidding contest or auction process.

While bidding contests may be good for targets, they are usually not in the best interest of bidders. The worry of bidders is that they will end up with the winner's curse, where the bidder who wins the contest overpays and is cursed with an overpriced acquisition.

In Chapter 2 we briefly discussed the winner's curse of takeovers. The analogy mentioned was that of a professional sport where teams, such as basketball, football, and baseball, bid against each other for the services of star (and some not-so-star-like) athletes and end up paying well beyond what the athlete's services are worth. Varaiya analyzed a sample of 91 matched, buyer-seller acquisitions. He found that the winning bid premium "significantly overestimates the capital market's estimate of the expected takeover gain."[2] This was true in 67% of the cases examined in this research. In estimating the capital market's forecast of the expected takeover gain, he considered a target's preacquisition profitability as well as its cash flow availability. The Variya study provides some support for the role that hubris plays in contested auctions. Such processes result in values in excess of the market's valuation of the companies prospects. Clearly, the winning bidder's management believed that the market was wrong and they were right. Unfortunately, there are an abundant supply of deals where management was wrong and the market was right.

## Bidding Contests and Hubris

In Chapter 2 the role that hubris played in creating a situation where bidders overpay for a target company was discussed. Although there has not been a definitive study on the number of merger failures that were exclusively caused by hubris, there is convincing evidence that hubris plays a role in many of them. The market regularly values companies. The average premium varies over time based on market conditions as well as industry factors. When the buyer's management decides that it can afford to pay a value in excess of what the market would offer for such a company, then either management is correct and the market is wrong or management incorrectly believes that its own valuation is more accurate than the market's. Such incorrect analysis can also lead managers to assume debt levels beyond what they can really service. This is sometimes true in debt-financed acquisitions that rely on post-sale asset sales to pay down the acquisition debt and lower debt service pressure. This was the case in the 1988 recapitalization of Interco, a St. Louis–based conglomerate with major brand names (e.g., London Fog, Florsheim Shoes, Converse Shoes, Lane, Broyhill and Ethan Allen furniture, and many other well-known business units). The recapitalization plan, which the company put together in opposition to a hostile bid from the Rales Brothers, which was to be financed by Drexel Burnham Lambert, was dependent on being able to sell major assets at aggressive prices—just as the economy and the M&A boom was coming to an end. The overvaluation of the company and its business units, which was done by some leading investment banking firms, led to the bankruptcy filing of the company.

In the bankruptcy case that followed the Chapter 11 filing of Interco, a bankruptcy examiner, Sandra Mayerson, was critical of company officials who breached their fiduciary duties. However, she was especially critical of the solvency opinion issued by American Appraisal Associates, which stated that Interco was solvent following the recapitalization.[3] The report exonerated the investment bank of Wasserstein Perella & Co., because it found that the bank was misled by company officials. However, the examiner found that while the work of the different investment banks, Goldman Sachs and Wasserstein Perella, working on the project was consistent with standards in the field of investment banking, these standards were in her opinion "abysmally low." For example, two investment banks working for the same client but refusing to share information with one another. This became problematic as Goldman Sachs was hired by Interco to find buyers for the divisions while Wasserstein Perella was hired to place a value on the company.[4]

The Interco case is an example of a bidding contest that went out of control. It was also one where the investment bankers clearly did not do enough to prevent the situation from getting so far out of control while the company incurring more debt that it could pay. There was certainly more than enough blame to go around.

## Campeau Acquisition of Federated Stores

On October 31, 1986, Robert Campeau, a Canadian-based real estate magnate, established a major foothold in the U.S. department store market with the acquisition of one of the largest department store chains in the United States—Allied Stores. At first this may seem like a deal well across industry boundaries in which the two business areas have little in common, but this is too strong a statement, although there is certainly some truth to it. Department stores are often located in shopping centers and often serve as in malls, anchor stores for a given mall. Therefore, knowledge of the real state business can be helpful in the acquisition of department stores.

Campeau acquired Federated Stores in 1988. As a result, he came to control both Federated Department Stores, Inc. and Allied Stores Corporation. Unfortunately, both of these entities were forced to file for bankruptcy on January 15, 1990. Each housed major department store chains. For example, Federated featured Bloomingdale's, one of the leading upper-end department stores in the United States. The combined companies included other large department store chains such as Abraham & Strauss and Lazarus. If the individual business units of the companies that were acquired were all valuable, then where did Campeau go wrong when he did the deal? The answer, in part, lies in an overvaluation of the price for Federated and the assumption of too much debt to finance this inflated value.

Before the Campeau bid, Federated's stock traded in the range of up to $33 per share. In January 1988, Campeau made a takeover bid of $47 per share, which was a premium over the late 1987 market price. Campeau then got into a bidding contest with Edward Finkelstein of Macy's as both bid for the prized department store chain. Campeau was determined to succeed and gain control over this company and would not back down. Finkelstein seemed to have similar emotions but knew (or at least his advisors did) when to fold when the price got too rich to be justified. Federated would be a valuable prize for Finkelstein, but there was only so far he was willing to go to get the prize.

Campeau would not be stopped and kept bidding until his offer reached $73.50 per share—a 124% premium! The bidding contest started out at a reasonable premium with some room for increases. The price implied an enterprise value in excess of $8 billion. Robert Kaplan of the University of Chicago has estimated the extent to which Campeau has overpaid for Federated, and this is shown in Exhibit 4.3.

**Exhibit 4.3**
Actual and Market-Adjusted Value of Federated Department Stores

Actual and market-adjusted value[a] of Federated Department Stores under pre-Campeau management, Federated assets under Campeau Corporation, and the purchase price paid by Campeau Corporation. Values of Federated under Campeau are the sum of asset sales, interim cash flows, and the value of remaining Federated assets. All values are in billions of dollars.

| Federated market value December 31, 1987[b] | Three valuation estimates of Federated under Campeau as of December 31, 1989[c] | Price paid by Campeau (including fees)[d] |
|---|---|---|
| | *(A) Actual value* | |
| $4.25 | Conservative: $6.20 | $8.17 |
| | Most likely: $7.35 | |
| | Optimistic: $8.49 | |
| $4.25 | *(B) Value market-adjusted to December 31,1987* | $7.67 |
| | Conservative: $5.28 | |
| | Most likely: $6.08 | |
| | Optimistic: $6.88 | |

a. Market-adjusted values equal the actual values discounted from the month in which they occur to December 31, 1987, by the actual return on the S&P 500. If invested in the S&P 500 on January 1, 1988, the market-adjusted value would equal the actual value in the month the cash flow occurs.

b. Federated market value on December 31, 1987, equals the sum of the market value of equity and the estimated market value of Federated debt. Details are provided in the text.

c. Value of Federated assets under Campeau equals the sum of asset sales, interim cash flows, and the value of remaining assets for the most likely case, conservative case, and optimistic case valuations. Asset sales are the value of the divisions sold by Federated from May 1988 to February 1989. Interim cash flows equal earnings before interest, taxes, depreciation, and amortization (EBITDA) less capital expenditure and the increase in net working capital.

d. Purchase price paid by Campeau is the sum of the market value paid for all equity and the fees paid in May 1988, and the book value of Federated debt outstanding on January 30, 1988.

While Kaplan gives us various different valuations of Federated based on different values of its divisions, they fall below the $8.17 billion price Campeau paid. Federated may have been undervalued as of the end of 1987, and both bidders were probably well aware of that. What made them continue on with the bidding contest into a range well beyond what the company was worth is a puzzle that can only be explained by hubris. The problem was greatly compounded by the manner in which the deal was financed. Campeau effectively financed 97% of the Federated purchase with debt (including assumed Federated debt)." These are the kinds of highly leveraged transactions that we rarely see today. When the cash flows from the various divisions within Federated could not support the great pressures of the huge debt service, the deal collapsed. If the deal had not been almost totally financed with debt, it may not have resulted in a Chapter 11 filing. If there had been a greater equity cushion, debt service pressures would have been less. Regardless, at the value placed on Federated by Campeau, the deal was destined to be a failure.

Was Robert Campeau simply a naive investor who lacked expert assistance and made a multibillion-dollar mistake? If this was the answer, then we would have easily isolated the problem, but it is not that simple. Campeau was advised by the investment banks First Boston Corp. and Wasserstein Perella (formed by these two former First Boston executives). We certainly cannot conclude that Campeau made such a valuation in isolation. He had the assistance of legal and financial experts who aided him in doing one of the biggest megaflops in history. So there is plenty of high-priced credit and blame to go around. It cannot be that there was not enough financial expertise available to create an accurate valuation mode. If the expertise is not enough to help us, what will? Maybe a little common sense.

If Campeau and some of the providers of capital were big losers in the Federated deal, were there any winners? Yes. The shareholders who received the hefty premium that Campeau could not afford were big winners. Campeau "paid $296 million in fees to complete the tender offer and an additional $133 million in fees as part of the merger."[5] Advisors profited handsomely for advice that helped complete one of the bigger mega-flops in merger history.

The fact that the Federated transaction was financed with so much debt was troubling in light of the fact that Campeau was already highly leveraged in advance of that acquisition. Kaplan puts the value of Campeau Corp. debt as of January 31, 1988, at $4.57 billion, while the book and market value of its equity was $0.09 billion and $0.07 billion, respectively. Its U.S. subsidiary, which housed the Allied Stores chain, also had much debt.

Following the leveraged acquisition, Campeau proceeded with the contemplated asset sales that are necessary in such deals to try to pay down the debt and reduce the burdensome debt service pressures. Exhibit 4.4 shows Kaplan's summarization of the asset sale prices and the buyers for the nine divisions that were sold off. It is interesting to see that R. H. Macy, the rival bidder, bought the Bullocks and I Magnin chains for a total of $1.1 billion. This illustrates how companies may profit from M&As if they are patient. Macy's lost the contest for Federated but was able to win some of the Federated divisions it prized. (We will see later that they really did not win anything, but instead ended up losers.)

The deal began to unravel shortly after the acquisition, and the proceeds from the asset sales were not enough to prevent a liquidity shortfall. Total proceeds from the asset sales were $4.04 billion. The investment bankers, notably including First Boston, were unable to refinance the $2 billion bridge loan they had given Campeau to bridge him over the period between when he needed the money to help finance the acquisitions and when he could refinance after the deal through high-yield bond sales. The junk bond market had weakened considerably by this time, another miscalculation by the investment bankers, and the demand for these bonds was not there when it was needed. In fall 1989, Campeau went to Toronto-based real estate developers, Olympia and York, who provided a $250 million loan, but this proved to be only a stopgap measure. By the end of that year, Campeau Corp. had to admit that it could not service the debt and would be forced to file Chapter 11.

Exhibit 4.4

Division sold, month of sale, purchaser, sale price, and market-adjusted sale price for divisions of Federated Department Stores sold after Federated's acquisition by Campeau Corporation in May 1988.

| Division sold | Month sold | Purchaser | Actual sale price ($ billions) | Market-adjusted sale price ($ billions)[a] |
|---|---|---|---|---|
| Bullock's | May 1988 | R.H. Macy | | |
| I.Magnin | May 1988 | R.H. Macy | $1.10 | $1.03 |
| Filene's | May 1988 | May Department Stores | | |
| Foley's | May 1988 | May Department Stores | $1.50 | $1.41 |
| Filene's Basement | July 1988 | Management buyout | $0.13 | $0.11 |
| Ralph's Supermarkets | August 1988 | Spin-off, buyout | $0.90 | $0.85 |
| Gold Circle | October 1988 | Liquidated | $0.30 | $0.27 |
| Main Street | November 1988 | Kohl's Department Stores | $0.09 | $0.08 |
| The Children's Place | February 1989 | Management buyout | $0.03 | $0.02 |
| | | Total Proceeds | $4.04 | $3.77 |

[a] Market-adjusted sale price is the sale price discounted from the month of sale to December 31, 1987 by the total return on the S&P 500. If invested in the S&P 500 on January 1, 1988, the market-adjusted sale price would equal the sale price at the month of sale.

Several lessons can be derived from this acquisition failure. The interplay between a bidding contest and a hubris-driven CEO, unconstrained by a board of directors or his financial advisors, is a dangerous combination. Such individuals have trouble backing away from a bidding contest that has gotten so rich. The second lesson is the troubling impact of highly leveraged acquisitions. High leverage puts great pressure on the cash flows of a company, and there is little equity cushion to absorb unplanned downturns. One additional lesson is that there has to be a recognition of the precarious position that such highly leveraged acquisition puts a company in. One cannot assume that the markets for asset sales are going to stay strong and that the debt financing markets also will be thriving. There appears to not have been much of a scenario analysis, where these factors were incorporated into the valuation model and the impact of such events were shown. We cannot assume that strong conditions will remain steadfast and not have any contingency for weakening. If a deal cannot withstand such weakening in the post-takeover period, then its risk must be recognized, and the corporate governance process has to step in and restrain the headstrong CEO and his compensation-driven advisors. This did not occur here, and the bankruptcy filing is testimony to that failure.

One note of humor is that boards need to be wary of deals made on odd dates. Campeau bought Allied on October 31, 1986, Halloween, and he bought Federated on April 1, 1988, April Fool's Day. The significance of these dates and the outcome of the purchases is noteworthy.

We would be remiss if we did not comment on how Macy's fared after its involvement in the ill-fated bidding contest. The debt that it incurred in the $1.1 billion acquisition of Bullocks and I Magnin, along with the debt it had from the $3.58 billion leveraged buyout it conducted in 1986, forced the company to file for Chapter 11 bankruptcy protection in 1992. We can get a sense of how good Macy's valuation process was when we consider that as part of its reorganization plan the company closed the entire I Magnin division. Ironically, Macy's and Federated merged in 1994.

## MATTEL: STRATEGIC VISION, OVERVALUATION, AND HUBRIS

Some targets have greater value to certain bidders than to others. For some companies, a target may be such a good strategic fit and add so much to its future value that will "overpay." While overpaying can hardly be recommended, it is clear that some targets are more valuable to certain bidders compared to others. We also have to realize that hubris may cloud a bidding CEO's vision so that it may believe that its valuation is superior to the market. This seems to have been the case in 1999 when Mattell paid $3.5 billion for the Learning Company—an educational software company. In 2000 Mattell sold off this acquisition and received virtually nothing in exchange! In February 2000, Julie Barad announced she was stepping down as CEO of the toy company. Her disastrous acquisitions proved to be her downfall. Yet just one year before Mattell bought the Learning Company Ms. Barad was at the top of the corporate world as underscored by a cover story about her in *BusinessWeek*. She assumed the role of CEO in 1997 and was quickly touted as one of the leading female executives in the United States.

Mattell had done some aggressive acquisitions prior to Barad taking the helm. They had bought Tyco Toys and Fisher Price which helped the company offer a broad product line. However, when Barad took the reigns of the company that brought Barbie to young girls across the country, she applied a vision that was hard to comprehend. Computer-based learning products for children was not similar to the toy products that had made the company so successful. In buying the Learning Company Barad paid a hefty price for an uncertain gain. The market and the board were quick to recognize its error and Barad was asked to step aside.

## TOE HOLDS AND BIDDING CONTESTS

One partial antidote to the adverse effects of auction bidders is for them to establish a toe hold. Toe holds are prebid ownerships of target company shares. They provide certain specific benefits for bidders. For one, they may allow the bidder to acquire shares at lower prices than what would apply after a bid has been announced. Bidders in the United States are somewhat limited in their use of toe holds in that Section 13d of the Williams Act requires the filing of a Schedule 13D within 10 days on acquiring 5% or more of the target's shares.[6] In addition, the market may learn on its own the identity of any acquirers of a large amount of shares even independent of the Williams Act requirements. In addition, if a bidder gets involved in the losing end of a bidding contest, it may be able to still gain by enjoying the difference between the winning bid price and the actual price paid for the shares acquired for the toe hold. Some research evidence suggests that toe holds may restrain potential bidders from making a competing bid and starting an auction for the target.[7]

## BIDDING CONTEST PROTECTIONS

The best protection for potential bidders in bidding contests is not to get involved in them in the first place. Such auctions are in the best interests of targets and usually not in the interests of acquirers. However, a bidder does not always know if it is going to ultimately be involved in a bidding contest when it first makes an offer—even a friendly deal. When an acquirer makes an offer for a target to merge with it, even if it tries to deter it by entering into *a no-shop agreement,* where the target agrees not to shop its company to other bidders, such an agreement may be challenged by shareholders or other bidders. For example, this was done when Paramount Communications was trying to avoid a hostile takeover by QVC. Courts generally do not want to enforce such agreements when they work against the auction process and limit shareholder wealth.

Bidders cannot feel confident that, even if they have a no-shop clause in their merger agreement, other bidders still will not come out of the woodwork. Bidders usually realize that if they make an offer to acquire or merge with a company, that initial offer may stimulate an interest in the target. Potential acquirers do not want to invest the time and expense of making an offer only to have the company sell to another bidder. Sometimes this happens, but it is something bidders want to avoid. One partial solution to the problem is to enter into an agreement where the target agrees to compensate the bidder in the form of a breakup fee. This is a payment that a target agrees to pay to the initial bidder if the company is ultimately sold to another firm and the initial deal is broken up. The largest breakup fee of all time occurred when American Home Products (AHP), now called Wyeth, received a $1.8 billion payment when Pfizer Corp. made an alternative to acquire the target—Warner Lambert. AHP won the "consolation prize" of the $1.8 billion while Pfizer acquired Warner Lambert with its line of cash flow generating pharmaceutical products to add to its own. AHP, unfortunately, was not able to invest these monies into an alternative acquisition because it was forced to pour them, along with billions more, into payments to diet drug plaintiffs and their attorneys. These billions of external payments came at a time when the pharmaceutical industry was consolidating and many pharmaceutical companies were acquiring research and development and other capabilities to better compete against increasingly larger rivals. Wyeth, however, responded with its own effective research and development and continued to grow, although we will never know just how much the company would have grown if it had not been hampered by these unprecedented litigation obligations.

## Do Managers Knowingly Overpay?

In Chapter 2 we discussed the hubris hypothesis of takeovers where managers would inadvertently pay more than what a target was worth because of managers' overestimating their ability to value the target and believing it is superior to that of the market. They also may overestimate their ability to manage the target and extract value from it. Directors who are evaluating a proposed acquisition and premium offer need to assess the extent to which managers may be motivated by hubris when they propose a particular offer price. Another relevant issue is whether managers purposefully overpay. Could they be so motivated by their own self-interest that they would knowingly pay more for the target than what is in the interest of shareholders?

Nejay Seyhun conducted a study to try to determine whether managers would knowingly overpay for a target.[8] He did this by examining managers' own purchases for their personal equity accounts. If managers knowingly overpaid, then deals that would be expected to cause the bidder's stock price to fall would be expected to be associated with stock sales before the offer.[9] Seyhun analyzed a sample of 393 firms involved in takeovers. His analysis of managers' trading activity failed to support the notion that they knowingly overpay. He found some small increases in insider stock purchases and some small decreases in stock sales before the announcement of an offer. He did find that in cases where there were larger two-day announcement period excess returns that insiders tended to be more optimistic, as reflected by their trading activity, than in situations where there was a negative stock market reaction. This research seems to imply that managers are somewhat adept at anticipating instances where there will be a strong positive reaction to a bid. However, this research does not support the notion that managers knowingly overpay. Whether they overpay for hubris reasons or because of incompetence is another issue that has not been fully addressed by research.

## Premiums from Strategic Mergers

We have discussed various motives for M&As that are not in shareholders' interests. Deals that have more of a strategic focus should be more in shareholders' interests than those that are made without much strategic focus. Does the extent to which there is a strategic focus affect the value of the premium that bidders are willing to pay? Roach investigated whether the size of the control premium is greater for strategic mergers versus those transactions that lack such a strategic focus.[10] Nonstrategic acquisitions have been criticized as deals that add little value to the acquiring firm. In theory, if strategic deals are more valuable, then sellers should be in a better position to demand higher premiums. In a study of 1,446 transactions over the period 1992 to 1997, Roach failed to find any difference in the control premium for those deals where the merging companies have the same or different SIC codes. This implies that strategic focus is not a determinant of merger premiums. Whether it should be an important determinant is another matter.

## Does the Market Value Control Independent of Takeovers?

Having cited the abundant evidence supporting the existence of a control premium in takeovers, we should determine whether control provides a premium in the absence of takeovers. In a study designed to measure the premium paid for control, Lease, McConnell, and Mikkelson sought to determine whether capital markets place a separate value on control.[11]

Their study examined the market prices of common stocks of 30 companies with classes of common stock that pay identical dividends but that differ significantly in their voting rights. One group had substantially greater voting rights on issues related to the control of the firm, such as the election of directors. The two groups of securities provided the same opportunities for financial gain and differed only in their voting rights and the opportunities to control the company's future. Their results showed that for 26 firms that had no voting preferred stock outstanding, the superior voting common stock graded at a premium relative to the other classes of common stock. The average premium they found was 5.44%. It is important to remember that this is not inconsistent with the premiums cited earlier, because these other premiums are found in takeovers. This is expected, however, because the companies included in the Lease study were not involved in takeovers.

Four of the 30 firms considered in the study showed that the superior voting rights common stock traded at a discount relative to the other class of common stock. These firms differed from the other 26, however, in that they had a more complex capital structure that featured preferred stock with voting rights. Given the existence of this type of voting preferred stock, these four are not as comparable to the other 26 clear-cut cases. Another study that focused on specific industries, such as the banking industry, found control premiums in the range of 50% to 70%.[12]

## Reliability of Accounting Data

The reliability of earnings data has drawn much attention in recent years, particularly as it relates to M&As. The relevance to M&As has to do with not just the premerger valuation analysis but also the assessment of postmerger performance. Two areas of such manipulations that have received much attention in recent years are in-process R&D charges and restructuring charges. Utilizing such charges has raised some concerns about the consistency of the accounting treatment of mergers. In addition, there is also the concern that the reported numbers may be fraudulently inaccurate.

## OVERPAYING AND FRAUDULENT
## SELLER FINANCIALS

Buyers usually are able to rely on the audited financial statements of target companies to provide information necessary to apply the different valuation models we have already discussed. However, if the inputs used in these models, such as revenue or earnings levels, are fraudulently inflated, then the resulting value will be correspondingly inflated. Buyers who make bids based on such manipulated numbers may end up overpaying.

One example of such a fraudulent misrepresentation was revealed in 1998 when Cendant Corp. reported that its earnings were overstated. Cendant is a franchiser of Ramada hotels, Coldwell Banker real estate, Avis Rent-a-Car, and a marketer of membership clubs. It was formed with the December 1997 merger of HFS, Inc. and CUC International, Inc. The company was forced to report that CUC International, originally called Comp U Card, deliberately inflated revenues and decreased expenses. CUC marketed consumer products and had a network of consumers for which it supposedly offered the best prices on a wide variety of products such as washers, dryers, and televisions. The business had certain attractive features, and it was really a broker for these products and did not maintain inventories but was merely a middleman in an electronic shopping business. Hospitality Franchise Systems, Inc. (HFS) was a franchiser of hotels including Ramada, Howard Johnson's, and Days Inn. The company was also in other businesses such as car rental operations and vacation clubs.

The merger between HFS and CUC was supposed to provide synergies through cross-marketing of services to the joint customer bases. We have discussed how difficult it can be to actually realize such revenue-enhancing synergies. On paper this deal looked good, but the only problem was that the numbers were not accurate. The misrepresentation was reflected in the treatment of revenues from offered memberships for which customers can ask for a full refund. In its restated data, the company reported revenues reflecting a high 50% cancellation rate. Various estimates of the inflated profits ranged from $500 million to $640 million. The deliberate falsification of financial statements is an acquisition nightmare scenario. The market reacted negatively to this news, and the stock price of Cendant fell.

With the new protections put in place by the accounting scandals of the 1990s and early 2000s, we hope there will be fewer instances of such fraud. However, buyers can try to protect themselves by using some common sense when reviewing the financials of target companies. If the target is unusually profitable or has grown at an unusually high rate relative to its competitors, then it is either being managed very well, has other specific factors that may cause this, or is misrepresenting its financial data. The more impressive the target's financials, the more closely the buyer has to review the data. If it is too good to be true, then maybe it is not true. Buyers will never be able to eliminate the possibility of fraud, but they can work hard to protect against it. It is not unreasonable that if the target is asking for a very high premium as a result of its great financials, that the buyer be allowed to do even more detailed due diligence to make sure the numbers are correct. In a short buying process, there is only so much due diligence you can do. However, buying corporations owe it to their shareholders to take reasonable steps to ensure that they are not overpaying.

## VALUATION AND HIDDEN COSTS

One of the problems with conducting a reliable valuation of a target company is that sometimes there may be costs that are hard to measure accurately. Some costs may be totally unknown, such as unforeseen litigation liabilities that manifest themselves after an acquisition. This was the case for some companies that acquired firms that became the target of asbestos litigation. It was believed at one time that the problems of asbestos liabilities were contained but this changed in late 1990s and many otherwise viable companies were forced to file for Chapter 11 bankruptcy protection due to the pressures of mounting asbestos lawsuits. The acquirers of such companies did not foresee the extent to which the litigation process would change.

There are various ways that companies can try to deal with such hidden costs. One is to try to do better predeal due diligence. Acquirers and their advisors have become aware of specific areas that can be sources of hidden costs, such as environmental liabilities, and have adapted the due diligence process to try to discover such costs prior to completion of deals. In addition, companies may be able to obtain M&A insurance that may provide some protection from hidden costs. The better and more thorough the premerger due diligence process, the less likely such costs will manifest themselves after the deal closes. Although these costs can never be totally eliminated, they have to be reduced to as low a level as possible.

## POSTMERGER INTEGRATION COSTS— HARD COSTS TO MEASURE

In some cases postmerger integration costs can be difficult to measure. For companies that do many deals, such as serial acquirers like Cisco, this is less likely as they have postmerger acquisition processes that have been developed based upon their successful experience in integrating many acquired entities into their company. For companies that have little experience with M&A, these costs may add another element of risk. When the target is small relative to the acquirer, the risk may also be small. For targets that are large relative to the bidder, such as when NCR was poorly integrated into AT&T after its

### QUAKER OATS' ACQUISITION OF SNAPPLE

A classic example of overpaying was the acquisition of Snapple by Quaker Oats. In 1994 Quaker Oats had acquired Snapple for $1.7 billion. Just three years later, in March 1997, Quaker Oats announced that it was selling Snapple for $300 million to Triac Cos. Now that is value creation for you! The market reacted positively to this financial admission of what was well known to be a big mistake when on March 27, 1997, Quaker Oats stock closed at $37.75—up 25 cents.

How did Quaker Oats, a well-known and established company with major consumer brands, make such a huge error? Clearly it overvalued Snapple and thought that its growth, which before the acquisition had been impressive, would continue. Snapple used its prior growth to demand a high premium, as it should have done. Quaker should have more realistically evaluated Snapple's growth prospects and used a more modest growth rate when it valued Snapple.

At the time that Quaker made its rich offer for Snapple, many analysts questioned it and thought that Quaker was overpaying. The word at the time was that Quaker might be overpaying by about as much as $1 billion. But Quaker was not buying Snapple in a vacuum, and it was already successful in the soft or recreational drinks business with its Gatorade line. Gatorade was and still is a successful beverage and has carved out its own niche in this business that is separate and distinct from giants such as Coke and Pepsi. To a large extent, Snapple had already done the same thing. However, with the familiarity it already had with the beverage business through its experience with Gatorade, Quaker Oats should have known better. It would be one thing for Quaker Oats to have had no experience with this business and make such a mistake. While that would not have made the misvaluation excusable, it is even less excusable considering that they should have known this business and Snapple's prospects better.

Quaker Oats is an established company with a 100-year history in business. It has a diverse product line that ranges from pancakes and cereals to juices and sports drinks. Quaker had already done well with its Gatorade acquisition. One author reported, however, that the success of this acquisition for Quaker's CEO, William Smithburg, was based on luck and impulsive decision making rather than shrewd acquisition planning.[a] He was reported to have bought this company based on "his taste buds" rather than a more serious market and valuation analysis. Regardless of his reasoning, however, the Gatorade purchase was a big success. The business cost him $220 million, and he grew it into a $1 billion company. Based on this success, Quaker's board gave him more free rein for other acquisitions, and it was here that both he and the board made an error.

The Quaker Oats–Snapple debacle was compounded by the manner in which the deal was financed. In order to raise the capital to afford the Snapple acquisition, Quaker sold its "highly successful pet and bean divisions" to "raise $110 million of the $1.8 billion price tag."[b] It sacrificed a profitable, albeit boring, business to purchase an overpriced and mature business.

Triac was a company with its own acquisition history. It was run by Nelson Peltz and Peter May. Peltz was well known in the world of M&A, having led Triangle Industries, which was involved in some well-known leveraged transactions working with Drexel Burnham Lambert and Michael Milken in the fourth merger wave. Triangle grew from acquiring stakes in several can-making companies, consolidating them, and eventually selling them to a French company for $1.26 billion.

Quaker made more errors than just overpaying. After it bought Snapple, it changed its advertising and marketing campaign. Before its sale, Snapple used an odd set of advertisements that featured a Snapple employee named Wendy Kaufman. When Quaker bought Snapple, it changed this campaign to one that directly positioned Snapple behind Coke and Pepsi. This campaign, however, did little to help Snapple grow enough to justify its rich price.

In 2000 Triac packaged together its beverage operations, which included RC Cola, Mistic, and Snapple, and sold them to Cadbury for $1 billion plus the assumption of $420 million of debt. This was a great deal for Triac when one considers that it invested only $75 million in equity for Snapple and borrowed the rest of the $300 million. The fact that Cadbury paid $1.4 billion for this business in 2000 is ironic in that it passed on the Snapple acquisition a few years earlier because it believed that the business was too troubled to justify a much lower price than what it eventually paid.[c] Triac's success is yet another example of how one dealmaker's failure can be a source for other opportunistic buyers.

Why did Quaker Oats overpay? One factor that is clear is that it believed there was more growth potential in the Snapple business than what was really there. To review the reasonableness of Quaker Oats' assessment of Snapple's growth potential, one can consider the distribution into the market that Snapple already enjoyed in 1997. Snapple had grown impressively before that year. It had a high growth rate to show potential buyers. Buyers, however, needed to assess if that growth was sustainable. One way to do so would be to determine how many more food outlets Snapple could get into and how much more product it could sell at those that it had managed to get distribution into. Was it already in most of the food stores that it would be able to get into in the U.S. market? Could it really increase sales significantly at the outlets it was already in? If it was at a maturity position, in a noncarbonated beverage market that was growing significantly but where the growth was slowing, then this needed to be incorporated into the valuation model using either a lower growth rate for a DCF model or a lower multiple for a comparable multiples model. That is, if historical growth rates were extrapolated, this would result in an overvaluation. Obviously, Quaker Oats was using inflated parameters when it significantly overpaid for Snapple.

a. Paul C. Nutt, *Why Decisions Fail* (San Francisco: Berrett-Koehler, 2002), pp. 87–93.
b. Ibid., p. 245.
c. Constance Hays, "Cadbury Schweppes to Buy Snapple Drinks Line, *The New York Times* (September 19, 2000): C1.

1991 acquisition, postmerger integration can present more significant problems. Bidders with more M&A experience are usually better able to measure these costs. Those who lack such experience may seek the help of consultants and their investment bankers to make up for this knowledge gap.

One good example of major postmerger integration costs was the 1997 stock merger between Kroll Associates and O'Gara Company. Kroll is considered by many to be one of the leading investigative and security companies in the world, whereas O'Gara was known more for its armored cars and guard services. They were both part of a broadly defined security business, but once again the definition of "related" came into play in this deal. O'Gara, led by founder Thomas O'Gara, pursued Jules Kroll and his firm, which was the gem of the high-end investigation business. However, among the many differences between the two companies was a very different corporate culture that made integration problematic. While both companies provided services to major corporate clients, the nature of the services they provided and the specific groups within corporations that they interacted with were different. The integration problems between the two companies came to a head in 1999 with media reports of a falling out between the heads of the two business units. Part of these reported disputes had to do with their postmerger acquisition strategy where the two company leaders could not agree on merger candidates. By 2000, the integration and culture problems at the combined company became so pronounced that the company announced it was breaking up into three parts. This sharp U-turn in strategy came in part from not understanding the cultural differences between the two companies and the costs that would be incurred in trying to integrate such diverse cultures.

## CONCLUSION

The field of valuation is as much of an art as it is a science. Valuation models appear to be scientific and exact. However, they include many subjective assumptions that when changed can lead to a different value for a company. There are several different valuation methods, but two of the more commonly used for M&As are the discounted cash flow and the comparable multiples methods. With the DCF method, free cash flows are projected into the future for a period such as five years. They are discounted back to present value using a risk-adjusted discount rate. In the comparable multiples method, acquisition multiples for similar companies are selected and then applied to a relevant base. Various comparable multiples, such as P/E, are available to use to value businesses.

Because of the subjective nature of some of the inputs of the valuation models, an overly optimistic assessment of a company's prospects can cause some of these inputs or parameters to be skewed. For example, in a DCF model, this overoptimism can mean that the growth rate for the free cash flows is higher than it should be. It could also mean that the risk assessment is lower than appropriate. This may mean that the risk premium that should be added to the risk-free rate is lower than what it should be. Both situations will result in an overvaluation. Similarly, using higher comparable multiples will result in an overvaluation. The higher comparables may come from selecting comparable companies that are in better condition and have higher growth prospects than the target company. It may also come from applying the comparable multiple to a higher than appropriate base.

Another source of overvaluation is managerial hubris. Hubris-driven managers may be more likely to get involved in contested auctions and may not have the self control to back down when the price of the target gets bid too high. In such situations, boards have to be extra vigilant and monitor the valuation process. If the CEO lacks the self control to walk away from an overvalued bid, then the board needs to step in.

The discussion thus far assumes that the data used for a valuation are correct. However, when these values are inaccurate, the resulting value of the target company may also be inaccurate. The lessons of the 1990s have taught us that managers will sometimes, for a variety of reasons but mainly greed, falsify financial data. These false data may escape the attention of auditors. Various regulatory changes have been enacted that may provide greater assurance that data contained in audited financials filed by public companies will be more reliable.

# ENDNOTES

1. James Cooter and Marc Zenner, "How Managerial Wealth Affects the Tender Offer Process," *Journal of Financial Economics* 35 (1994): 63–97.
2. Nikhal Variya, "The Winners Curve Hypothesis and Corporate Takeovers," Managerial and Decision Economics 9 (1988): 209–219.
3. Floyd Norris, "Almost Everyone is Faulted in Interco Bankruptcy Case," *The New York Times* (October 25, 1991): D1.
4. Ibid.
5. Steven Kaplan, "Campeau's Acquisition of Federated," *Journal of Financial Economics* 25 (1989).
6. Other laws, such as the Hart Scott Rodino Antitrust Improvements Act may limit the ability to acquire a toe hold as they may require the approval of antitrust authorities before continuation of an offer once a certain dollar limit of share holdings, such as $50 million worth of stock.
7. Jeremy Bulow, Ming Huang, and Paul Klemperer, "Toeholds and Takeovers," *Journal of Political Economy* 107 (June 1999): 427–454.
8. H. Nejat Seyhun, "Do Bidder Managers Knowingly Pay Too Much for Target Firms," *Journal of Business* 63, no. 4 (October 1990): 439–464.
9. Note that the Section 16c of the Securities Exchange Act of 1934 prohibits short sales by insiders while 16 (b) requires the return of short swing profits from a sale and purchase within six months of each other. We also assume that we are not including trades motivated by violation of insider trading laws.
10. George R. Roach, "Control Premiums and Strategic Mergers," *Business Valuation Review* (June, 1998): 42–49.
11. Ronald C. Lease, John J. McConnell, and Wayne H. Mikkelson, "The Market Value of Control in Publicly Traded Companies," *Journal of Financial Economics* 11 (April 1983).
12. Larry McElcer and Maurice Joy, "Price Premiums for Controlling Shares of Closely Held Bank Stocks," *Journal of Business* 53 (1980): 297–314.

# Case Study

# AOL Time Warner

On January 10, 2002, American Online (AOL) and Time Warner announced the second largest merger in history. The initial valuation placed on the deal was $166 billion. The deal merged the world's largest Internet service provider, AOL, with Time Warner, one of the largest media companies featuring magazines, movies, cable networks, and music producers. Time Warner was a combination of a prior merger between Time, Inc. and Warner Brothers. The AOL–Time Warner deal proved to be a disaster for its shareholders, especially Time Warner shareholders. At the time, AOL shares were highly valued, thereby allowing those shareholders to receive 55% of the combined company, with Time Warner shareholders getting the remaining 45%. As bad as the stock of the combined company performed after the merger, AOL shareholders were probably better off being combined with Time Warner because that unit continued to perform well after the deal, whereas the AOL side suffered and pulled down the overall company. In light of this, we would expect that AOL shareholders would have been worse off if they had not had Time Warner's performance to offset their losses.

Therefore, it would seem that AOL could thank its chairman, Steve Case, for at least finding a good partner to merge with using its overvalued stock. He negotiated an all-stock, no-collar deal with Gerald Levin of Time Warner, who did this deal as his last hurrah. Time Warner shareholders probably wished he had retired earlier than April 2002 when he finally stepped down from the failing media giant. Levin, who had a 30-year history with the company and its predecessors, had a good track record up to that point. He could not pass up this huge deal and eagerly accepted overvalued AOL stock for his company. Those same shareholders, however, cannot thank him for managing the company well because its postmerger performance was very bad.

It was amazing that somewhere in the negotiation process Levin did not pause and consider that AOL stock was valued at 231 times cash flow![1] The deal was labeled a merger of equals, but as we have seen with other deals given that same label, one party usually quickly becomes the dominant entity. Levin and Time Warner wanted the combined company to be split 50:50, while Case offered a 60:40 split. Levin compromised with a 55:45 deal,[2] even though AOL added less than 20% of the total revenues and less than one-third of the combined company's cash flows.

At the onset of the deal, it was more of an acquisition of Time Warner by AOL than a merger of equals. Time Warner management reluctantly put up with this situation until AOL began pulling down the combined company.

## PRIOR DEALS BY THE MERGER PARTNERS

Before the AOL deal, Time Warner was involved in some large mergers that generally worked out well. The main one was the merger between Time and Warner in 1989. This deal become a hotly contested hostile battle as Paramount emerged with a counterbid and sought to transform the merger of equals into an auction. Paramount lost this argument in the Delaware courts and the deal went forward. Time Warner was run for a time by Steven Ross and Gerald Levin,

1. Richard Morgan, "The Big Picture," *The Daily Deal,* May 29, 2003.
2. Alec Klein, *Stealing Time: Steve Case, Jerry Levin and the Collapse of AOL Time Warner* (New York: Simon Schuster, 2003), p. 95.

**Exhibit A**
Time Warner Stock Price Growth during the 1990s

Source: finance.yahoo.com.

with Levin eventually becoming the sole CEO in December 1992. The company then merged with Turner Broadcasting in a $7.5 billion deal in September 1995, making Ted Turner its largest shareholder. Shareholders did well during this time period, as shown in Exhibit A. Part of this fine performance, however, was simply the runup of the stock market in general, which carried with it many such companies.

While Time Warner, or its various components, had a long history, AOL had only gone public in March 1992 when it raised $66 million. In 1999 it acquired Netscape, which was a major player in the Internet industry as a result of its 1994 introduction of its Netscape Navigator Web browser. Its contribution to AOL, however, was not what was originally anticipated when the deal was announced.

## STRATEGY BEHIND THE DEAL

AOL, being the world's largest Internet service provider, had 34 million customers. However, as of 2002, the number of subscribers was down to 32.5 million—still significant but indicative of the fact that the business was losing ground to competitors. However, this was a large audience to which many products could possibly be delivered online. The architects of the deal saw the AOL–Time Warner deal as a marriage of content, that which Time Warner had, and distribution, the contribution that AOL was supposed to provide. Time Warner had long looked at the Internet as a major emerging market in the media industry. It tried to enter part of this business on its own and invested hundreds of millions of dollars in its failed attempt to do so. Its Full Service Network, an interactive TV business, was a bust. From failures such as this one, Time Warner management realized it could not be successful going down the Internet road alone, but it believed that this road was the path to the future. Time Warner looked to AOL to take it down the Internet path—and it certainly got a ride for its money.

When we look back at AOL's growth to becoming the leading Internet service provider, we see that it did not face formidable competition in its ascent to the number-one position in the industry. The number of subscribers rose with the growth of PC sales and the proliferation of the Microsoft Windows operating system. AOL went from 1 million subscribers in 1994 to 10 million just three years later. Although this growth is impressive, the performance of its two main rivals, Compuserve and Prodigy, can hardly be considered impressive. By 2000 AOL doubled its subscribers and had six times the number of its number-two rival—Earthlink. As the technology became available, the market rewarded the best of the main Internet service providers, and AOL prevailed while Compuserve and Prodigy let opportunities slip through their grasp and into AOL's waiting clutches. Eventually, Microsoft, and to some extent cable companies, would step into the market and provide more meaningful competition.

At the end of 1996, as part of its growth strategy, AOL switched to a flat-rate pricing system, which provided unlimited usage for a fixed fee. This was designed to spur growth, but it imposed major capacity burdens on its undersized network. This lack of capacity created annoyed customers, who looked elsewhere for Internet service. Eventually, AOL would lose its appeal to more savvy computer users, who would switch to Microsoft MSN or other Internet services providers. AOL rapidly expanded its network and used $100 million in cash from a deal with Telesave in 1997. The company also introduced the Instant Messenger product, which was popular and helped fuel growth while holding competitors partially at bay. At the same time, AOL aggressively and successfully pursued advertising dollars, which enhanced its cash flow. However, subscriber fees constituted 70% of AOL revenues, with advertising providing an important but comparatively minor share of revenues. At the same time, the market was growing in a speculative boom that pushed up AOL's stock value. A shrewd Steve Case now controlled valuable equity, which he would use to engineer a valuable acquisition. His timing was perfect because AOL's growth was showing signs of slowing, and its stock was greatly overvalued. It was time to convert this lofty stock value into other, non-Internet assets.

The Time Warner side of the business was a valuable combination of various forms of media and entertainment. Among them were the following business units:

- *Time, Inc.* This unit was the world's largest magazine publisher, which traces its roots back to Henry Luce, who founded the company in 1932. It featured more than 30 popular magazines, including *Time, Sports Illustrated, People,* and *Life.* Although magazine publishing is a competitive business that has been attacked by nonmagazine forms of competition, this unit was an industry leader.

- *Warner Music Group.* Album sales have steadily been weakening. However, Warner Music had a CD manufacturing unit that could possibly be sold off for as much as $1 billion.

- *Warner Brothers movies.* This Burbank, California, movie studio business had marketed some major winners, including the Harry Potter, Lord of the Rings, and Matrix series. On the other hand, one risk factor was the great uncertainty caused by video piracy.

- *Time Warner Cable.* While this unit was a major cable company, it eventually fell way behind Comcast, which grew to more than 20 million subscribers while Time Warner had approximately 11 million. As AOL–Time Warner's post-deal troubles mounted, some called for the spin-off of this business.

- *Turner Broadcasting.* This business included the world-renowned CNN as well as the TBS Network. However, rivals such as Fox

News had made inroads into CNN's market and were gaining market share, while TBS was in need of further development.

- *HBO.* This was still a major cable channel, with 30 million subscribers, and it boasted an impressive track record, including award-winning shows *Sex and the City, The Sopranos,* and *Six Feet Under.*

The listed units within Time Warner featured many valuable products. However, the company was not without its own problems. Its debt level was high while some divisions, such as Warner Music, faced an uncertain future.

With all of the valuable content in the various Time Warner units, the question was whether the Internet would become a major distribution arm for these various products. Could it enhance the normal distribution channels through which these valuable Time Warner products were already being marketed to the public? As we look back on the deal years after the merger, we see that little meaningful growth came from the Internet. The Time Warner units largely continued to grow after the merger, but this growth was not meaningfully enhanced by their association with AOL. The robust premerger talk of synergies had always been vague and nonspecific. The deal makers went full speed ahead to complete one of the largest mergers in history without having a clear vision of how the synergies were going to be exploited. So many well-paid senior managers worked on this deal and yet none of them was able to formulate a strategy that specifically articulated how the combination of the two companies would produce any synergies. The whole strategy was vague at best, and this was its undoing. The fact that the marriage also presented a major culture clash was but one additional flaw that stood a distant second to the flawed strategy.

Another potential source of synergy between the two companies was Time Warner's ownership of broadband cable lines. While AOL had many subscribers on dial-up lines, it worried about its access to high-speed broadband cable connections. Time Warner could conceivably provide content to AOL but also help with AOL's own distribution. Finally, the deal proponents alleged that the combination could realize up to $1 billion in the usual premerger proposed cost savings derived from reducing administrative overhead and other sources. Never discussed was the possibility of record losses that would be recorded.

## PERFORMANCE OF THE POSTMERGER AOL TIME WARNER

Almost right from the beginning of the marriage, and not unlike the DaimlerChrysler deal, the merger soured. AOL's performance was poor and got worse, pulling down Time Warner with it, to the chagrin of former Time Warner, now AOL Time Warner, shareholders. The collapse of the company's stock price is shown in Exhibit B.

## POSTMERGER CULTURE CLASH

In addition to various other problems, the marriage of AOL and Time Warner was a major culture clash. AOL being the dominant company in the merger had managers at the senior levels headed by Case, while Time Warner was led by Levin, Robert Pittman, and Richard Parsons. After the merger, Case was chairman while Levin was CEO. Parsons had a laidback style and would prove to be the long-term survivor of the whole group, as the board eventually looked

**Exhibit B**
Stock Prices of AOL Time Warner, December 1999 to September 2004

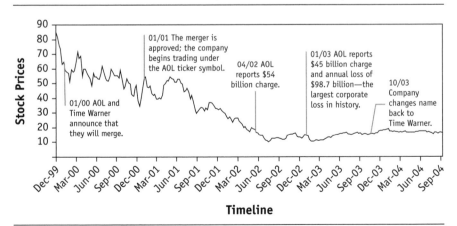

*Source:* finance.yahoo.com.

to him to take over the entire company as it fell on bad times. AOL was a loose culture in which its managers had a "fly by the seat of your pants" management style. It was a relatively new company in a rapidly growing high-tech industry that made long-term strategy planning difficult at best. Time Warner's culture was much more structured and conservative. It did not respond well to being thrust together with AOL's unconventional and brash executives. When AOL's performance faltered, Time Warner management rebelled and refused to accept a subordinate position to AOL, which they felt was pulling down the whole company. The rebellion was also spurred on by the news of accounting irregularities at AOL, which was accused of improperly booking $190 million in revenue.

Over time Levin grated on Case and major shareholder Ted Turner, and both wanted Levin ousted.[3] Levin was reported to have failed to show sufficient respect for Case. When the combined company suffered, Levin, its CEO, received much blame for the debacle. Having alienated Case and Turner, whose wealth had suffered greatly during Levin's reign at the combined company, Levin found himself on the chopping block.

## LESSONS FROM THE AOL TIME WARNER DEAL

The strategy and how its proposed synergies were going to be exploited needed to be clearly set forth. This deal had a strategy that was vague at best and more accurately was confused and nonexistent. Levin and his colleagues wanted to exploit the Internet distribution channel of AOL but did not really know how they were going to do it. What benefits would this strategy bring, and how valuable would it be? This was a huge question that they never came close to answering. How can Time Warner's board say that they were satisfied with the answers they got to this all-important question?

The overriding lesson we can take from this deal is that the strategy should be clear. Synergistic gains are difficult enough to realize when we think we see the path to their realization clearly. The future is always uncertain, and it can place many unforeseen obstacles in the

---

3. Ibid., pp. 269–270.

pursuit of corporate success. When we cannot even see the path, how do we know if one exists, or even where it leads? If management does not clearly delineate the path to the synergistic gains to the directors, then it needs to hoist a red flag and send managers back to the drawing room.

# 5

## Corporate Governance: Part of the Solution

The topic of corporate governance has attracted much attention in recent years, and most of it has been directed at the numerous large-scale accounting scandals. As a result of scandals at companies such as Enron, Adelphia, and WorldCom, there have been significant changes in laws as well as in general corporate practices. However, much of this attention has been directed at accounting manipulations of financial data and the prevention of inaccurate and misleading disclosure. There has been less focus on changes in governance related to M&As. Given the problematic track record of M&As, it seems that much improvement is still needed in corporate governance in this area of oversight.

In this chapter we discuss how corporations are governed. We will explore the role of the board of directors and how they oversee management. We will review the composition of boards and the selection of directors. As part of this review, we will see how the board is composed of a group of insiders and outside directors. The makeup of the board and the director selection process plays an important role in how the directors hold managers responsible for their actions and the results they generate for shareholders. Abundant evidence suggests that the oversight process works best when more directors are independent of the CEO. Independence may enable them to make objective decisions that are in the interest of shareholders to whom they have a fiduciary responsibility. Also in this chapter, we will review the status of boards as well as the abundant research on the issues of how boards affect shareholder wealth.

## GOVERNANCE FAILURE

The recent cases of major failures in corporate governance have captured the headlines for several years as investors learned how management failed to look after their interests and how directors did not prevent the process from happening. The Enron debacle was perhaps the most extreme case. Here one of the largest companies in the world created fictitious earnings while using special purpose entities (SPEs), partnerships formed by the company, to create a false image of a profitable company with much less debt than it actually had.[1] Unfortunately, the Enron scandal was not an isolated event. The trial and subsequent conviction of executives at Adelphia highlighted the extent to which some members of this company engaged in various manipulations, such as creating imaginary customers. The number of customers is one measure used to value cable companies. In a federal trial, John J. Rigas and his son and heir apparent, Timothy Rigas, were convicted of conspiracy and fraud involving Adelphia.[2]

Sunbeam, led by Al "Chainsaw" Dunlap, was accused of inflating sales by shipping appliances to customers who would accept the deliveries in warehouses supplied by Sunbeam even if these deliveries were never actually cash sales. Still another major corporate scandal and governance failure was the one that led to the failure of WorldCom. We will devote a specific case study to WorldCom, but we will mention at this point that this company grew rapidly and impressively from M&As, but when the M&A-fueled growth could not be sustained, the company, led by its CEO Bernie Ebbers, may have resorted to other means to create a profitable image. It is alleged that this included booking capital expenditures as operating expenses.

The fallout from these and other scandals gave rise to various regulatory changes as well as a whole new focus on corporate governance. Unfortunately, the discussion of corporate governance has focused more on the accounting frauds and less on the need to more closely monitor the M&As in which companies may engage. However, this is an important governance function, and an increased focus on this area is needed. Throughout this book we have discussed the reasons why some M&As, including those that required large investments for bidder companies, were a product of poor corporate strategy. In some instances they were motivated mainly by managerial hubris. Many of these deals could have been prevented by better corporate governance and more diligent directors. In this chapter we will discuss how that process could be better designed so that fewer merger-related governance failures occur.

## REGULATORY CHANGES

Several regulatory changes were enacted in the wake of some of the major corporate scandals of the late 1990s and early 2000s. One of the most focused of these changes was the Sarbanes-Oxley Act, which was quickly passed in response to the public outcry at the magnitude of some of the leading scandals.

### Sarbanes-Oxley Act

Enacted in July 2002, this law changed the way companies reported their financial statements and the way they had their financials audited for public release. The law sought to remove opportunities for conflicts of interest. As part of this process, it put guards in place to separate the various ways that auditors could profit from other work, such as consulting assignments, with the companies they were auditing. This limited their ability to be influenced by pecuniary gain other than through their time and expenses devoted to the audit. In doing so, auditors are now required to be more independent than they had been before the passage of this law. Independence will be a regular theme in this chapter. In addition, other parts of this same law focused on conflicts of interest by other parties, such as investment bankers, and their potential role in trying to influence research reports that a securities firm might prepare. It was recognized that there was a potential for conflict through any close association between the marketing investment banking services as the supposedly objective research reports that a securities firm might issue. This has always been a source of conflict for companies that seek to objectively advise clients on the investment benefits of a security while also hoping they would purchase that security from them so they could derive a commission on the sale. This law did not eliminate this conflict, but it did put more pressure on companies that might be inclined to deceive investors.

Another major change brought on by Sarbanes-Oxley was that the CEO and CFO have to personally certify the financial statements being released to the market and verify that they are not aware of any material misstatements contained in them. The law requires that the CEO and CFO will forfeit bonuses and compensation if the statements have to be subsequently restated because of material inaccuracies contained in them. The statements also have to provide clearer disclosures, especially with respect to off-balance items that would affect how an investor would interpret the data contained in them. This was designed to prevent Enron-like deceptions through the release of financial statements that were not sufficiently complete.

## Other Regulatory Changes

In addition to those changes brought on by formal laws, the accounting industry responded with its own changes in professional standards. As part of this process, the Public Company Accounting Oversight Board (PCAOB) was created. This entity is a nonprofit corporation that oversees the auditing of public companies. Each firm doing audits needs to register with the PCAOB. This entity also oversees the auditing committee at public companies and requires that there be some demonstration of expertise on each public company's auditing committee.

The accounting profession has also devoted new attention to correct and accurate disclosure, and this attention has been focused all the way down to the education and training of accountants as the profession has learned to place greater focus on more rigorous auditing standards.

The various legal and professional changes, however, are not really directed at the governance problems that relate to M&As. These problems are much more difficult to regulate. They are not as obvious as finding false numbers in financial statements. They involve preventing deals that are not in shareholders' interests from being completed. Part of this process is making sure that a company pursues its best long-term growth strategy. This is not always easy to regulate. The solution to better governance as it relates to M&As lies in putting in place better, more vigilant, and knowledgeable directors who take their duties seriously and who are willing to closely monitor management to make sure that companies work in shareholders' interest.

## CORPORATE GOVERNANCE

Corporations are one of three general forms of business organizations: sole proprietorships, partnerships, and corporations. Corporations trace their roots back many centuries as a business form that was designed to encourage the investment of capital into potentially risky ventures, such as oceangoing trade, which was subject to major risks (e.g., bad weather or theft from those such as pirates). The Dutch East India Company is one notable example of an early corporation.

Shareholders in corporations have their losses limited to their investment in the entity, and usually their personal assets are shielded from exposure to litigation. This is different from sole proprietorships and partnerships, where the owners' personal assets are at risk. However, in recent years, alternatives to simple partnerships have been formed, which limit the exposure and liability of partners in certain partnerships. As Exhibit 5.1 shows, the most common form of business is corporations, and this percentage accounts for the vast majority of the dollar value of businesses.

One of the problems that shareholders in corporations face is that they have to select others to represent their interests. This is usually done by utilizing a board of directors who are elected by shareholders. The directors, in turn, then select managers who run the company on a day-to-day basis (see Exhibit 5.2).

Exhibit 5.1   Employee Enterprise Establishments

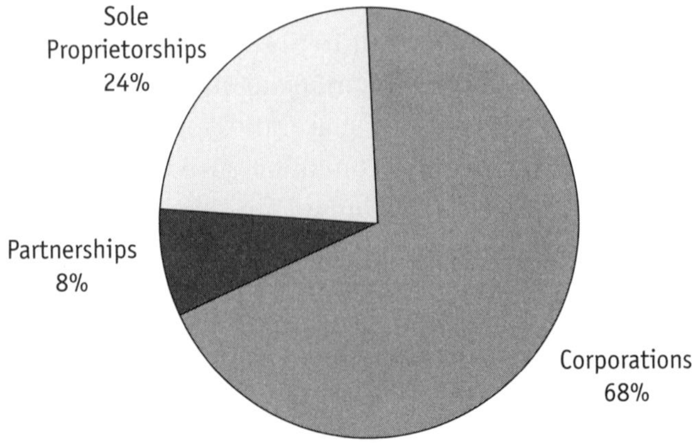

Sole Proprietorships 24%

Partnerships 8%

Corporations 68%

*Source:* Special Tabulations of 2000 County Business Patterns, United States Census.

Exhibit 5.2   Management, Directors, and Shareholders Flow Chart

> **Management**

↑

> **Board of Directors**

↑

> **Shareholders**

## Agency Costs

When shareholders are also the managers of the company, such as in the case of smaller closely held businesses, there is less of a concern that the managers will take actions that are not in the best interests of shareholders. However, as we move from smaller privately held corporations to the larger publicly held companies, each shareholder holds a relatively small percentage of the total shares outstanding. As the percentage of shares owned declines, shareholders have less and less incentive to devote time to overseeing the operations of the company. In addition, as the shareholders' percentage of total shares outstanding decreases, shareholders have a reduced ability to influence the operations of the company—even if they wanted to devote time to doing so. For this reason, shareholders must trust that managers will really run the business in a manner that maximizes shareholder wealth. One of the concerns that shareholders have is that managers will pursue their own personal goals and will not run the company in a manner that will maximize their gains as shareholders. Corporate governance issues arise when we consider that shareholders in large corporations with widely distributed equity bases are usually not in a position to do much to change the actions of managers when they do not approve of them. This is why they rely on the board of directors to oversee management and make sure they act in shareholders' interests. That is the essence of their fiduciary duties. When directors are insufficiently diligent and do not require managers to act in shareholders' interests, they violate these fiduciary duties.

In the 1970s and 1980s, agency costs were a hot topic in corporate finance, and it is ironic that this issue remains in the forefront as we go through the 2000s. This seems to be a function of human nature and the inability of some to put their ethical obligations ahead of their own personal ambitions. Shareholders are not in a position to manage a large company on a day-to-day basis and elect directors to look after their interests. It has been noted that these directors select managers who oversee their performance. The directors are not generally monitoring the company on a daily basis but receive periodic updates from management and review their performance as reflected in various financial statements such as quarterly reports. One survey of directors reported that on average there were 5.6 board meetings per year, and that they devoted an average of 19 hours per month on board issues.[3]

When managers, the agents of the shareholders, pursue their own self-interest at the expense of shareholders, the owners of the company are said to incur *agency costs*. Shareholders will never be able to eliminate agency costs, and they will always exist to some level. The goal is to limit them to some minimal or acceptable level. One of the solutions that has been used to try to control agency costs is to create incentives for managers to act in the interests of shareholders. This is sometimes done by giving management shares or stock options that would enable them to profit when shareholder values increase, thereby aligning the interests of both managers and shareholders.[4] One of the more extreme cases of profiting from exercising options was Disney's Michael Eisner, who in 1997 exercised more than $500 million in options in Disney. At one time, stock options were touted as the solution to the agency costs problem. However, with the various highly publicized accounting scandals of the late 1990s and 2000s, many have questioned the large offerings of stock options, and the popularity of this method of reducing agency costs has diminished. To some extent, this solution became more of a problem than the problem it was designed to solve.

## Agency Costs, CEO Compensation, and Corporate Governance

There have been many vocal critics of the very high CEO compensation levels that exist in corporate America, which tend to be higher than many other parts of the developed world. For example, according to data compiled by Towers Perrin, the average CEO compensation at 365 of the largest publicly trading corporations was $13.1 million in 2000. In the United States CEO compensation was 531 times the average employee's compensation, compared to Brazil, the second highest multiple, where CEO compensation was 57 times the average employee compensation. Developed economies such as that of the United Kingdom was only 25 times, while Germany was 11 times, and Japan was a multiple of 10.[5] Other surveys have documented the magnitude of the differences between CEO compensation in the United States compared to the rest of the developed world. Canyon and Murphy found that CEOs in 500 of the largest corporations in the United Kingdom earned in the aggregate £330 million (£600 million each) and £74 million from exercising options, whereas the top 500 CEOs in the United States earned £3.2 billion (£6.3 million each) and £2 billion from exercising options.[6]

The cross-country differences between the United States and the rest of the world cannot be explained by cost of living factors, and even when one considers the fact that the U.S. economy is the richest in the world, the pay gap between CEOs in major economies such as Japan and Germany compared to the United States cannot be explained by economic differences. The United States has become accustomed to paying its CEOs very well by international standards, and shareholders have a right to expect superior performance in exchange.

If higher CEO compensation provides commensurate benefits for shareholders, then it may be money well spent. However, when such compensation does not provide such benefits, it becomes a taking by management and is symptomatic of agency costs and poor corporate governance. The question then is how effective is corporate governance at reining in CEO avarice? A study by Core, Holtausen, and Larker sheds much light on this issue.[7] They looked at 205 large companies over a three-year period that were mainly employed in 14 different industries. They measured CEO compensation and then examined various different measures of board independence. In the case of the boards of directors, they looked at several characteristics of effective boards from a corporate governance perspective.

Core, Holtausen, and Larker assumed that larger boards were less effective and more susceptible to CEO influence.[8] This conclusion is intuitive  because in a larger board each director constitutes a smaller percentage of the total voting power. In addition, Holtausen and Larker not only looked at the percentage of outside directors on the board, but they also looked at the amount of "grey" directors. These were directors whose companies received financial benefits from the company whose board they were serving while also being personally paid for their director's services. It was also assumed that if the director was appointed to the board after the CEO was in place, that the CEO played a role in that decision. Interlocked directors were also highlighted as being those who may be weaker from a corporate governance perspective (interlocked boards will be discussed in greater detail later in this chapter). They also assigned a negative value to CEOs being older (over 70) and being on too many other boards.[9]

The Core, Holthausen, and Larker findings are exactly what anyone who understands human nature would expect. They found an inverse relationship between CEO compensation and the percentage of outside directors on the board. As hypothesized by the researchers, CEO compensation was positively related to board size as well as the percentage of the board that was appointed by the CEO, those who were grey, those who were over age 69, and those who served on three or more boards. There was also an inverse relationship between CEO compensation and the amount of shares that the CEO owned. In addition, they found that CEO compensation (remember that CEO compensation is our proxy for agency costs) was lower when there were external blockholders who owned 5% or more of the outstanding shares.

Their findings are instructive if we want to determine how we can keep agency costs down through proper construction of the board of directors. Boards are more likely to control agency costs and to govern companies better when:

- The members of the board are not appointed by the CEO or through any other incestuous process.
- Boards are not interlocked.
- Directors do not serve on too many boards.
- Most of the board members are independent.

Having discussed these board characteristics, let's talk about two of them some more: board independence and interlocking boards.

***Agency Costs, Perks, and Shareholder Value.***   There is evidence to suggest that the accumulation of perks by management may have costs well in excess of the direct cost of the benefits themselves. One study by David Yermack indicated that companies that provided personal use of corporate aircraft and which disclosed this benefit underperformed the market benchmarks by four percent annually.[10] Yermack's study focused on 237 large companies over the period 1993–2002. The loss of market value was well in excess of the actual monetary costs of this specific perk. At a minimum, these results imply that the market is concerned about managers who may be gaining at shareholder's expense without creating value that would offset these costs.

***CEO Involvement in Director Selection.***   Should CEOs be allowed to play a role in the selection of directors? Given that directors will be charged with monitoring their performance, will they try to install directors who will rate them favorably? Once again, human nature tells us they will if they are given the chance. In a study of over a thousand first time director appointments over the period 1994–1996, Shivdasni and Yermack found that when the CEO serves on the nominating committee, or when there is no such a committee, those companies appointed fewer independent directors.[11] Even when independent directors were appointed in such a process, the market tended to react negatively to the announcements. It is not surprising that we now see a trend away from such CEO involvement in director selection. If we want better corporate governance, and better monitoring of corporate M&A strategy, directors who are not beholden to the CEO will perform better.

***Board Independence.*** One of the problems we have had with corporate governance lies in the close relationship boards sometimes have with managers. Boards have two subcomponents: the inside board and the outside board. The inside board are those members who are also management. For example, the CEO of the company may also be a board member, along with possibly a couple of other members of senior management. As Exhibit 5.3 shows, a 2003 survey conducted by *Corporate Board Member* magazine found that the average number of inside directors is 2.7, while the average number of outside directors is 7.2, giving us an average size of a board of 10 directors.[12] This same survey found that 70% of the time the CEO does not sit on

Exhibit 5.3   Board Size by Inside and Outside Directors

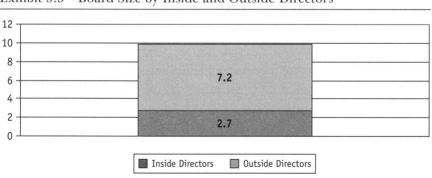

*Source:* What Directors Think Study 2003, *Corporate Board Member Magazine.*

the board. However, the directors surveyed by *Corporate Board Member* were somewhat divided on the issue of whether the positions of chairman of the board and the CEO should be split into separate positions. Fifty-seven percent said they should not be split and the remainder (43%) said they should.

Research has shown that boards of directors that are dominated by outsiders tend to increase the value of the shareholder wealth of their companies when they are taken over or when they merge with another company.[13] One study by Rosenstein and Wyatt noted that stock prices of companies tend to rise when an outside director is added to a board.[14] Perhaps the reason for these findings is that inside directors are always considering the trade-offs they experience when they are confronted with conflicting interests of their managerial position and their director's oversight role. In takeovers, for example, inside directors may consider their relative gains and losses from a takeover that could cause them to possibly lose their positions and related compensation. They then may be trading off these losses against the gains they would receive from a premium on any shares they may own. Clearly, they are fiduciaries, and they should not be considering such issues. However, research in this area implies that perhaps they do. If this is the case, then the vast majority of boards should be composed of outsiders, and only a small component should feature inside board members who are there for the greater information they may provide their co-directors. The research implies that the higher the percentage of outside directors, the greater gains from takeovers for potential target shareholders. However, one must keep in mind the obvious point that boards function for reasons other than considering M&As. The regular operations of the company have to be a much more important issue than considerations relating to M&As. In fact, if boards find that they are devoting a significant amount of their time to considering merger-related issues, then, in light of the track record of many mergers, they may want to take significant steps to make sure that M&As becomes a much lesser part of the company's overall activities.

The monitoring of the CEO function of boards seems to work better when insiders have less influence on the board. When we consider some of the prominent instances in which CEOs have been removed, prominent outside directors played a key role. This was the case when John Smale led the board of General Motors when it removed Robert Stempel from his CEO position. Smale held great stature in the corporate world from his years of being CEO of Procter & Gamble. When Smale asserted that GM would benefit from a change at the helm, the corporate world took him seriously. This seems to be a theme behind many of the CEO overthrows. Robert Morrow, CEO of Amoco, led the ouster of Paul Lego of Westinghouse. The same was the case when James Burke, former CEO of Johnson & Johnson, led the overthrow of IBM CEO John Akers. Each of these situations has some important common characteristics. In each case, the situation called for a change at the wheel. In each instance, the company was lagging behind where it should have been, and the position of CEO was a prominent one that was very much in the public eye. The markets had been critical of the company's performance, and thus indirectly, if not directly, of the CEO's performance. There was outside pressure on the board, and there was a need for clear and bold action. In each of these CEO terminations the impetus came, at least partially, from a prominent role by these particular independent directors, who each were CEOs of companies that were comparable in size and stature.

Board independence can be helpful by not only having more independent directors but also by having some directors who have had positions that were comparable to that of the CEO who might need disciplining. This is not to say we need a board composed solely of such directors. Much can be said for a mixed board composed of not just inside and outside directors but also of outside directors of diverse backgrounds who can bring a wide range of expertise and experience to the management monitoring process.

Michael Weisbach showed that boards with a greater percentage of outside directors were more likely to discipline their CEO for performing poorly than those boards on which insiders played a more prominent role.[15] The inside-dominated boards may be so close to the CEO that they find it more awkward to pursue the actions that need to be taken when a company is not being run properly. Outside directors are often less close to the CEO and can react more objectively. One possible exception to this is in the case of interlocking directorships that may create more of a club atmosphere and reduce objectivity.

***Interlocking Boards.***    Interlocking boards are situations where directors sit on each other's boards of directors. For example, we may have a CEO of Company X who sits on the board of Company Y while the CEO of Company Y is on X's board. This can be a very chummy situation, and one can imagine how uncomfortable it would be for one CEO/director to agree to discipline the other CEO/director. The dynamics of how these interests play out was seen in a study by Hallock, who analyzed a data set of 9,804 director seats covering 7,519 individuals and 700 large U.S. companies.[16] He found that 20% of the companies in his sample were interlocked. He defined interlocked to be where any current or retired employee of one company sat on another company's board where the same situation was the case for the other company. He found that approximately 8% of CEOs are reciprocally interlocked with another CEO.

Hallock had several findings that are of interest from a corporate governance perspective. First, interlocked companies tended to be larger than noninterlocked firms. Second, CEOs of interlocked companies tended to earn significantly higher compensation. He controlled for firm characteristics, such as firm size, and still found a pay gap, albeit one that was smaller. Interlocking boards are clearly not optimal. If we believe that the supply of quality directors is so limited and that we need to tap into the supply of CEOs in an interlocking manner, then such interlocked companies would be a necessity. However, probably few people believe that this is the case—other than CEOs who may seek to secure their own positions through such relationships. There may be situations where business relationships between companies are such that interlocking directorships provide a benefit. When this is not the case, however, interlocking directorships provide few, if any, benefits and may work against shareholder wealth maximization.

## Are Smaller or Larger Boards More Effective at Corporate Governance?

Evidence exists that there is an optimal size board of directors and that boards greater than a certain size do not function as effectively from a corporate governance perspective. Kini, Krawcaw, and Mian found that board size tended to shrink after tender offers for firms that were not performing well.[17] This implies that disciplinary take-overs—or at least the threat of such takeovers—tend to reduce the size of boards to one that the market believes may be more effective. David Yermack of New York University attempted to determine if there was a relationship between the market valuation of companies and board size. He analyzed a sample of 452 large U.S. corporations over the period 1984 through 1991. The average board size for his sample was 12 directors.[18]

Yermack found that an inverse relationship existed between market value, as measured by Tobins q, a valuation measure introduced in Chapter 4, and the size of the board of directors. Smaller boards were associated with higher market values and larger boards tended to be associated with lower valuations. As we can see in Exhibit 5.4, the higher valuations really come from relatively smaller boards, such as

Exhibit 5.4    Board Size and Tobin's q: Sample Means and Medians

Sample means and medians of Tobin's q for different sizes of boards of directors. The sample consists of 3,438 annual observations for 452 firms between 1984 and 1991. Companies are included in the sample if they are ranked by *Forbes* magazine as one of the 500 largest U.S. public corporations at least four times during the eight-year sample period. Utility and financial companies are excluded. Data for board size are gathered from proxy statements filed by companies near the start of each fiscal year. Tobin's q is estimated at the end of each fiscal year as *Market value of assets/Replacement cost of assets*. The estimation of q follows the $q_{PW}$ specification of Perfect and Wiles (1994), which is described more fully in the text.

*Source:* D. Yermack, "Higher Market Valuation of Companies with a Small Board of Directors," *Journal of Financial Economics* 40 (1996): 185–211.

those with fewer than 10 members. Yermack also looked at other operating efficiency and profitability measures and found that they were
also inversely associated with board size. He found that smaller boards
were more likely to replace a CEO following a period of poor performance. He also found some evidence that CEO compensation was
more closely linked to performance, especially poor performance,
when boards are smaller.

## Are Busy Directors Good for Corporate Governance?

It is not unusual for the CEO of a Fortune 500 to sit on the board of
another large corporation. One wonders does running a large corporate enterprise really leave one with extra free time to oversee the
operations of another large business? It is also not unusual for directors to serve on the board of several companies. Ferris, Jagannathan
and Pritchard found that 16% of all directors hold two or more seats
while 6% have three or more director positions.[19] They found that the
better the performance of the firm whose board they served on, the
more likely they would receive other directorship offers. While their
study did not find a negative relationship between having busy directors, those with three or more directorships, and firm performance,
later research which addressed certain econometric issues related to
their study, did.  Fich and Shivdasani examined a sample of 508 large
companies over the period 1989–1995.[20] They found that when a
majority of the directors served on three or more boards, those companies exhibited lower market-to-book ratios. Perry and Peyer's study
of 349 public companies which had announced that one of their executives was taking a director position at another firm showed negative
announcement effects.[21] These effects occurred when the managers
in question had low managerial ownership in the company that
employed them and when that company did not have a majority of
independent directors. In sum, it appears that busy directors are not
good for corporate governance and shareholder wealth creation.

## Takeovers and the Interests of Directors

We have noted that directors are the fiduciaries for shareholders.
As such, they have been retained to maximize shareholder wealth and,

# HOLLINGER INTERNATIONAL

The 2004 probe of Hollinger International, into what it referred to as a "corporate kleptocracy," was released at the end of summer 2004. The report issued by a special committee of the Hollinger board of directors found that the company's CEO, Conrad Black, and ex-president, David Radler, "siphoned off more than $400 million through aggressive looting of the publishing company."[a] Hollinger International is a publishing company that publishes various newspapers, including the *Chicago Sun-Times* and the *Jerusalem Post*. Black controlled Hollinger through a holding company he owned, Ravelston, which owned 78% of the stock of a Canadian company, Hollinger, Inc., which in turn owned 68% of the voting shares in Hollinger International. Through his control of a 68% interest in Hollinger International, Black was able to effectively influence the board of directors.

One astounding finding of the report was that the total cash taken equaled "95.2% of Hollinger's entire adjusted net income during the period 1997-2003!"[b] The probe of the activities of Hollinger's CEO and ex-president was headed by former Securities and Exchange Commission (SEC) chairman Richard Breeden and was filed with the federal courts and the SEC. Black and Radler engaged in lavish spending that included $24,950 for "summer drinks," $3,530 for silverware for their corporate jet, which they put to regular personal use, thousands of dollars for handbags, tickets for the theater and opera, as well as very generous donations made by the company but to charities and establishments favored by Black and his wife, columnist Barbara Black. The couple threw lavish dinner parties for friends, including Henry Kissinger who was, coincidentally, on the board of directors. Birthday parties for Mrs. Black were thrown at the company's expense. One such party for 80 guests cost the company $42,870. Other examples of a looting of the company were a 10-day vacation to Bora Bora at a cost of $250,000 and refurbishing work on Black's Rolls-Royce, which cost $90,000.[c] Black and Radler took compensation from the company in several ways, including $218 million in management fees, which they derived over the period 1997 to 2003. Management fees were paid to Ravelston, while Hollinger International also paid "noncompete" fees to other entities controlled by Ravelston. In addition, Hollinger sold newspapers to entities controlled by Lord Black and his associates for below-market values.

These included the sale of the *Monmouth Times,* in Monmouth Lakes, California, which went for "$1 when there was a competing bid of $1.25 million."[d] The report called the board and the audit committee's monitoring of payments such as these management fees "inept."

The board of directors included some prominent names in international diplomacy. Among its members were former secretary of state, Henry Kissinger, as well as former assistant secretary of defense in the Reagan administration Richard Perle and James Thompson, former governor of Illinois who headed the company's audit committee. While such individuals may be world renowned, it is not clear what special expertise they brought to the board of directors of a publishing company. Clearly, if one wanted to talk foreign affairs at a board meeting, this was probably one of the boards to be able to do that with. If you were looking for corporate oversight, however, the track record of these directors was dismal at best. The report of the special committee particularly singled out Perle for "repeatedly breaching his fiduciary duties as a member of the executive committee of the board, by authorizing unfair related party transactions that enabled Black and Radler to evade disclosure to the audit committee. The report calls for Perle to return $3 million in compensation he received from the company."[e]

The board also included friends and family members. For example, Lord Black's wife, Barbara Amiel Black, was on the board along with family friend Mrs. Kravis, the wife of financier Henry Kravis of Kohlberg, Kravis and Roberts. Clearly, Black pushed the appointment of directors to an extreme. This became possible because Black controlled the votes required to place individuals on the board. The hand-picked board was kept as much in the dark as Black could manage, and they did not go to any great lengths to remove themselves from any clouds that he surrounded them with. They were being taken care of very well by Black and Hollinger and did not seem to want to rock the boat.

The following passage from *The Wall Street Journal* describes one Hollinger board meeting and is instructive of the atmosphere in Hollinger's board room:

> Gathered around a mahogany table in a boardroom high above Manhattan's Park Avenue, eight directors of the newspaper publisher, owner of the *Chicago Sun Times* and the *Jerusalem Post,* dined on grilled tuna and chicken served on royal blue Bernardaud china, according to two attendees. Marie-Josée Kravis, wife of financier Henry Kravis, chatted

about world affairs with Lord Black and A. Alfred Taubman, then chairman of Southeby's.

Turning to business, the board rapidly approved a series of transactions, according to the minutes and a report later commissioned by Hollinger. The board awarded a private company, controlled by Lord Black, $38 million in "management fees" as part of a move by Lord Black's team to essentially outsource the company's management to itself. It agreed to sell two profitable community newspapers to another private company controlled by Lord Black and Hollinger executives for $1 apiece. The board also gave Lord Black and his colleagues a cut of profits from a Hollinger Internet unit.

Finally, the directors gave themselves a raise. The meeting lasted about an hour and a half, according to minutes and two directors who were present."[f]

One lesson we can learn from the Hollinger scandal is that a board should not be too close to the CEO and definitely should not be handpicked by the CEO. The board needs to be somewhat at arm's length from those whom they will be monitoring. If they are indebted to the CEO, then how objective will they be in pursuing the interests of shareholders?

a. Mark Heinzl and Christopher J. Chipello, "Report Slams Hollinger's Black for Corporate Kleptocracy," *The Wall Street Journal* (September 1, 2004): A1.

b. Ibid.

c. Geraldine Fabricant, "Hollinger Files Stinging Report on Ex-Officials," *The New York Times* (September 1, 2004): 1.

d. Ibid.

e. See note a, p. A4.

f. Robert Frank and Elena Cherney, "Lord Black Board: A-List Cast Played Acquiescent Role," *The Wall Street Journal* (September 27, 2004): 1.

as far as the oversight of the corporation is concerned, should monitor management and the affairs of the company in a manner that pursued this goal. However, from a corporate governance perspective, we have to be aware that directors are human and also think about their own interests. How are directors affected by takeovers? Directors of target companies are usually not retained after the takeover by a company. The bidder has its own board, and their directors usually remain overseeing the combined company after the takeover.

The personal adverse financial impact of a target director approving a merger or hostile takeover has been documented in a study by Harford of 1,091 directors of Fortune 1000 companies over the period 1988 through 1991.[22] He found that, in general, directors of target companies not only are rarely retained after the merger or acquisition, but they are less likely to have a director's position in the future. This is true for both inside and outside directors. It seems that such seats are difficult to replace when they are lost in a merger or takeover. However, Harford found one exception that is of interest: that directors of poorly performing companies that are able to engineer a merger or takeover do not seem to be exposed to this adverse effect of a lower frequency of future directorships. Conversely, he found that directors of poorly performing companies that are part of an antitakeover process that successfully prevents a takeover are less likely to be directors of companies in the future. These findings are remarkable because they imply that the market for directors seems to be pretty efficient in weeding out those directors who may place their own interests ahead of those of shareholders. The process would be improved, however, if it could be accomplished on a more timely basis.

## MANAGERIAL COMPENSATION AND FIRM SIZE

It has long been postulated by economists that managers run companies in a manner that is more consistent with revenue maximization than profit maximization.[23] This is based on the purported relationship between managerial compensation and firm size. As Exhibit 5.5 shows, the optimal firm size may be less than that which would maximize revenues. Companies may produce an output such as $x_1$ which is greater than optimal output, $x^*$, but which generates a minimal profit that may be enough to avoid the ouster of management. The reason why researchers theorize that management would want to have a larger than optimal company is the positive relationship between firm size and managerial compensation. Senior management of larger companies tend to earn more than their smaller corporate counterparts.[24] Lambert, Larker, and Weigelt[25] have shown that this positive association exists for most major levels of management, such as those shown as follows:

- *Corporate CEO.* The manager with the greatest authority in the company
- *Group CEO.* A manager who has authority for various different subgroups with the overall corporation
- *Subgroup CEO.* Senior manager of one of the individual subgroups
- *Divisional CEO.* Senior manager of a division or corporate unit
- *Plant manager.* Senior manager of a cost center

The Lambert, Larker, and Weigelt results for these broad categories of management may help explain why there may not be as much managerial resistance to the recommendations of senior management who advocate transactions that result in greater corporate size but not necessarily greater profitability. Their findings are not unique to this field of research. In fact, executive compensation research finds that a good relationship exists between company size and executive compensation, but a poor one exists between compensation and corporate performance.[26]

Exhibit 5.5   Gains from Eliminating Agency Costs

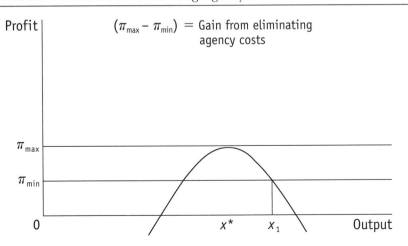

## MANAGERIAL COMPENSATION, MERGERS, AND TAKEOVERS

Managers often personally gain from M&As. That is, many CEOs and other senior management have employment agreements that provide them with large payouts if a control change takes place. Sometimes such agreements are called *golden parachutes*. An example of such payouts is the change of control provisions in Caesar's Entertainment's CEO, Wallace R. Barr's employment agreement that has been reported to provide total compensation of almost $20 million in accelerated options and stock awards.[27] In early July 2004, Harrah's announced that it would acquire Caesar's for $5.2 billion. Usually shareholders do not have a lot to say against such large payouts. The theoretical basis for them is that target shareholders may stand to gain from the premiums offered by a bidder. However, target management may stand to lose their positions and their compensation if there is a change in control and the bidder replaces them. Control share employment agreements provide a financial incentive for management to support value-enhancing takeovers that may cost them their jobs. That is how it works in theory. A cynic, however, might say that the real incentive is for management to recommend the quick takeover so they receive their high payouts and ride off into the sunset with their money in their pocket. This seemed to be the position of the California Public Employees Retirement System (CALPERs) when it voted against the merger of two health care companies—Anthem, Inc. and WellPoint Health Networks. Total executive compensation from the change of control provisions equaled approximately $200 million. Leonard Schaeffer, WellPoint's CEO, alone was to receive $47 million in various severance agreements.

The issue becomes even more interesting when we consider the role that target CEOs play in negotiating their own postmerger positions and compensation. It is well known that this is an important part of the premerger negotiating process. It has been reported that the failure of the American Home Products (now called Wyeth) and Monsanto merger came down to neither CEO being willing to let the other take control of the merged company.[28] Sometimes the CEO who is forced to leave the combined entity is provided with enhanced compensation in order to accept such a defeat.

Hartzell, Ofek, and Yermack analyzed 311 primarily friendly transactions over the period 1995 to 1997.[29] They found that target CEOs enjoyed mean wealth increases between $8 million to $11 million. The bulk of these financial gains came from increases in stock and options, as well as from golden parachute payments. Some CEOs even receive last-minute increases in their golden parachute agreements —presumably in order to get them to advocate the deal. They also found that about one-half of the CEOs became officers in the buying entity, although their departure rates over the three years following the merger were very high. Even for these exits, however, the former target CEO received enhanced compensation. The Hartzell, Ofek, and Yermak study cannot be used, however, to definitely determine if the bountiful compensation enjoyed by target CEOs comes at the expense of target shareholders. In order to come up with a reliable measure of the target shareholder wealth effects, they would need to also be able to consider a sample of both completed and rejected deals so that we would be able to include the effects of the premiums that target shareholders receive as well as to try to measure the "lost premiums" from those deals that did not go through because target CEOs could not come up with a sufficiently rich compensation package for them to accept the proposal.

One of the potential limiting factors that hinders unscrupulous managers from expanding their own compensation beyond what would be prudent is the threat of takeovers. Managers who dip into the corporate till beyond what they should may create an opportunity for an outside bidder to acquire the company in a hostile takeover and correct this inefficiency. Agrawal and Knoeber examined a sample of 450 corporations and looked at the compensation of their CEOs.[30]

They divided their sample into two subgroups: (1) where the CEO was protected by a golden parachute agreement and (2) where the CEO lacks such protections. In the protected group, the CEO might not experience personal financial losses in the event that he or she was removed following a takeover. Their research sought to determine the relative strengths of two opposing effects as they relate to takeovers and upper management. The *competition effect* is where takeovers put pressure on CEOs and thereby lower compensation. With the *risk effect*, management demands more compensation when they are employed by companies that are more likely to be takeover targets. They were able to detect and measure both of these opposing effects. They determined that the net effect was positive meaning that the risk effect dominates. This confirms that being removed as a result of a takeover is something that CEOs are mindful of and require that they be compensated for. Nonetheless, takeovers and the threat of them can serve to help keep management on their toes.

## DISCIPLINARY TAKEOVERS, COMPANY PERFORMANCE, AND CEOS AND BOARDS

The board of directors, as fiduciaries of shareholders, need to be ready to discipline the CEO and upper management of poorly performing companies and make them run the company in a manner that is consistent with investors' reasonable expectations. When the board fails in its duties, the market is sometimes forced to take action. Sometimes this action takes place in the form of takeovers of the poorly performing company. Kini, Kracaw, and Mian analyzed a sample of 244 tender offers and looked at the effects that these hostile bids had on CEO and director turnover.[31] They found an inverse relationship between post-takeover CEO turnover and pre-takeover performance. That is, targets that performed poorly before the takeover were more likely to have their CEO replaced. However, this finding was not true across all types of boards. For those targets that had insider-dominated boards, the findings were clearly true, but not for those with outside-dominated boards. This seems to imply that the acquirers concluded in cases where the board was dominated by outsiders that the problem of performance could not be fixed by replacing the CEO, but the hostile bidder did not seem to think along the same lines as the insider-dominated boards, which obviously did not see fit to replace the CEO before the takeover.

The Kini, Kracaw, and Mian study also found that board composition tended to be changed following disciplinary takeovers. They found that for insider-dominated boards, the number of insiders decreased following the takeover. Interestingly, for outsider-dominated boards, the number of insiders actually increased. This gives support to the common-sense notion that there is an optimal mix of insiders and outsiders on the board and that bidders seek to try to move to that optimal level and do not believe that the pretakeover board had the right mix.

Some evidence indicates that the effect of disciplinary takeovers is greatest in more active takeover markets. A study by Mikkelson and Partch of the University of Oregon found a greater rate of CEO, president, and board chair turnover for companies that were performing poorly in an active takeover market relative to a less active takeover market.[32] Specifically, they found that 33% of the companies in the "poor performer" sample experienced complete turnover of the CEO, president, and board chair during the 1984 to 1986 time period, a very active takeover market. This was almost double the 17% rate they found for comparable performing companies during the less active 1989 to 1993 time period. So we see that takeovers can play an important role in weeding out poor managers, and they can play this role even if the company is not taken over. A high level of takeover activity may be all that is needed to accomplish this change. However, this process works more sluggishly in times of low M&A volume. Other research has already shown that management turnover is greater when companies are actually taken over.[33] Other studies have shown that takeover pressures alone on a particular company can bring about turnover of top management.[34] However, the Mikkelson and Partch research showed that this process may work even if the company is not a takeover target as long as the takeover market is active. This implies that active takeover markets can be good for corporate governance. Conversely, it also implies that a sluggish takeover market may not be best for shareholders who are interested in improving corporate governance.

## MANAGERIAL AND DIRECTOR VOTING POWER AND TAKEOVERS

Companies can be vulnerable to takeovers when they have valuable assets, have performed poorly, and where the market has responded to the performance by bidding down their stock price. The more the shares of the company are in hands of investors who are less loyal to the company, the more vulnerable the company is. Conversely, the more shares that are controlled by groups interested in keeping the company independent, the more the company may be insulated from the cathartic benefits that the takeover market can provide. Shareholders and directors need to be mindful of this when they allow large blocks of shares to come under the control of groups who may pursue their own interests at the expense of those of shareholders. With this in mind boards may want to periodically examine the distribution of the company's shares and consider whether the current distribution is in the best interest of shareholders. If it determines that too many shares are controlled by individuals or groups who may be working against the majority of shareholders, it may consider altering the distribution of shares. This, however, is not that clear cut decision. The directors are fiduciaries for shareholders—theoretically all shareholders. Therefore, they must have compelling reasons to try to emphasize the interests of some shareholders while opposing the interests of others.

## SHAREHOLDER WEALTH EFFECTS OF MERGERS AND ACQUISITIONS AND CORPORATION ACQUISITION DECISIONS

One question that needs to be considered is if the structure of managerial compensation was related to the tendency of managers to engage in M&As. If this is the case, then does the market react differently when these deals are pursued by managers who receive a significant percentage of their compensation from equity-based components? Dutta, Dutta, and Raman analyzed a sample of 1,719 acquisitions made by U.S. companies over the period 1993 to 1998.[35] This was a time period when there were large increases in stock option–based compensation for senior executives. Therefore, it is an excellent time period to test market reactions as a function of the extent to which the managers pursuing the deals will gain in a similar manner to shareholders. If the deals are value reducing to equity holders, then managers would stand to personally lose from value-reducing deals. They found that companies with managers having high equity-based compensation tended to receive positive stock market responses to the announcement of their acquisitions, whereas those with lower equity-based manager compensation tended to receive negative reactions.

Dutta, Dutta, and Raman also looked at the magnitude of the premium paid by acquiring firms. When managers are potentially playing with their own money, because of the impact that a premium may have on their equity-based compensation, were the premiums different based on the percentage of equity in their compensation? Interestingly, they found that companies with higher equity-based compensation tended to pay *lower premiums*. Once again, when managers are playing with their own money, to some extent, they are more frugal with exchanging premiums, whereas when they are playing with house money—shareholder wealth—they will tend to be more generous and more liberally give away corporate wealth when they do not personally lose from such largesse. Dutta, Dutta, and Raman also found that high equity-based compensation managers tended to acquire targets with higher growth opportunities than their lower equity-based counterparts did. That is, they tended to acquire companies with a greater likelihood of generating equity-based gains for both themselves and shareholders. Moreover, they found that lower equity-based compensation managers and companies significantly underperformed their higher equity-based counterparts.

The Dutta, Dutta, and Raman study implies that if management's interests are aligned with shareholders, they tend to do better deals and pay less. It also seems to be reasonable to assume that such managers may try harder to pursue value-reducing deals. The market is aware of this fact and reacts more positively when such managers announce deals but penalizes acquiring shareholders when they, and their board of directors, allow managers to push deals when they do not have their own compensation at risk.

## POST-ACQUISITIONS PERFORMANCE AND EXECUTIVE COMPENSATION

Is the compensation of senior management affected by the success or failure of acquisition programs? For companies that engage in large-scale acquisition programs where M&As are an integral part of their growth strategy, then linking managerial compensation to the success of those deals makes good sense. Schmidt and Fowler analyzed a sample of 127 companies, of which 41 were bidders that used tender offers to make acquisitions, 51 were non-tender offer acquirers, and 35 were control firms.[36] Consistent with research previously discussed, bidder companies, those that would more likely be involved in initiating hostile takeovers, showed a significant decrease in post-acquisitions shareholder returns. This was not the case for acquirers who did not use tender offers as well as for the control group. Also interesting from a corporate governance perspective was that both bidders and acquirers showed higher managerial compensation than the control group. Takeovers pay dividends for management in the form of higher compensation while they generate losses for shareholders of those companies that use tender offers and hostile takeovers to pursue the acquisition strategy. Takeovers may be good for the personal wealth of managers, but they may not be in the interests of shareholders; therefore, boards must be extra diligent when overseeing managers who may be acquisition-minded. There is a greater risk of shareholder losses and managers, in effect, gaining at shareholder expense. For this reason, the board needs to ensure that the deals will truly maximize shareholder wealth and not just provide financial and psychic income for managers.

## LESSONS FROM THE HEWLETT-PACKARD–COMPAQ MERGER: SHAREHOLDERS LOSE, CEOS GAIN

In February 2005 the board of Hewlett-Packard announced that it had terminated the employment of its colorful CEO—Carly Fiorina. Ms. Fiorina, formerly of AT&T and Lucent, had orchestrated the $25 billion stock financed merger between Compaq and Hewlett-Packard in September 2001. This merger was strongly opposed by leading shareholders such as Walter Hewlett, son of the company's founder. Fiorina barely won shareholder approval of the deal. When we look back on the merger, we see that the concerns of the market and opposing shareholders were well founded. The gains that Ms. Fiorina projected when the operations of the rival computer makers were combined never materialized. While revenues at Hewlett-Packard rose steadily over her tenure, profitability had been weak. Fiorina caused the company to move even more deeply into the PC business which it has not been able to manage profitability unlike its rival Dell.

## PROPER BOARD DUE DILIGENCE—COCA-COLA PROPOSED ACQUISITION OF QUAKER OATS

While it seems that many boards simply rubber-stamp M&As proposed by their CEOs, some boards have the foresight and the courage to stand up to the CEO and question proposed deals. This was the case when a $15.75 billion offer for Quaker Oats was proposed to Coca-Cola Company's board of directors in November 2001. Quaker Oats had a certain appeal to Coca-Cola because it included its popular Gatorade line, which might fit in well with Coke's other soft drink products. Gatorade commands more than 80% of the sports drink market, whereas Coke's own Powerade brand accounted for just over 10% of that market. The whole sports drink business had grown significantly, and Powerade had a distant second position to the leader Gatorade, and Coke was having great difficulty gaining ground on the leader. We have already discussed the major disadvantages that competitors who have a dominant rival with a large market share face. Acquiring Gatorade through an acquisition of Quaker Oats could have been a quick solution to this problem. However, the acquisition also presented another problem because Coke most likely would have been forced by antitrust regulators to divest Powerade in order to have the deal approved.

Coke was not the first bidder for Quaker Oats. On November 1, 2000, Pepsi made an initial offer for Quaker following negotiations between Robert Enrico, Pepsi's CEO, and Robert Morrison, Quaker's CEO. However, after Quaker could not get Pepsi to agree on improved terms, including a stock collar provision, Pepsi and Quaker's negotiations broke down. Quaker was then "in play," and other potential bidders, such as Coke and French food giant Group Danone, expressed interest in the U.S. food company. Both companies made competing bids, which featured improved terms over Pepsi's bid, yet Pepsi held fast and declined to exceed its prior offer. Coke's CEO assured Quaker Oats that he had been keeping his board appraised of the bid's progress and had asked and received agreement from Quaker to exclusively negotiate with just Coke. Coke's CEO Douglas Daft, however, did not count on the negative response of the market to the deal (see Exhibit A).[a] The board, however, was mindful of the market, and after a long meeting on November 21, 2000, it forced Daft to go back to Quaker Oats and inform it that Coke was pulling out of the negotiations. The market loved this, and the stock price immediately rose.

**Exhibit A**
Coca-Cola Stock Price Response to Quaker Oats Bid

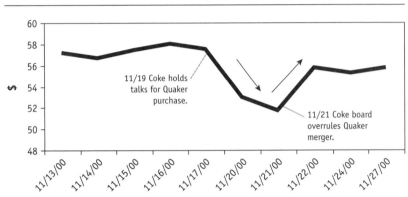

*Source:* finance.yahoo.com.

There were some clear problems with the deal that Coke's board obviously paid attention to. As already noted, the market did not like the proposed acquisition, and it voiced its displeasure by dropping its valuation of Coke's stock. In the years before the Coke bid, the company had experienced problems with other failed acquisitions, and the spotlight was on its merger strategy. Right at the start, management faced an uphill battle. Another problem with the deal was that the acquisition would require Coke to be able to effectively manage the component of Quaker Oats' business that was outside of Coke's soft and sports drink business lines. These were Quaker Oats' food brands, which included Captain Crunch cereals, Rice-A-Roni, Aunt Jemima pancakes, as well as other snack products such as rice cakes and granola bars. Some of Quaker's brands were impressive, but they were a little far afield from Coke's core business. Another problem with the deal was its defensive nature. Coke's bid was in response to Pepsi's original offer. It was not a product of Coke's own strategic plan. Such defensive responses are not the best motive for a merger or acquisition.

One of the reasons why the Coke board stood up to this proposal lies in the nature of its board and its relationship with the CEO. Coke had a CEO, Robert Goizueta, who was highly acclaimed. Unfortunately, after many successful years at the helm of the soft drink giant, Goizueta passed away in October 1997 at a relatively young age. Goizueta was succeeded by Douglas Investor, who resigned at the end of 1999 and was replaced by Douglas Daft, who was well thought of but could not draw on the track record of success that Goizueta enjoyed. Perhaps if Goizueta had brought this deal to the board, it might have considered it more seriously. Nonetheless, there is little reason to believe that the board would have ultimately approved it no matter who brought the deal because it considered the deal generally flawed.

Coke's board featured some leading business figures, including the reknowned Warren Buffet, who is considered by many to be one of the market's shrewdest investors. In this case, this strong board featured leading business figures and a new CEO who was looking to make a mark for himself. This board, however, would have none of it.

The board of directors is one of the last lines of defense against poorly conceived merger strategies. In order for it to work with maximum effectiveness, the board needs to be knowledgeable and strong willed. However, it is not enough that a board be composed of individuals who are strong willed and capable of standing up to the management leaders of the company. Knowledge of the industry and the company's operations are also essential to being an effective director. Management, who runs the company on a day-to-day basis, should have a distinct advantage over board members who are engaged full-time in other activities, such as running their own companies, and have not invested nearly as much time as management in studying the company. However, there is a certain minimum level of knowledge that the board must have in order for it to function properly. When considering the commitment of billions of dollars in merger costs, the board needs to get whatever resources it needs to be able to effectively evaluate management's proposals. If this means retaining outside consultants to study the proposal in-depth, then this should be done. This is sometimes difficult to do because the proposals may be time sensitive and require a quick response. Nonetheless, the board must apply all of the necessary resources to reach an enlightened and impartial decision. The bigger the deal, the more work and research the board needs to do. However, in the case of Coke's offer for Quaker Oats, the board's studied response was clear and strong. In properly exercising its fiduciary responsibilities, it saved shareholders from a possibly costly acquisition.

---

a. Pepsi's Bid for Quaker Oats (B), Harvard Business School, 9-801-459, August 5, 2002.

Ms. Fiorina was not content to focus on HP's more successful business segments such as printers. Instead it expanded into areas where it would be a major player—but not one which would make a meaningful contribution to shareholder value. In merging with Compaq, it was adding a company that also had some similar troubles. Compaq itself was the product of a prior merger between Compaq and Digital Equipment. It is ironic that while shareholders have suffered under Fiorina's reign, she will profit handsomely from her five-year stint at the company. At the time of her dismissal, it was estimated that she would enjoy a severance package in excess of $20 million. In addition, Michael Capellas, the former CEO of Compaq, who served as president of the postmerger Hewlett-Packard, received in excess of $15 million when he left even though he was only with the combined entity for a relatively short period. The merger was the most significant action that Ms. Fiorina orchestrated at HP and it was a clear failure. However, the board, which had been very supportive of Fiorina during much of her time there, rewarded her handsomely for a strategy that was a clear failure. When CEOs receive great rewards for eroding shareholder value, there are few incentives for them to pursue different strategies. One solution would be to tie CEO compensation to the achievement of specific targets. If a CEO very aggressively pushes a major merger in which the success is predicated on the achievement of certain measurable performance targets, then let the board only agree if the CEO's compensation and bonuses are also tied to the achievement of these targets. This should be particularly true for deals that face strong opposition as this one did. If the CEO does not agree to that, then maybe the likelihood of these goals being achieved is questionable.

## CEO POWER AND COMPENSATION

Research has shown that the greater the CEO's power, the greater his or her compensation. Cyert, Kang, and Kumar analyzed a sample of 1,648 small and large companies and found that the average CEO was 55 years of age and had served as CEO for an average of eight years.[37] They also found that in 70% of the cases, the CEO was also the board chairman. They found that equity ownership of the largest shareholder and the board of directors as well as default risk are all negatively correlated with CEO compensation. They found that equity ownership of the board members was a more important factor in determining CEO compensation than the size of the board or the percentage of outside directors. When board members are also owners of the company, they demonstrate a greater tendency to control the efforts of the CEO to increase his or her compensation at shareholder expense. Once again, human nature comes into play. When the board's own financial wealth is more at risk, they seem to monitor management better. Also, the presence of a larger shareholder may help keep the CEO in check and maintain his or her compensations within reasonable limits. The takeover market also helps control CEOs. Bertrand and Mullainathan found that when a company is allowed to install antitakeover defenses that insulate the company from the takeover market, the CEO enjoys increased compensation.[38] Boards need to be aware of such incentives and be extra cautious about installing takeover defenses that will allow to entrench themselves. A check-and-balance system needs to be put in place to ensure that CEOs manage the company in a manner that is in shareholders' interests and that they do not help themselves to gain at shareholders' expense. Greater equity ownership of those who are in a position to monitor the CEO—the board along with the presence of a large blockholder—can help this process work better.

## DO BOARDS REWARD CEOS FOR INITIATING ACQUISITIONS AND MERGERS?

Given what we have seen of the track record of many M&As, one would wonder why boards were not more reluctant to allow their CEOs to engage in such transactions. The research that has been presented in Chapter 3 has shown that targets gain from such deals, but often acquirers fail to realize significant benefits and may, in fact, lose from the deals. If this is the case, it would seem logical that boards would display some reluctance to allow their companies to enter into such transactions or would at least install certain safeguards that would require CEOs to make a convincing demonstration of the benefits of the deal before allowing them to go forward. We would expect that boards would overrule CEOs' acquisition proposals more frequently than what we are aware of. However, with the exception of the Coca-Cola board's strong rejection of the Quaker Oats deal in 2000, we find that such actions are relatively infrequent. What is truly ironic is that research has shown that rather than limit CEOs' acquisitive tendencies, boards sometimes actually encourage them.

An interesting study on CEO compensation and mergers was conducted by Grinstein and Hribar, both of Cornell University.[39] They examined 327 large M&As over the period 1993 to 1999. This sample included many of the big deals of the fifth merger wave. They examined proxy statements that identified the components of CEO compensation and sought to find which of these statements attributed part of the CEOs' compensation to their ability to complete certain M&As. Specifically, they found that in 39% of cases they considered, the compensation committee cited completion of a deal as the reason they provided certain compensation. Other firms gave bonuses following deals but did not specifically cite the ability to complete the deal as the reason for the bonus. This implies that the real percentage of boards that gave bonuses for mergers was even higher than the 39% that overtly cited this as a reason.

Grinstein and Hribar noted that bidder announcement period returns were negative for their sample, as they have tended to be in many other studies, which were reviewed in Chapter 3. What is interesting is that the negative reaction was most pronounced in cases where the CEOs have the greatest corporate power, as reflected by the CEO also being head of the board of directors. The market often seems to not only not like acquisitions, but they really do not like acquisitions done by CEOs whose power is subject to fewer limitations by the board of directors. Conversely, the market seems to prefer power limitations on the CEO and will penalize companies less for doing acquisitions when they know that a group of directors is potentially capable of preventing CEOs from doing deals that might not be in the company's best interest. Whether the board actually does this or not is another issue.

One other interesting finding of the Grinstein and Hribar study is that not only did the market react more negatively to deals done by CEOs with more power, but they also noted that managers of companies who had more power got higher bonuses and tended to do bigger deals. Their power was less checked and they seemed to personally gain from this situation—at the expense of shareholders. Once again, we find abundant evidence of the role of managerial hubris in most losing M&As.

## CEO Compensation and Diversification Strategies

In Chapter 2 we saw that diversification strategies generally cause the shareholders of companies pursuing such strategies to lose value. There are clearly major exceptions to this generalization, such as for large diversified companies (e.g., GE and 3M). We have also already seen that some types of diversifications, such as related diversifications, can enhance shareholder value. Nonetheless, we do know that there is actually a diversification premium, meaning that research has shown that the CEOs of diversified companies earn on average 13% more than CEOs of companies that operate in only one line of business. However, it has also been noted that Rose and Shepherd found that when they traced the relationship between changes in compensation and the pursuit of a diversification, such a strategy was associated with lower, not higher, CEO compensation.[40] This implies that boards are slow to stop diversification deals recommended by CEOs and penalize them after the fact in the form of lower compensation. An improvement in corporate governance would be to have boards act quicker and stop certain M&As before they go through, rather than pay CEOs who pursue such deals less after they make ill-advised deals. The key is to enhance shareholder value, and the compensation paid to the CEO is but one relatively small aspect of that value. Changing CEO compensation after the bad deals is not enough. Boards need to make sure they can identify good and bad deals in advance of their completion.

We should also note that not all diversifying deals are bad for shareholder wealth. We also showed in Chapter 2 that related diversifications tended to improve shareholder wealth, whereas unrelated deals did not. Therefore, boards have to exercise some caution here and consider deals that may have some degree of relatedness while being wary of those that bring the company outside of its overall line of business. The key is defining relatedness that brings with it common elements of which acquirers can take advantage. We should also note that some of this discussion may not apply in cases of companies that have proven that they can successfully manage a portfolio of companies within their corporate umbrella. This seems, however, to be a challenging managerial task at which many companies are not successful.

## Agency Costs and Diversification Strategies

One theory about why there are so many diversifying M&As is because of the *agency cost hypothesis*. This is the idea that the agents of the owners, the managers, derive private benefits that are greater than their own private costs from doing these deals. That is, these deals may provide managers with greater prestige and what economists called *psychic income*. Denis, Denis, and Sarin[41] analyzed a sample of 933 firms starting in 1984. They looked at the degree of ownership owned by managers and related them to the tendency of managers with different percentages of equity ownership to engage in diversifying deals, which research has shown often tend to reduce shareholder value. They found that diversification, moving the company into other business segments, was more likely to reduce shareholder values when CEO ownership was lower (e.g., less than 5% of the outstanding shares). Such deals, however, had a mild positive effect when the CEO's ownership shares were greater than 5%. Similar effects were found when they looked at the combined share percentages owned by overall management.

They also found that there was a strong relationship between decreases in diversification and external control threats. Almost one in five of the decreases in diversification, such as selling off diversified divisions, were preceded by a takeover bid. In other words, decreases in diversification were associated with market pressure. This implies that management often may not be willing to sell off prior acquisitions that reduced shareholder value until they were faced with an outside bidder that may be taking advantage of reduced stock values relative to the underlying value of the divisions if they were sold separately on the market. If the diversification strategy reduces value, it made the company vulnerable to a takeover, and when the takeover threats materialized, management financially responded by refocusing.

The tendency to diversify and the reaction to outside threats supports the agency cost hypothesis. However, we do not have to rely just on outside market forces to limit these costs. Once again, the board of directors is in an even better position to prevent deals that will reduce shareholder value. Directors need to be aware of the track record of certain types of deals and make sure that management and the CEO does not complete them. They also need to be aware of the company's own track record of deals. Some companies, such as AT&T and Daimler, have a poor track record in the M&A arena. Boards of these companies need to be especially wary.

## CORPORATE GOVERNANCE AND MERGERS OF EQUALS

In mergers of equals, two companies combine in a friendly deal that often features extensive negotiations between the managers of the two companies. As discussed in Chapter 3, research shows that bidders do better in mergers of equals, while targets do worse when compared to more traditional M&As. In Chapter 3 we reviewed the study by Wulf, who showed that bidder shareholders enjoyed more of the gains in these types of takeovers. She discussed the role of the negotiation process between the management and directors of the respective companies. The negotiation process for these types of deals plays an important role in explaining why the results of mergers of equals is different from that of other deals.[42] Wulf found that the abnormal returns that target shareholders received were lower when target directors received equal or even greater control of the combined entity! This result raises corporate governance concerns. Are target directors, fiduciaries for target shareholders, trading off returns for their shareholders just so they can gain positions and control of the combined entity? We have to also acknowledge that such positions come with compensation and prestige that is important to these directors. If it was not important, they would be serving for free, and that is not consistent with the way the for-profit corporate world is overseen.

Another interesting finding of the Wulf study—and one that has important ramifications for corporate governance—is that she found shared corporate governance was more common for larger and more poorly performing target companies and ones that were in industries that were undergoing restructuring. CEOs of target companies that may not have been doing well or that are in industries that are consolidating may pursue mergers of equals to prevent a bid that might not provide them with any continued control. These companies may see a friendly merger of equals deal as their best option, even though it may be self-serving and not in the best interests of shareholders.

## ANTITAKEOVER MEASURES AND CORPORATE GOVERNANCE

Companies that are concerned about being the target of hostile takeovers may choose to implement certain antitakeover defenses that make it more difficult for the company to be taken over without the consent of the target. These takeover defenses can be characterized as coming in two forms: active and preventive.[43] *Preventive defenses* are implemented in advance of a possible hostile bid to prevent that kind of takeover. Among the more common preventive measures are corporate charter amendments and poison pills. *Active defenses* are deployed in the midst of a takeover battle. These range from targeted share repurchases to the filing of lawsuits.

Of all the kinds of defenses, poison pills are probably the most effective form of preventive takeover defense. Although different variations exist, poison pills are rights offerings that are issued to target companies' shareholders and that often allow them to use these rights to purchase shares in either their own company or the combined entity if it is taken over by an outside bidder. Essentially, they are 50% off coupons that may allow the rights-holders to purchase $200 worth of the relevant stock for $100. To complete a takeover with poison pills in place, the bidder has to purchase the target shares and then is faced with rights-holders, the former shareholders, who then have the right to buy back certain shares at a low price. This defense makes completing a takeover prohibitively expensive unless the target can be persuaded to dismantle the poison pill. Targets may be willing to do so, but only if the deal is one that they would approve. Presumably, this approval will be based on getting a good value for target shareholders as opposed to getting other concessions that mainly are of value to the target board and management. The power of the poison pill defense was underscored in the 2004 takeover battle between Oracle and Peoplesoft where Oracle was kept at bay for 18 months by Peoplesoft's poison pill. Peoplesoft was able to use its poison pill as leverage to get Oracle to increase its offer to $26.50, which was a 75% premium above Peoplesoft's stock price prior to Oracle's initial bid.

## Board Composition and Antitakeover Defenses

A study by Brickley, Coles, and Terry found that board compensation affected the likelihood that a company would adopt a poison pill defense.[44] In some time periods, the market has seemed to react negatively to the adoption of poison pill defenses.[45] These studies drawn from the fourth merger wave seem to support the notion that such a takeover defense was being used by management, without board approval, because poison pills do not usually need to be approved by shareholders, to entrench management. However, a later study by Comment and Schwert, which used data through 1991, found that this was initially the case, especially when poison pills were first popularized in the mid-1980s, but the negative response was tempered in later years as the market seemed to adapt to these defenses, which had by then proliferated.[46] Thus such defenses were more associated with higher premiums for selling shareholders. It seems that strong defenses can improve the target's bargaining position without altogether preventing takeovers. What we do not know, however, is how many deals did not go through due to strong defenses. We do not have a measure of lost takeover premiums and shareholder wealth as a direct result of antitakeover defenses.

The Brickley, Coles, and Terry study analyzed the role that the composition of the board might play in any negative reaction the market might have to the adoption of poison pills by 247 companies over the period 1984 to 1986. This was a period during which prior research had shown that the negative market reaction to poison pills was the greatest. They found a statistically significant positive relationship between the stock market's reaction to the adoption of poison pills and the percentage of the board accounted for by outside directors. The market's reaction was positive when the board was dominated by outsiders and negative when it was dominated by insider board members. This implies that the market tended to believe that when an outside-dominated board adopted a strong antitakeover defense like a poison pill, it did so to advance shareholder wealth. However, when an insider-dominated board took the same action, the market seemed to believe that it was doing this to entrench managers and insulate them from the disciplinary forces of the takeover market. The market was also saying that it believes that outside directors represent shareholders' interests better than insider directors.

## CONCLUSION

The corporate governance process has received significant attention in recent years. Much of this attention has centered on financial fraud and manipulations of data contained in statements disseminated to the public. Various reforms, such as those that have been required pursuant to the Sarbanes-Oxley Act, have been implemented to address these governance problems. However, insufficient attention has been paid to limitations in the corporate governance process as they relate to M&As. The track record of many M&As has been poor, and many of these failures can be related to breakdowns in the oversight process. This is an additional area where corporate governance reforms could be helpful.

Boards of directors are the main force that needs to monitor management and the CEO and ensure that the company is run in a manner that maximizes shareholder wealth. When that board is more independent and less close to the CEO, the process works best. When the board is closely aligned with the CEO, the monitoring process is less reliable. Abundant evidence suggests that when CEOs are unchecked, some will tend to pursue their own goals. Sometimes these goals will be increased compensation and perks. Other times they will be manifested in the building of a larger corporate empire, which may be motivated by CEO hubris rather than shareholder interests. Independent boards, and ones that are not interlocked, work best in holding such CEOs in check.

When boards fail to make sure that their CEOs avoid value reducing deals, the takeover market is ready to step in to take corrective action. Value reducing deals make acquirers vulnerable to takeovers. These takeovers often result in managerial and director changes as well as post-deal restructuring.

## ENDNOTES

1. Bethany McLean and Peter Elkind, *The Smartest Guys in the Room: The Amazing Rise and Scandalous Fall of Enron* (New York: Portfolio/Penguin, 2003).

2. Barry Meier, "2 Guilty in Fraud at Cable Giant," *The New York Times* (July 9, 2004): 1.

3. "What Directors Think Study 2003," *Corporate Board Member* (July 2003).

4. Michael Jensen and W. H. Meckling, "The Theory of the Firm: Managerial Behavior, Agency Costs and Ownership Structure," *Journal of Financial Economics* 3 (1976): 305–360.

5. "Spreading the Yankee Way of Pay," *Business Week Online* (April 18, 2001).

6. Martin J. Canyon and Kevin Murphy, "The Prince and the Pauper? CEO Pay in the United States and the United Kingdom," *The Economic Journal* 110 (November 2000): F640–F671.

7. John E. Core, Robert W. Holtausen, and David Larker, *Journal of Financial Economics* 51 (1999): 371–406.

8. See David Yermack, "Higher Market Valuation for Firms with a Small Board of Directors," *Journal of Financial Economics* 40 (1996): 185–211.

9. A. Shivdasani, "Board Composition, Ownership Structure and Hostile Takeovers, *Journal of Accounting and Economics* 16 (1993): 167–198.

10. David Yermack, "Flights of Fancy: Corporate Jets, CEO Perquisites and Inferior Shareholder Returns," New York University Working Paper, September 2004.

11. Anil Shivdasani and David Yermack, "CEO Involvement in the Selection of New Board Members: An Empirical Study," *Journal of Finance*, 54, no. 5 (October 1999): 1829–1853.

12. "What Directors Think Study 2003," *Corporate Board Member* (July 2003).
13. J. Cooter, A. Shivdasni and A. Zenner, "Do Independent Directors Enhance Target Shareholder Wealth During Tender Offers," *Journal of Financial Economics* 43 (1997): 195–218.
14. S. Rosenstein and J. Wyatt, "Outside Directors, Boards Independence and Shareholder Wealth," *Journal of Financial Economics* 26 (1990): 175–192.
15. Michael Weisbach, "Outside Directors and CEO Turnover," *Journal of Financial Economics* 37 (1988): 159–188.
16. Kevin Hallock, "Reciprocally Interlocked Boards of Directors and Executive Compensation," *Journal of Financial and Quantitative Analysis* 32, no. 3 (September 1997): 331–344.
17. Omesh Kini, William Krackaw, and Shehzad Mian, "Corporate Takeovers, Firm Performance and Board Composition," *Journal of Corporate Finance* 1 (1995): 383–412.
18. David Yermack, "Higher Market Valuation of Companies with a Small Board of Directors," *Journal of Financial Economics* 40 (1996): 185–211.
19. Stephen P. Ferris, Murali Jagannathan, and A.C. Pritchard, "Too Busy to Mind the Business? Monitoring by Directors With Multiple Board Appointments," *Journal of Finance*, 58, no. 3 (June 2003): 1087–1111.
20. Eliezer M. Fich and Anil Shivdasani, "Are Busy Boards Effective Monitors?," University of North Carolina Working Paper, February 2004.
21. Tod Perry and Urs Peyer, "Board Seat Accumulation by Executives: A Shareholder's Perspective," Unpublished Manuscript, February 2003.
22. Jarrad Harford, "Takeover Bids and Target Director Incentives: The Impact of a Bid on Director's Wealth and Board Seats," *Journal of Financial Economics* 69 (2003): 51–83.
23. William Baumol, *Business Behavior: Value and Growth* (New York: McMillan, 1959), p. 46.
24. S. Finkelstein and D. Hambrick, "Chief Executive Compensation: A Study of the Intersection of Markets and Political Processes," *Strategic Management Journal* 10 (1989): 121–134.
25. Richard A. Lambert, David F. Larker, and Keith Weigelt, "How Sensitive is Executive Compensation to Organizational Size," *Strategic Management Journal* 12, no. 5 (July 1991): 395–402.
26. H. L. Tosi and L. R. Gomez-Mejia, "The Decoupling of CEO Pay and Performance: An Agency Theory Perspective," *Administrative Science Quarterly* 34 (1989): 169–189.
27. Gretchen Morgenson, "No Wonder CEOs Love Those Mergers," *The New York Times* (July 18, 2004): Sec. 3, p. 1.

28. Thomas M. Burton and Elyse Tanouye, *The Wall Street Journal* (October 13, 1998): B1.
29. Jay Hartzell, Eli Ofek, and David Yermack, "What's in It for Me? CEOs Whose Firms Are Acquired," NYU Working Paper, August 2002.
30. Anup Agrawal and Charles R. Knowber, "Managerial Compensation and the Threat of Takeover," *Journal of Financial Economics* 47 (1998): 219–239.
31. See note 15.
32. Wayne H. Mikkelson and M. Megan Partch, "The Decline of Takeovers and Disciplinary Managerial Turnover," *Journal of Financial Economics* 44 (1997): 205–228.
33. K. J. Martin and J. J. McConnell, "Corporate Performance, Corporate Takeovers and Management Turnover," *Journal of Finance* 46 (1991): 671–687.
34. David. J. Denis and Diane. K. Denis, "Ownership Structure and Top Management Turnover, *Journal of Financial Economics* 45 (1997): 193–222.
35. Sanip Dutta, Mai Iskandar-Datta, and Kartik Raman, "Executive Compensation and Corporate Acquisition Decisions," *Journal of Finance* 56, no. 6 (December 2001): 2299–2336.
36. Dennis R. Schmidt and Karen L. Fowler, "Post-Acquisitions Financial Performance and Executive Compensation," *Strategic Management Journal* 11, no. 7 (November–December 1990): 559–569.
37. Richard M. Cyert, Sok-Hyon Kang, and Pravenn Kumar, "Corporate Governance, Takovers and Top-Management Compensation: Theory and Evidence," *Management Science* 48, no. 4 (April 2002): 453–469.
38. M. Bertrand and S. Mullainathan, "Is There Discretion in Wage Setting? A Test Using Takeover Legislation," *Rand Journal of Economics* 30 (1999): 535–554.
39. Yaniv Grinstein and Paul Hribar, "CEO Compensation and Incentives: Evidence from M&A Bonuses, *Journal of Financial Economics* (2003): 535–554.
40. Nancy L. Rose and Andrea Shepard, "Firm Diversification and CEO Compensation: Managerial Ability or Executive Entrenchment," *Rand Journal of Economics* 28, no. 3 (Autumn 1997): 489–514.
41. David J. Denis, Diane K. Denis, and Atulya Sarin, "Agency Problems, Equity Ownership and Corporate Diversification, *Journal of Finance* 52, no. 1 (March 1997): 135–160.
42. Julie Wulf, "Do CEOs in Mergers Trade Power for Premiums? Evidence from Mergers of Equals," University of Pennsylvania Working Paper, June 2001.

43. Patrick A. Gaughan, *Mergers, Acquisitions, and Corporate Restructurings,* (New York: John Wiley & Sons, 2002).

44. James A. Brickley, Jeffrey L. Coles, and Rory L. Terry, "Outside Directors and the Adoption of Poison Pills," *Journal of Financial Economics* 35 (1994): 371–390.

45. Paul H. Malatesta and Ralph A. Walking, "Poison Pill Securities: Shareholder Wealth, Profitability and Ownership Structure, *Journal of Financial Economics* 20 (1988): 347–376 and Michael Ryngert, "The Effect of Poison Pill Securities on Shareholder Wealth, *Journal of Financial Economics* 20 (1988): 377–417.

46. Robert Comment and G. William Schwert, "Poison or Placebo? Evidence on the Deterrent and Wealth Effects of Modern Antitakeover Measures," *Journal of Financial Economics* 39 (September 1995): 3–43.

# Case Study

# WorldCom

WorldCom is an excellent example of a good strategic merger plan that was pushed too far and ended up killing the company that was built through such mergers. Mergers enabled the company to grow to a size where it could compete effectively with the largest telecommunications companies in the U.S. market. At one time, WorldCom was one of the better M&A success stories. Over a 15-year period, the company grew from a tiny business to one of the world's largest telecom enterprises. However, this great story of corporate growth all came to a crashing end. In this case study, we discuss what went wrong and where the line should have been drawn and the M&A engine shut down.

## WORLDCOM'S M&A HISTORY

WorldCom traces it roots to a small telecommunications reseller called LDDS, which was founded in 1983. The telecom resale business grew in the wake of the breakup of AT&T that allowed other companies to come in and compete with the venerable telecom giant. At that time, AT&T offered price breaks for bulk buying of minutes on the AT&T long-distance network. Companies, including many small firms, would commit to buying bulk minutes from AT&T and then pass along some of the discount they would receive to customers they would solicit. These customers would be able to receive lower rates than they might get on their own. As a result, a whole industry of resellers grew. However, such companies were limited in their profit opportunities because they had to incur switching and access costs at both the origination and end of a call. The reseller industry eventually grew into subgroups: switchless and switch resellers, as some of the resellers purchased their own switches so they could avoid some of the costs they would incur going to and from the long-distance network. The industry then grew through M&As, and one of the companies that used this method to grow was a Mississippi-based reseller—LDDS Communications. The head of that company was Bernie Ebbers, who was far from being a major figure in the deal-making business.

The idea for what would become WorldCom can be traced back to 1983, when Bernie Ebbers and a few friends met at a diner in Hattiesburg, Mississippi, to discuss the concept of forming a long-distance company now that the breakup of AT&T was moving toward a reality. Mr. Ebbers prior experience included work as a basketball coach and an owner/manager of some motels in the Jackson, Mississippi area. Ebbers was initially an investor in the business, but he took the reins when the company began to perform poorly. Within six months he transformed this losing operation into a profitable one. In doing so, he showed that he had the management skills to run a small business efficiently. Years later he would demonstrate that these same management skills could not be translated to a multibillion-dollar telecommunications business. Ebbers would show that he could effectively build a large company through M&As, but when it came to running such an enterprise profitably, he failed.

The business went on to grow, and in 1989 it went public through an acquisition with the already public firm Advantage Companies. As a result of this deal, LDDS now had operations in 11 different states, mainly in the South and Midwest United States. The next major step in LDDS's history was a 1993 three-way deal in which LDDS would merge with Metromedia Communications and Resurgens Communications Group. Each of these companies was a full-service long-distance firm. Ebbers had established momentum in his growth through an M&A strategy and he would not be slowed. LDDS was still a comparatively small company compared to giants such as AT&T and MCI, but there was no denying the company's meteoric growth path. Ebbers continued on this path when, on the last day of 1994, he completed the acquisition of IDB Communications Corp., and on January 5, 1995, the acquisition of the WilTel Network Services took place. The IDB deal moved LDDS more clearly into the international telecommunications market because that company had more than 200 operating agreements in foreign countries. WilTel operated a national digital fiber-optic network and was one of only four companies in the United States to do so. Using this network, LDDS would be able to transfer some of its traffic and save outside network costs. With these deals, LDDS then changed its name to WorldCom because it considered itself to be a major U.S. telecommunications company but also a presence in the world telecom market. M&A had now helped the company continue with its exponential growth, as shown in Exhibits A through C.

**Exhibit A**
WorldCom Revenues, 1991–1995

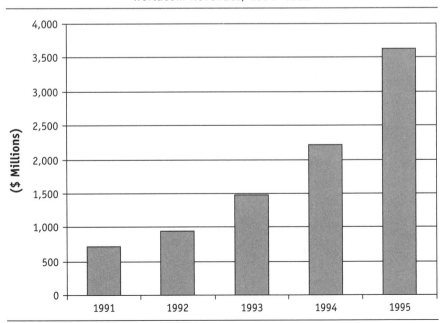

*Source:* WorldCom Annual Report.

**Exhibit B**
WorldCom Operating Income

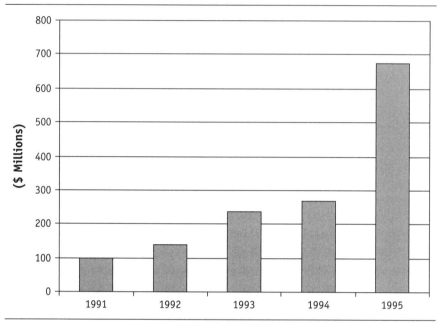

*Source:* WorldCom Annual Report.

In December 1996, WorldCom completed its first megamerger when it merged with MFS Communications in a deal that was valued at approximately $14 billion. This deal brought several valuable capabilities to WorldCom. For one, MFS had various local networks throughout the United States and in Europe. Second, the deal brought with it UUNet, which was a major Internet service provider, thus expanding the package of services that WorldCom could offer customers. However, Ebbers was not content to sit on his laurels. He was determined to make WorldCom an industry leader. He continued in 1997 to seek out other merger partners to help him fulfill this dream.

At the beginning of 1998, WorldCom completed three more deals: mergers with BrooksFiber, a company in the local exchange business, Compuserve, and ANS Communications, Inc. Compuserve was acquired from H&R Block. This sale by H&R Block was the undoing of a failed prior deal because H&R did not derive significant benefits from its ownership of Compuserve. However, in the fall of 1998,

**Exhibit C**
WorldCom Minutes Billed

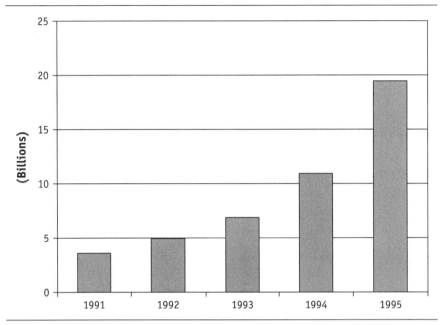

*Source:* WorldCom Annual Report.

WorldCom announced a deal that would vault the company to a leadership position in the world telecommunications business. In September 1998, WorldCom merged with MCI in a transaction valued at $40 billion. By 1999 the company would have revenues of more than $37 billion, with the growth coming from M&As as opposed to organic processes. As rapidly as the company was growing in the early 1990s, the end of the decade made that progress seem modest (see Exhibit D). However, while the revenue growth over the period 1995 to 1998 was impressive, profits were not, although they appeared to move in the right direction in 1999 (see Exhibit E). Unfortunately, this revenue growth leveled off, and it appeared that growth through mergers was providing diminishing returns while adding to the financial pressures on the company (see Exhibit F).

The MCI deal put WorldCom on a new level. However, Ebbers was not satisfied to stay put. His expertise was doing deals, and he sought out even more transactions. He reached an agreement to acquire Sprint in a $155 billion stock transaction. However, almost immediately,

**Exhibit D**
WorldCom Revenues, 1995 to 1999

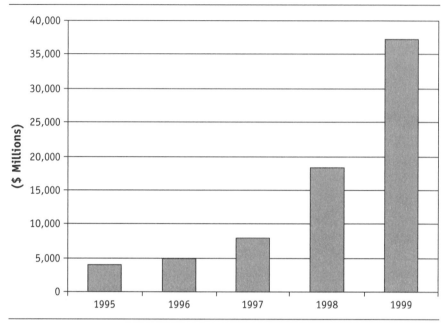

*Source:* WorldCom Annual Report 2000.

antitrust concerns began to materialize. The market was skeptical that the Justice Department would approve this acquisition, and this skepticism proved warranted when in July 2000 the Justice Department stopped the merger. By this time, however, the stock had already begun its slide, from which it would never recover until the company had to file for bankruptcy (see Exhibit G). Amazingly, Ebbers kept right on doing deals. In July 2001, WorldCom announced that it was acquiring Intermedia Communications.

Although Ebbers seemed to keep trying to grow the company through M&As virtually right up to the end of his tenure with the company, an irreversible slide had now begun. The SEC, fresh from dealing with major accounting frauds at companies such as Enron and Adelphia, now began an investigation into WorldCom accounting practices. It questioned the company's revenue recognition and other accounting policies. It appeared that many of the revenues and profits that the company was booking were fictitious. Ebbers was

## Exhibit E
### WorldCom Net Income, 1995 to 1999

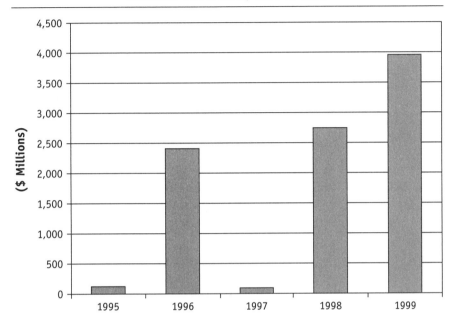

## Exhibit F
### WorldCom Quarterly Revenue Growth and Key Acquisitions

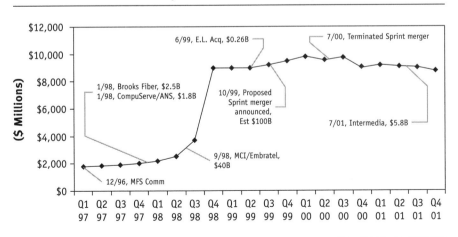

*Source:* Dick Thornburgh, "First Interim Report of Dick Thornburgh, Bankruptcy Court Examiner," November 4, 2002.

# Exhibit G
## Stock Price Growth and Fall at WorldCom: 1989 to 2002

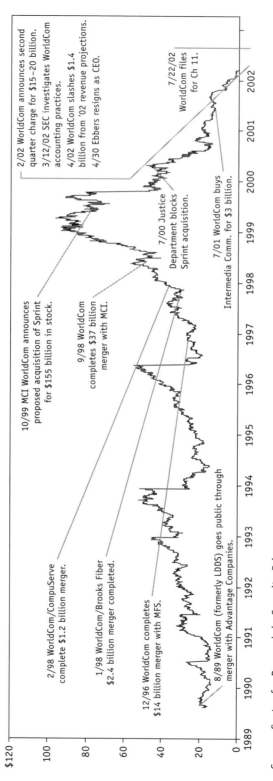

*Source:* Center for Research in Security Prices.

forced to resign from the company on April 30, 2002. The demise of WorldCom resulted in the largest corporate bankruptcy in history. From this bankruptcy a new company, now called MCI, would emerge.

## WHAT WENT WRONG WITH WORLDCOM'S STRATEGY?

There were several flaws in WorldCom's growth through mergers strategy. The fact that it eventually failed so miserably, after such an impressive growth period, can be attributed to several reasons, of which we will now discuss a few.

### Ebbers's Management

Ebbers was great at doing deals and building up his company to be a leading player in the world telecommunications business. The telecommunications industry has natural economies of scale, which can be exploited through growth. His performance at achieving growth through mergers has to rank up there with leaders in American business history. So where did it all go wrong? It went wrong in several ways. The obvious one was the accounting manipulations and other alleged improprieties. However, from a strategy perspective, the problem was that Ebbers and the company could not turn off the M&A binge. This really was what Ebbers was good at, but he also proved that he was not good at managing a large company on a day-to-day basis. Reports of him micromanaging at company headquarters are amusing, as the following passage relates:

> It was billed as a strategy meeting not to miss. WorldCom, Inc. senior executives from around the globe gathered two months ago at the telecom giant's headquarters in Clinton, Miss. They had come to hear CEO Bernard J. Ebbers reveal his grand vision for rescuing a company mired in debt, sluggish growth, and rising controversy about its accounting practices. What executives heard instead was their boss thundering about the theft of coffee in the company's break room.
>
> How did Ebbers know? Because he had matched brewing filters with bags, and at the end of the month, filters outnumbered bags. Henceforth, Ebbers commanded, his executives would follow a check-list of priorities now referred to as "Bernie's seven points of light."

They would count coffee bags, make sure no lights were left on at
the end of the day, and save cooling costs in the summer by turning the thermostat up four degrees, say three former and current
executives. "Bernie is running a $40 billion company as if it were
still his own mom and pop business," says one WorldCom exec who
attended the meeting. "He doesn't know how to grow the company,
just save pennies."[1]

Other reports state that Ebbers installed video cameras outside
of company facilities to record the length of employee smoking
breaks. Still other reports talk about his approving expenditures above
$5,000 and of personally reviewing all press releases the company
would issue. Running a large company was not what Ebbers was good
at. The skills that one needs to run a small company or to initiate cre-
ative and aggressive deals are not the same skills that one needs to
manage a multibillion-dollar company. With the exception of his
grand-scale deal making, Ebbers gave all the signs of being a small
company CEO. Running a company as though it was a small, closely
held enterprise also contributed to his own personal woes. Before his
resignation from the company, Ebbers borrowed $366 million from
the company to bail him out when personal loans he had taken had
come due and he would have had to sell some of his WorldCom shares
at a time when the price was not favorable. It is not unusual for CEOs
of closely held companies to cause the company to function for their
own personal benefit. However, when a company is mainly owned by
public shareholders, it has to be run for their benefit, and it is no
longer the founding shareholder or CEO's personal fiefdom.

Ebbers and his management also did a poor job of managing the
capital structure of the telecom giant. The company had assumed
significant amounts of debt that had risen to $30 billion by 2002. In
that year, interest payments were $172 million but were scheduled to
rise dramatically to $1.7 billion in 2003 and $2.6 billion in 2004.[2]
Ebber's dealmaking contributed to a highly leveraged capital structure which raised the company's risk level.

---

1. Charles Haddad and Steve Rosenbush, "Woe Is WorldCom," *Business Week*
   (May 6, 2002): 86.
2. Ibid.

In addition, investment bankers were reporting that the company had negative cash flow in 2001. The company's increased debt service pressures came at a time when the company's market share and cash flows were under pressure. The company had more than $1 billion in cash on hand and had a line of credit with banks of up to $8 billion. However, credit lines periodically come up for renewal, and banks will reexamine a company liquidity position at such times. WorldCom was heading for a liquidity crisis, and deal maker Ebbers had no answers. The wrong man was at the wheel, and he kept the company on course for disaster.

## Analyst Recommendations

One problem that was highlighted in WorldCom's rapid growth through acquisitions strategy is that it made the company difficult for investors to evaluate. When a company is doing so many acquisitions, it is more difficult to discern how much of this growth is coming from organic sources as opposed to just the additive effects of M&As. The high volume of deal making that the company engaged in made it popular with investment bankers, who derived generous fees from this work. This led to concerns that the analyst reports being issued by firms that benefited from WorldCom's deals were not sufficiently objective. This was underscored by a complaint that was filed by the New York Attorney General alleging that Solomon Smith Barney received more than $107 million in fees while its telecommunications industry analyst, Jack Grubman, issued "extremely favorable" reports on the company.[3] Mr. Grubman consistently maintained that WorldCom:

> [R]epresented the cheapest S&P large-cap growth stock at the time, remained the "must own" large-cap growth stock in anyone's portfolio, represented one of the premier large-cap growth companies in any industry, and represented the single best idea in telecom. Mr. Grubman urged investors to "load up the truck" with WorldCom stock. In fact, he declared any investor who did not take advantage of current prices to buy every share of WorldCom should seriously think about another vocation.[4]

---

3. First Interim Report of Dick Thornburgh, Bankruptcy Court Examiner, November 4, 2002, p. 87.
4. Ibid., p. 91.

Even when its price began to collapse, Grubman continued to support the stock and recommended that investors buy more shares. Investors simply need to be wary of companies that are pursuing such rapid growth through serial acquisitions.

## WorldCom's Board

As we have seen with many other merger failures, WorldCom's board was not diligent in evaluating Ebbers and his strategy. In fact, they provided him with extremely generous rewards that escalated while the company's fortunes waned. These rewarded included unusual retention bonuses of $10 million to Ebbers and his CFO Scott Sullivan. The compensation committee made loans to Ebbers that totaled $400 million.[5] It is not clear if the full board was aware of the extent of these loans or if the compensation committee did not share this information with the other board members. It also seemed that the board was aware of analyst reports about the company. In fact, the board seemed to have an unusually close relationship with industry analysts. This was underscored by the presence of Grubman at board meetings—something that should have raised eyebrows.

## Strategy and the Market

Over a 15-year period, WorldCom completed more than 60 acquisitions. The fuel that is used for this growth through M&A strategy was its stock. It wanted to ensure that this currency maintained its value, if not appreciated. The Thornburgh reports states the following:

> WorldCom grew in large part because the value of its stock rose dramatically. Its stock was the fuel that kept WorldCom's acquisition engine running at a high speed. WorldCom needed to keep its stock price at high levels to continue its phenomenal growth.
>
> WorldCom did not achieve its growth following a predefined strategic plan, but rather by opportunistic and rapid acquisitions of other companies. The unrelenting pace of these acquisitions caused the Company constantly to redefine itself and its focus. The Com-

---

5. Robert A. G. Monks and Nell Minow, *Corporate Governance* (Malden, MA: Blackwell Publishing), 2004, p. 510.

pany unceasing growth and metamorphosis made integration of its newly acquired operations, systems and personnel much more difficult for investors to compare the Company's operations to historical benchmarks.[6]

When it is clear that the company has gotten all it is going to get out of a growth through M&A strategy, and the company is at an efficient size, then the deal-making process needs to be, at least temporarily, turned off. At that point, organic growth needs to be the focus, not more deals. The board let shareholders down by not stopping Ebbers and putting someone else in place to run the business. The outcome is a sad one because the growth Ebbers achieved was impressive, but many will now only know him for allegations of improprieties and the bankruptcy of the company. Who knows what would have happened if the board had been vigilant and asked him to step aside before they got close to bankruptcy? Would a good manager have been able to maintain and grow the business Ebbers built?

## LESSONS OF THE WORLDCOM STRATEGY

The lessons of the WorldCom disaster are many, but a few of the principal ones are outlined as follows:

- *Deal-making CEOs need to be controlled by the board.* There will come a time that deal making may need to be paused and possibly stopped. Acquisitive CEOs need to be held in check. They also need to demonstrate that they can run a company and do something other than acquisitions.

- *Deal making and managing are two different skills.* Some managers are capable of doing both, but some are better at one than the other. Boards need to put in place the right people with the right skills. Having a deal maker in place greatly increases the likelihood that he or she will do deals. If that is not what the company needs, then get someone else in the leadership position.

---

6. Dick Thornburgh, Bankruptcy Court Examiner, p. 7.

- *Investors need to be extra wary of serial acquirers.* Companies that engage in many M&As in rapid succession are difficult for analysts to evaluate. Therefore, investors need to exercise added caution. In such instances, it is difficult to pick out how much of the growth in revenues and profits is attributable to organic sources as opposed to deals.

- *Deals have to fit the strategy, not the other way around.* A company needs to have in place a strategy for growth, and M&A may be a tool it uses to achieve its strategic goals, but it should not be changing its strategy to fit the changes required by its prior deals.

In February 2005, while Bernie Ebbers was defending himself in a criminal lawsuit, the post-bankruptcy MCI (the company assumed the MCI name after its accounting troubles became overwhelming) reached agreement to be acquired by Verizon (pending regulatory approval), one of AT&T's offspring. Verizon, itself formed with the merger between Nynex and Bell Atlantic, two of the regional holding companies spun off from AT&T, reached agreement to acquire MCI for $6.8 billion, a fraction of what WorldCom paid just a few years earlier.

# 6

## Reversing the Error: Sell-Offs and Other Restructurings

Assuming at some point that management and the board come to a decision that a prior merger or acquisition was a mistake, then a sell-off of that business unit may be a means of reversing the error. It may be a means for the company to recoup some or even all of its losses and devote the capital it may receive to more fruitful activities. However, the question arises: How do we know that a sell-off of the entity in question is the financially superior option relative to its retention? To help answer this question, we will review the research in the area of sell-offs, divestitures, and other forms of downsizing, such as equity carve-outs. We will review the various forms of restructuring that are available to managers and discuss how such restructuring may best be accomplished. Following the introductory discussions, we will then review the research on the shareholder wealth effects of such sell-offs and the other forms of downsizing. Companies should be mindful of this research when trying to determine if a company would be better off with a sell-off of some form or whether it would be better to retain the unit and try to make the best of a deal that may not have turned out well.

In certain instances where a company's prior mergers or acquisitions have not lived up to expectations, sell-offs and downsizing may be the appropriate route to go. However, managers must have a systematic process to follow to enable them to make that decision objectively. They also need to be aware of what the research shows about the shareholder wealth effects of such forms of downsizing. When we review a large volume of this research, we form a compelling picture of the benefits of downsizing in certain situations. The key is identifying those situations and taking advantage of them so as to maximize shareholder gains.

## DIVESTITURES

The most basic form of a sell-off is a simple divestiture. This is where a company sells a division or unit to another firm. In every year, there are a large number of divestitures in the United States and elsewhere (see Exhibit 6.1). For the selling company, the process is a form of contraction, while for the buyer it is a means of expansion. Buyers of prior failed M&As may be able to find a good value—especially when the unit could be more valuably combined with the new buyer's business and be more productive than as part of the seller's firm. One caveat is when a buyer of a company has run it so poorly that some of its value may have eroded. It can be even worse if the buying company had paid a high premium for the acquired entity and then proceeded to manage it in a manner that diminished its value. In such instances, a quick divestiture may be a way out of the situation.

### Historical Trends in Divestitures

Exhibit 6.2 shows more than four decades of divestiture data for the United States. A couple of trends are immediately apparent. First, divestiture volume was relatively small in the third merger wave while companies were busy assembling large conglomerates—highly diversified entities with little strategy behind their combinations. As discussed in Chapter 1, the end of the 1960s featured the third merger wave in U.S. history. During that period the number of divestitures and sell-offs was relatively small as a percentage of the total number

Exhibit 6.1  Number and Dollar Value of Divestitures

| Year | Number | Year | Dollar Value of Divestitures |
|------|--------|------|------------------------------|
| 1965 | 191 | 1988 | 69,614.9 |
| 1966 | 264 | 1989 | 70,843.7 |
| 1967 | 328 | 1990 | 42,179.8 |
| 1968 | 557 | 1991 | 29,256.1 |
| 1969 | 801 | 1992 | 50,400.1 |
| 1970 | 1,401 | 1993 | 48,153.4 |
| 1971 | 1,920 | 1994 | 84,892.1 |
| 1972 | 1,770 | 1995 | 96,487.6 |
| 1973 | 1,557 | 1996 | 117,629.7 |
| 1974 | 1,331 | 1997 | 172,667.7 |
| 1975 | 1,236 | 1998 | 191,460.7 |
| 1976 | 1,204 | 1999 | 255,592.6 |
| 1977 | 1,002 | 2000 | 276,548.1 |
| 1978 | 820 | 2001 | 268,323.4 |
| 1979 | 752 | 2002 | 209,001.2 |
| 1980 | 666 | 2003 | 184,651.3 |
| 1981 | 830 | | |
| 1982 | 875 | | |
| 1983 | 932 | | |
| 1984 | 900 | | |
| 1985 | 1,218 | | |
| 1986 | 1,259 | | |
| 1987 | 807 | | |
| 1988 | 894 | | |
| 1989 | 1,055 | | |
| 1990 | 940 | | |
| 1991 | 849 | | |
| 1992 | 1,026 | | |
| 1993 | 1,134 | | |
| 1994 | 1,134 | | |
| 1995 | 1,199 | | |
| 1996 | 1,702 | | |
| 1997 | 2,108 | | |
| 1998 | 1,987 | | |
| 1999 | 2,353 | | |
| 2000 | 2,501 | | |
| 2001 | 2,914 | | |
| 2002 | 2,691 | | |
| 2003 | 3,188 | | |

*Source: Mergerstat Review,* 1989, 1998, and 2004.

Exhibit 6.2    Dollar Value of Divestitures

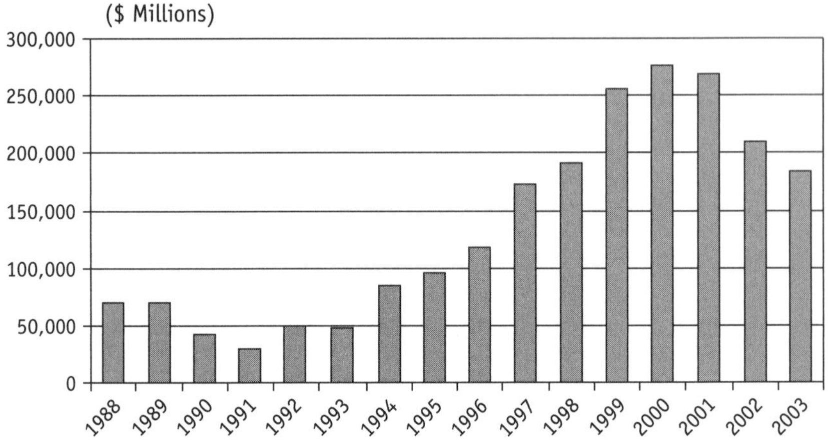

Source: Mergerstat Review, 1989 and 2004.

of transactions. During the third wave, the economic climate was such that companies were seeking to expand and engaged in various M&As as a means to help them do so. As the economy slowed in the late 1960s and 1970s and the market declined, companies responded in various ways, including selling off prior acquisitions as well as other entities. However, a high level of divestitures is not only noticeable in times of low M&A volume and economic pressure. When we look at the fifth merger wave, for example, we see a high number of divestitures that were caused by companies fine-tuning their strategic goals as opposed to trying to realize short-term gains. We should bear in mind that one of the characteristics of this merger wave was that it featured more strategic deals as opposed to some of the financial manipulations that occurred in the fourth wave. Remember that the fourth wave featured many short-term, financially motivated deals that were designed to achieve near-term gains and were often pressured for and pursued by aggressive investment banks. Drexel Burnham Lambert was a leading culprit. Things were somewhat different in the 1990s, when companies sought deals more for their strategic value than for short-term gains that could be achieved. Divisions that did not fit the strategic goals were often sold off, thus increasing the number of divestitures, while business units that could enhance corporate value became the target of acquisition bids or merger proposals.

## SALE OF MILLER BREWING BY PHILIP MORRIS COMPANIES

In 2002 Philip Morris Companies was a somewhat diversified company with major operations in tobacco, food, and beer, with a smaller presence in financial services. The Philip Morris tobacco business is divided into two separate corporate entities: Philip Morris USA and Philip Morris International. Each company faces its own unique issues, with the U.S. division being the target of over a thousand tobacco-related lawsuits. Philip Morris Companies was already one of the largest food companies in the world through its Kraft division. This entity was formed through a series of major acquisitions that included buying General Foods in 1985 and later Kraft Foods in 1988. The company then bought Nabisco in 2000 to become an even larger player in the worldwide food industry (see Exhibit A). This left the company with significant debt, but it

**Exhibit A**

Philip Morris Operating Income by Division

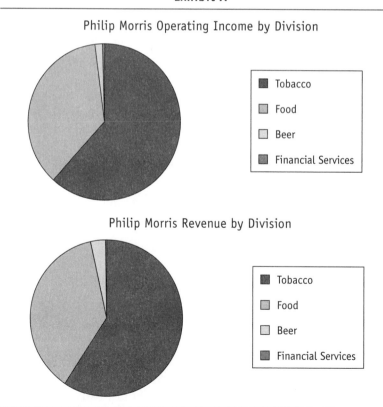

| | |
|---|---|
| ■ | Tobacco |
| ▨ | Food |
| ☐ | Beer |
| ■ | Financial Services |

Philip Morris Revenue by Division

| | |
|---|---|
| ■ | Tobacco |
| ▨ | Food |
| ☐ | Beer |
| ■ | Financial Services |

*Source:* Altria 2003 Annual Report.

was able to offset this leverage by doing a public offering of 16% of Kraft, which brought in $8.7 billion in equity capital to the company.

Being a major food company, Philip Morris Companies, which later changed its name to Altria, sought to move out of businesses that did not fit its current strategy or contribute sufficiently to its overall profits. As part of this strategy, it announced in 2002 that it would sell its Miller Brewing subsidiary to South African Breweries. The sale was valued at $5.6 billion. The sale brought in valuable capital for Philip Morris Companies and enabled it to leave a business that it was not satisfied with in terms of its overall contribution to the parent company. The beer business is a competitive one that requires significant expenditures in marketing and promotions. Although Miller was a major beer brand, it competed with other leading beer producers, such as Anheuser Busch. For Anheuser Busch, beer was its key product, and the company's complete operations revolved around its various beer brands. For Philip Morris Companies, beer was a division and one that was something of a disappointment. By selling off the beer unit, the company was able to increase its focus and concentrate on those businesses where it had a strong core presence. In both food and tobacco, it had a major presence and could use its market shares to pursue gains that are available to such major players in these respective markets.

One of the advantages of the Miller deal was that, at least initially, it appeared to provide good benefits for both parties. While allowing Philip Morris Companies to exit from the beer business, the sale enabled South African Brewers to become a major player in the worldwide beer industry. By increasing its scale of operation, South African Brewers became one of the largest beer marketers in the world. The sale, however, was matched by other deals by competitors as they responded to the increased size of South African Brewers.

## Divestitures and Poor Performance of Acquisitions

Many critics of corporate acquisitions use the record of the divestitures following poor acquisitions as evidence of ill-conceived expansion planning. Using a sample of 33 companies during the period from 1950 to 1986, Michael Porter showed that these firms divested 53% of the acquisitions that brought the acquiring companies into new industries.[1] Based on this evidence, he concludes that the corporate acquisition record is "dismal." The adverse implications of movement into other industries outside of the acquirer's own industry, which is shown in this research by Porter, is a common theme in this book. A wide variety of research shows that these types of acquisitions are much more difficult to achieve success in. At the point when the acquirer recognizes that the deal may be a mistake and takes the tough decision to reverse the error, it may then be able to move in a more fruitful direction. The Porter results were also supported by Ravenscraft and Scherer, who found that 33% of acquisitions made during the 1960s and 1970s were later divested.[2] While this percentage is lower than the majority value of the Porter study, it is still relatively high. As we continue our discussion of the research in this area, we see that more recent studies support some of these early findings of Porter and Ravenscraft and Scherer.

## Divestiture Likelihood and Prior Acquisitions

Kaplan and Weisbach conducted a study to try to determine if a relationship exists between the incidence of divestitures and prior acquisitions conducted by the divesting entity. They analyzed 271 large acquisitions completed during the period between 1971 and 1982.[3] Almost 44% (43.9%), or 119, of these acquisitions were divested by 1982 (see Exhibit 6.3). When we think that an acquisition is usually a long-term, strategic investment, or in most cases it should be, then the 44% value seems high. These researchers found that the divested entities were held for an average of seven years.

Kaplan and Weisbach investigated the pattern of the divestitures in search of a common motive for some of the sell-offs. They found that diversifying acquisitions are *four times more likely* to be divested than nondiversifying acquisitions. This result is consistent with other research discussed in Chapter 2. In that chapter we highlighted the abundant research that showed how many diversifying acquisitions fail to pay benefits for acquirers and how more focused transactions, or those that only diversified into related industries, tended to pay greater benefits. The Kaplan and Weisbach study showed that the most often cited reason for the divestitures was a change in focus

Exhibit 6.3    Acquisitions and Divestitures

| Year | Number of Acquisitions | Median Target Value as Percentage of Acquirer Value | Number Divested | Percentage Divested | Median Years Held |
|------|------|------|------|------|------|
| 1971 | 8 | 36.0 | 5 | 62.5 | 15.6 |
| 1972 | 4 | 28.9 | 1 | 25.0 | 16.9 |
| 1973 | 9 | 22.3 | 7 | 77.8 | 11.6 |
| 1974 | 7 | 19.6 | 2 | 28.6 | 7.7 |
| 1975 | 7 | 34.1 | 4 | 57.1 | 11.5 |
| 1976 | 16 | 19.8 | 8 | 50.0 | 8.3 |
| 1977 | 30 | 26.1 | 12 | 40.0 | 8.8 |
| 1978 | 39 | 28.0 | 16 | 41.0 | 7.6 |
| 1979 | 45 | 28.1 | 23 | 51.1 | 6.5 |
| 1980 | 30 | 25.7 | 12 | 10.0 | 6.3 |
| 1981 | 34 | 28.4 | 17 | 50.0 | 6.5 |
| 1982 | 42 | 24.6 | 12 | 28.6 | 4.5 |
| Total | 272 | 25.6 | 119 | 43.9 | 7.0 |

*Source:* Steven N. Kaplan and Michael N. Weisbach, "The Success of Acquisitions: Evidence from Divestitures," *Journal of Finance* 47, no. 1 (March 1992).

or strategy. In addition, the admission of an unprofitable acquisition and an outright mistake was cited in 22 of the 103 transactions they studied (see Exhibit 6.4). Clearly, a large percentage of divestitures are reversals of failed M&As. When we review the research on sell-offs and other forms of downsizing, we will see that such decisions make good sense because they tend to provide quick financial benefits for shareholders.

## Issuing a Tracking Stock

An intermediate step that is not as drastic as an outright sell-off is the issuance of a tracking stock. As the name implies, this stock tracks the performance of the specific entity that the company is isolating. It is a tax-neutral transaction that is sometimes referred to as a *pseudo-divestiture*. Sometimes such shares are referred to as *lettered stock or even targeted shares*. Tracking shares were first issued in 1984, but they became more popular in the fifth merger wave. Telecom companies,

Exhibit 6.4    Reasons for Divestitures

| Reason | Number of Divestitures |
|---|---|
| Change of focus or corporate strategy | 43 |
| Unit unprofitable or mistake | 22 |
| Sale to finance acquisition or leveraged restructuring | 29 |
| Antitrust | 2 |
| Need cash | 3 |
| To defend against takeover | 1 |
| Good price | 3 |
| Divestitures with reasons | 103 |

*Source:* Steven N. Kaplan and Michael N. Weisbach, "The Success of Acquisitions: Evidence from Divestitures," *Journal of Finance* 47, no. 1 (March 1992).

such as Sprint, seized onto this financing vehicle when they issued PCS tracking stock to help fund the multibillion-dollar capital spending program of its wireless division. This particular tracking stock was initially successful, but many of the other tracking shares did not fare as well.

Shareholders investing in tracking stocks do not have the same rights that shareholders typically have. They only have a claim to the earnings of the tracked entity and do not have other corporate democracy rights, such as the right to elect directors who would oversee the management of the company.

The stock is issued by the overall company, and the dividends paid by the shares that are issued are a function of the performance of the specific entity that is tied to the tracking stock. Tracking stocks are sometimes issued when the company perceives that the overall company's stock is not trading at values that reflect the overall company. One possibility related to our current discussion of divestitures is where the market does not approve of a prior acquisition and is registering this disapproval through lower market price of the overall company. In effect, the bad prior acquisition is depressing the value of the equity in the combined business. Of course, many other possibilities could result in a company issuing a tracking stock. However, the first instance of a tracking stock came from an acquisition. This occurred in 1984 when General Motors issued a tracking stock that would reflect the performance of its recently acquired Electronic Data Systems (EDS) subsidiary. The issuance of this stock was GM's way of dealing with EDS shareholder concerns about exchanging their high-growth EDS shares for slower-growth GM shares. By getting this newly created tracking shares, Class E shares, EDS shareholders would gain or lose mainly based on the performance of just this division—not the overall parent company.

Another more recent example of a tracking stock occurred when Loews Corporation issued shares in what is called the Carolina Group (see Exhibit 6.5). The Carolina Group shares reflect the performance of just the Lorillard division of Loews Corporation. Loews Corporation is a diversified parent company that includes several dissimilar entities such as CNA Insurance. The value of Loews stock was burdened by the large litigation liabilities of the U.S. tobacco entity it owned. This entity was the target of more than 1,000 tobacco lawsuits, which brought with them uncertain liabilities. By issuing Carolina Group shares, the market could better assess the trade-off between the cash flows that this division generated in relation to the liabilities that it brought.

Another prominent example of a tracking stock, and one that is related to a failed acquisition strategy, was the issuance of shares in AT&T Wireless by AT&T. In April 2000, AT&T was able to raise $10.6 billion in a public offering of shares in its wireless entity. In doing this transaction, the company was able to try to adjust for the depressing effects that AT&T's prior acquisition program had on the

Exhibit 6.5    Carolina Group Tracking Stock Prices

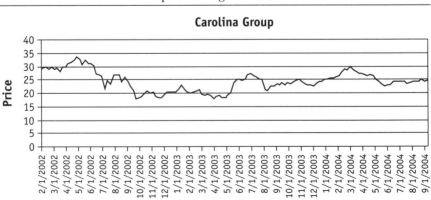

Source: finance.yahoo.com.

company. Like many other tracking stocks, such an intermediate step as issuing a tracking stock, as opposed to selling off the division, was only a short-term fix. The market never really accepted the combination of the wireless company with the rest of AT&T's telecommunications business. The market also had to be aware of the company's dismal acquisition record and generally is skeptical when such companies engage in other large-scale deals when they have done so poorly in the deal market. AT&T's acquisition woes were to continue, and a tracking stock was merely a small bandage on a large wound that would only be fixed with major corporate surgery in the form of still another restructuring program. The real question was, in light of the company's failure with acquisitions, why was the market so willing to accept its other large-scale acquisitions and not look at them with a jaundiced eye when considering the company's track record?

Tracking stocks are often merely a temporary solution. When a company engages in acquisitions or has other divisions whose value is not reflected in the stock price, then a tracking stock may provide some short-term relief, but it usually is not the solution to the problem. It is important to note that this is not always true for tracking stocks. This is not the reason why Loews Corp., for example, issued a tracking stock. That was done because of the unique aspects of that company's cash flows and liabilities that are very different from the rest of the company. With a tracking stock, the market can more clearly assess the Carolina Group and Lorrilard's future cash flow generation capability and liabilities and to some extent separate them from the rest of the Loews' business, which had many other valuable and different business segments, such as CNA Insurance. However, companies that are contemplating creating a tracking stock to deal with poor prior acquisitions that are depressing its stock price may find that a tracking stock can give the company a temporary respite from stock market pressures. This may temporarily relieve market pressures while the company pursues other options such as a sell-off or an even more major corporate restructuring. If the market finds this approach acceptable, then the parent company's stock price may rebound. In a sense, a tracking stock allows the market to follow and separately profit from the tracked entity while the parent company still owns the division.

Unfortunately, issuing a tracking stock may not be a permanent solution. Often, the real solution will be to separate the two entities and have them not just trade separately but make them completely separate businesses. Sometimes issuing a tracking stock may put even more pressure on the company to take the ultimate steps of separating the two entities and selling off the divisions. The advantage of a tracking stock is that it can buy time while the parent company finds the most opportune moment to sell off the division. If the market is not right for such a sale, issuing a tracking stock may allow the stock market to recognize the value of the rest of the company while it may still take a dim view of the outlook for the tracked entity. It may also allow certain groups of investors to register their positive assessments of their company in the form of increased demand for its shares, while other investors with different preferences may do the same for the tracked entity. If this works out that way, a tracking stock is a win-win situation. If it does not, the parent company still has the option to sell off the division at an advantageous time.

Later in this chapter we will discuss the shareholder wealth effects of various forms of sell-offs through a review of the research literature in this field. Studies also address the shareholder wealth effects of the issuance of tracking stocks. However, in the interests of continuity, we will postpone this review until after the shareholder wealth effects of the various different forms of sell-offs have been discussed. We would be remiss, however, if we did not mention that some of the long-term financial results of tracking stocks are less than stellar. This is underscored by a fall-off in tracking stock issuance as well as the removal of some of them from the market. For example, Sprint announced in March 2004 that it would fold its tracking stock back into the parent company, thus ending the run of one of the more successful tracking stocks.

## DECISION: RETAIN OR SELL OFF

The decision to retain or sell off a division should be preceded with a rigorous financial analysis of the division. This should include a projection of the future financial benefits that the division would provide. For a company that is considering selling off, or otherwise disposing of, a division, such as when a company has decided that a prior acquisition no longer fits into the acquirer's strategic plans, it needs to pursue a systematic process to ensure that this decision will prove to be a wiser one than perhaps the original acquisition or merger decision. The decision can be approached in its simplest form—what is the financial contribution of the division as part of the parent company and comparing that value to what could be achieved in a sale of the division. It is important to recognize that these two values will each change over the passage of time. That is, the company could have paid a certain price for the entity at a moment in time, but this value would reasonably change over time as the market and the earning power of the entity varied. Many of the situations where a company is considering selling a division are ones where the performance of the division has been a disappointment. In other situations, the parent company simply changed strategic direction and the acquired entity may no longer fit in with the company's plans, possibly because of factors outside of the company's control, such as changes in market conditions. It could be a situation where management pursued a diversification strategy that was not well received by the market. Such was the case when Sears decided to try to extend its well-known brand name and leverage its customer traffic by acquiring companies in the real estate and securities businesses. Here the market registered its doubts about the strategy in the form of weak demand for the stock. Sears eventually reversed the strategy and went "back to basics."

Particularly in situations where the unit in question is a significant part of the overall company, the value of the combined entity as well as the value of the business without the unit need to be analyzed. When doing the latter valuation, one needs to also take into account the use to which the selling company would put the proceeds of the sale. In situations where the target has been a major disappointment, its value in the marketplace may be less than what the acquirer paid for it. If continued ownership of the entity is eroding its value, the acquirer may need to consider that it may want to cut its losses and move on. Sometimes a poorly performing division can be not only a financial drain but also a managerial distraction occupying upper management, who could more profitably devote their time in other business areas. If a division does not fit the overall strategy of the parent company, then perhaps it would be better off on its own or in the hands of another company for which it is a better fit. Again, the analysis needs to be broken down into numbers where the return is computed with and without the business unit. If the rate of return generated by the division is less than the rate of return that the proceeds generated from the sale of the division could earn, then an outright sale needs to be considered along with other options, such as what it may take to fix the problem. The financial analysis is briefly summarized in the following section.

## Financial Evaluation of Divestitures

The financial evaluation of a subsidiary by a parent company contemplating divestiture should proceed logically. The following general steps form a basis for a general process of evaluation:

1. *Estimation of after-tax cash flows.* The parent company needs to estimate the after-tax cash flows of the division. This analysis should consider the interrelationship between the subsidiary and the parent company's respective capabilities to generate cash flows. If, for example, the subsidiary's operations are closely related to the parent company's activities, then the parent company's cash flows may be positively or negatively affected after the divestiture. Thus, this needs to be factored into the analysis at the start of the evaluation process.

2. *Determination of the division's discount rate.* The present value of the division's after-tax cash flows needs to be calculated. To do so, a division-specific discount rate must be derived, taking into account the risk characteristics of the division on a stand-alone basis. The cost of capital of other firms that are in the same business and approximately the same size may be a good proxy for this discount rate.

3. *Present value calculation.* Using the discount rate derived in step 2, we can calculate the present value of each projected after-tax cash flow. The sum of these terms will represent the present value of the income-generating capability of the division by itself.

4. *Deduction of the market value of the division's liabilities.* Step 3 of this process did not take into account the division's liabilities. The market value of these liabilities needs to be deducted from the present value of the after-tax cash flows (see Equation 6.1). This results in the net liability value of the division, which is the value of the division as part of the parent company, assuming it maintains ownership of the division.

$$NOL = \sum_{i=1}^{n} \frac{ATCF_i}{(1+k)^i} - MVL$$

Where

$NOL$ = the net of liabilities value of the present value of the after-tax cash flows

$ATCF$ = the after-tax cash flows

$k$ = the division-specific discount rate

$MVL$ = the market value of the liabilities          (6.1)

5. *Deduction of the divestiture proceeds.* The proceeds that the parent company can derive from a sale of the division *(DP)* are then compared with the value developed in step 4. As shown following, if the divestiture proceeds, net of selling costs, are higher than the value of keeping the division, the unit should be sold:

$DP > NOL$   Sell division

$DP = NOL$   Other factors will control decision

$DP < NOL$   Keep division

This five-step description is simplistic. Each situation will present its own additional factors that need to be considered and other steps that need to be taken. Thus, this five-step process is a skeleton of a framework that needs to be created in order to perform a complete analysis.

## SPIN-OFFS

In addition to an outright divestiture, a company that is considering downsizing and separating a particular division from the overall company has more alternatives available to it than merely a divestiture. Two alternatives are spin-offs and equity carve-outs. Each is very different from divestitures and from each other. In order to make an enlightened decision, we need to explore the strengths and weaknesses of each alternative.

Spin-offs have become one of the more popular forms of corporate downsizing. The dollar volume of spin-offs grew dramatically in the United States over the second half of the 1990s and through 2000–2001. Spin-off volume peaked in 2000 at $190 billion and remained at a very high level ($163 billion) in the following year (see Exhibit 6.6). However, the dollar volume of spin-offs declined dramatically in the years that followed, which is consistent with the turndown in M&As.

We have had some major spin-offs in corporate finance, and one of the biggest was the AT&T spin-off that broke up AT&T in the 1980s. Another was the spin-off of the international conglomerate ITT. In 1995, ITT initiated a $12.4 billion spin-off of the international conglomerate's assets into three separate entities. ITT was a storied conglomerate that grew dramatically in the 1960s under the leadership of Harold Geneen. He helped build a vast international conglomerate that operated in many different fields but had little synergy. It took decades to disassemble this corporate giant, and the 1995 spin-off of

Exhibit 6.6    Spin-Off Volume, 1998 to 2003

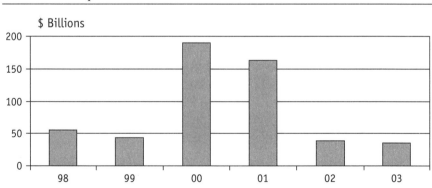

*Source:* Thomson Financial Securities Data.

the company's assets into three separate divisions was part of that downsizing, increased focus process. The ITT spin-off was motivated by the fact that the overall company was composed of various valuable assets and divisions, but the company's overall equity value was not reflecting the underlying values of its combined assets. This can be a problem because the breakup value of the assets may be greater than the enterprise value that constitutes the combination of the company's liabilities and the depressed equity value. With these market-based pressures in mind, ITT sought to implement a downsizing but one that was in the best interests of shareholders. Its solution to this problem was to do a spin-off. Part of the benefits that a spin-off was able to provide to shareholders is the tax treatment that can be available with a spin-off but may not be available with other forms of downsizing.

## INVOLUNTARY SPIN-OFFS

Before we proceed further with our discussion of spin-offs, we should differentiate between voluntary spin-offs and those that are imposed on a company—involuntary spin-offs. The heralded AT&T spin-off that was mentioned earlier was an example of an involuntary spin-off. This spin-off came as a result of an antitrust suit that was originally filed in 1974 by the Justice Department. The result was that the government and AT&T reached an accord to break up the large telecommunications company. The parties entered into an agreement that became effective on January 1, 1984, and provided for the breakup of the telecom giant into 22 operating companies, which would be organized within seven regional holding companies. This spin-off gave rise to many other M&As as AT&T's former telecommunications business consolidated and transformed itself into a new market-based combination that quickly did not resemble the one that was initially created by the initial spin-off.

   In this famous spin-off, the 22 holding companies focused on local telecommunications service, while the new AT&T became exclusively a long-distance telecommunications company. Shareholders in the original AT&T then came to hold shares in the operating companies as well as the long-distance firm. Specifically, the deal provided that for every 10 shares that each shareholder had in the original AT&T, shareholders received one share in each of the seven regional holding companies.[4] Those shareholders who had fewer than 10 shares received a cash value for their shares rather than shares in the regional holding companies. They would still be shareholders in the post-spin-off AT&T.

While the giant AT&T spin-off of the 1980s is a fascinating and historical transaction, it is not typical of the spin-offs we are focusing on. We are mainly considering spin-offs that are part of a strategy that is designed to maximize shareholder value through a restructuring process. That is, we are interested in situations where a company may be able to enhance shareholder value through a transaction such as a voluntary spin-off. In such a transaction, we would need to compare the gains the company may realize from a spin-off, as opposed to other forms of downsizing, such as a divestiture and equity carve-out, with the value that shareholders would receive if the company stayed in its combined form.

## DEFENSIVE SPIN-OFFS

In addition to discussing involuntary spin-offs, deals that are less relevant to our strategy discussions, it is also useful to briefly mention defensive spin-offs. A corporation may utilize this form of restructuring to defend itself against a hostile takeover. Companies may choose to spin off divisions to make the company less appealing to a hostile bidder. A well-known example of this occurred in January 1987, when Diamond Shamrock's board of directors decided to approve a restructuring plan that would spin off two core businesses and form a new company—Diamond Shamrock R&M. In doing so, it would distribute R&M stock to its shareholders.[5] This is a drastic antitakeover defense. While one should be aware of these types of transactions, they are also not the types of deals in which we are most interested. We are assuming that the company is not under attack from a hostile bidder and that it is deciding on the best course of action for its shareholders in the absence of immediate pressure from a hostile bidder.

## TAX BENEFITS OF SPIN-OFFS

A major advantage that a spin-off has over other forms of corporate downsizing is that the transaction may be able to be structured in a manner that does not have an adverse tax impact on shareholders. This was the case with the spin-off of the regional Bells previously discussed. The exchange of shares in the various telecom companies that were formed with this deal did not create tax liabilities for the shareholders. In reviewing the transaction, the IRS did not consider that the deal provided shareholders with a gain or a loss. Thus, it was tax neutral. This is very different from the outcome that might occur if a company decided to sell off a division. With such an outright sale, the company may incur a gain that may have adverse tax consequences for its shareholders.

The rules covering spin-offs are set forth in Section 355 of the Tax Code. These regulations specify that both the parent entity and the spun-off company must be in business for at least five years before the transaction. In addition, the subsidiary that is spun off must be at least 80% owned by the parent company.

We see that the tax effects are very important considering that management and the board of directors must keep in mind when deciding which form of downsizing to pursue. In some instances, the tax benefits of spin-offs may offset any cash infusion that a company may receive from other forms of sell-offs. In other cases, the main goal is to separate the division from the parent company so as to have a more focused strategy, and the cash infusion from a sale is not the main impetus behind the deal.

## SHAREHOLDER WEALTH EFFECTS OF SELL-OFFS

Sell-offs allow companies to try to realize gains from reverse synergy. For companies that have divisions that may be detracting from their market value, a company may be able to release suppressed values that lie dormant within its equity by getting rid of the troubled divisions. As discussed earlier, a sell-off can be accomplished in several ways. It is useful to review some of the research studies that exist to see if they show that the market values necessary downsizings. When we do so, we see that the average shareholder wealth effects are consistently positive. These positive results are apparent in three decades of research in this area. The strength of the results is that they are persistent over a long time period, through many different markets, combined with the fact that the studies show consistently positive shareholder wealth effects (see Exhibit 6.7).

## RATIONALE FOR A POSITIVE STOCK PRICE REACTION TO SELL-OFFS

When a firm decides to sell off a poorly performing division, this corporate unit is transferred to another owner, which presumably will put it to a more valuable use than the selling company did. The seller receives cash (or sometimes other compensation) in place of the asset. When the market responds positively to this asset reallocation, as it so often does, it is expressing a belief that the selling firm will use this cash more efficiently than it was utilizing the asset that was sold. Moreover, the asset that was sold may have attracted a premium above market value, which should also cause the market to respond positively.

Exhibit 6.7    Average Stock Price Effects of Voluntary Sell-Offs

| Study[a] | Days | Average Abnormal Returns (%) | Period Sampled | Sample Size |
|---|---|---|---|---|
| Alexander, Benson & Kampmeyer (1984) | −1 through 0 | 0.17 | 1964–73 | 53 |
| Hite and Owers (1984) | −1 through 0 | 1.50 | 1963–79 | 56 |
| Hite, Owers & Rogers (1987) | −50 through −5 | 0.69 | 1963–81 | 55 |
| Jain (1985) | −5 through −1 | 0.70 | 1976–78 | 1,107 |
| Klein (1983) | −2 through 0 | 1.12 | 1970–79 | 202 |
| Linn and Rozeff (1984) | −1 through 0 | 1.45 | 1977–82 | 77 |
| Loh, Bezjak & Toms (1995) | −1 through 0 | 1.50 | 1982–87 | 59 |
| Rosenfeld (1984) | −1 through 0 | 2.33 | 1963–81 | 62 |

*Source:* Patrick A. Gaughan, *Mergers, Acquisitions, and Corporate Restructurings, 3rd Edition* (Hoboken, NJ: John Wiley & Sons, Inc., 2002).

The selling firm has a few options at its disposal when contemplating the disposition of the newly acquired cash. The firm can use the funds for internal investment in its core business. If the returns from that investment are not impressive, such as in the case of a mature business, then the company could choose to distribute the cash to stockholders in the form of a dividend, or it may repurchase its own shares at a premium. Both means can provide a quick benefit to shareholders. Another alternative would be to invest the monies in the company's core business. Still another option would be to use the funds to make another acquisition, such as in the core business area. The only concern we have here is that we have to make sure that such a transaction will truly increase shareholder value. We discussed at length in Chapter 2 that often times acquisitions fail to pay positive returns to shareholders. So while another acquisition is definitely a possibility, the company must proceed with great caution so that it isn't considering selling that acquisition as well in the years to come.

## WEALTH EFFECTS OF VOLUNTARY DEFENSIVE SELL-OFFS

We have already introduced defensive spin-offs while also highlighting the positive shareholder wealth effects of traditional sell-offs that are not motivated by factors such as antitakeover considerations. One question that immediately arises is whether defensive spin-offs provide shareholders with some of the same consistent positive benefits as traditional sell-offs. There is evidence in the research literature that such transactions do not provide positive benefits for shareholders. A study conducted by Loh, Bezjak, and Toms found comparable positive shareholder wealth effects of voluntary sell-offs as what other studies have noted, but they did not detect a positive shareholder effect for defensive spin-offs. These findings are consistent with the other research that has been already discussed.[6] In their study, Loh, Bezjak, and Toms examined a sample of 59 companies over the period of 1980 to 1987, 13 of which featured takeover speculation. They found cumulative average abnormal return equal to 1.5% over a one-day period up to the sell-off date. However, when they divided their sample into two subsamples, those with and without takeover speculation, the 13 firms that were the target of takeover speculation failed to show any significant changes in shareholder wealth. These results imply that when firms engage in sell-offs to prevent themselves from being taken over, the market treats the transactions differently and does not consider it a positive change.

## WEALTH EFFECTS OF INVOLUNTARY SELL-OFFS

Involuntary sell-offs are usually negative events in a company's history. They often come as a result of some adverse regulatory ruling that requires the company to sell off specific divisions. When this occurs as part of a preacquisition agreement with the Justice Department or the Federal Trade Commission, it will usually not be a surprise to the market. In other instances, when it is part of a long adversarial regulatory process where the company has come out the loser and regulators require strong remedial action in the form of sell-offs, the market considers this an adverse result. However, even here this may not be news to the market, which often anticipates events in advance of their actual occurrence. When the market has already correctly anticipated the event, then any downward stock price reaction usually occurred before the actual announcement of the ruling and the eventual sell-off. This is what occurred when Santa Fe–Southern Pacific received an unfavorable ruling requiring it to divest the Southern Pacific Railway. The company strongly opposed the divestiture, and the stock price declined in response. This stock price decline had other adverse side effects for the company as it made it a target of takeover speculation. Santa Fe–Southern Pacific was actually a diversified company that had significant assets beyond the railroad industry. It was also a major holder of real estate that could have provided valuable collateral for a financial bidder that was interested in leveraging the assets of the railway giant. The potential bidders wanted to take advantage of the declining stock price while the assets that the company maintained held their value and were unaffected by the regulatory ruling. The company had to respond with its own restructuring plan before a hostile bidder came in to implement its own.

## FINANCIAL BENEFITS FOR BUYERS
## OF SOLD-OFF ENTITIES

The various studies we have reviewed clearly point to benefits for companies that engage in sell-offs. We have also discussed at length the reasoning for why these companies realize these benefits. The question that arises is, if they are gains for sellers, are there also gains for buyers of these sold-off entities, or is it a zero-sum gain where the sellers profit at the buyer's expense? The impact on buyers of sold-off entities was reviewed in a study by Prem Jain. He used a large sample that included 304 buyers and 1,062 sellers (not all the buyers were known).[7] He found that the sellers earned a statistically significant positive excess return of 0.34%. We have seen that sellers register larger gains, but the point is that both sellers and buyers may gain, although sellers may have more to gain than buyers. The sellers' gain does not seem to come at the expense of buyers, who end up acquiring the sellers' problem. Perhaps the reason that both sellers and buyers often gain is that sellers are able to pursue a better strategy without the business unit while buyers are able to acquire an entity at perhaps a good value, especially if the value of the entity has been depressed while the seller owned it.

Remember, when we saw the gains that sellers registered we were really only looking at them as of the time of the announcement and not considering a longer-term view of companies that had paid a premium for an acquisition at one point in time and then later saw this value erode over time, as some of the long-term studies of acquisitions have showed. So when we say that the gains of the seller are not coming at the expense of the buyer, we have to also consider what a more complete analysis would show. This would be an analysis that may consider losses that a seller experienced over a longer time period, going back to when it pursued a poorly conceived acquisition that it may now be selling off. We should also bear in mind that while we are discussing the situation in the context of a prior acquisition that was sold off, most of the research studies of sell-offs reviewed only consider sell-offs and may not distinguish between those that were prior acquisitions and those that were not.

## SHAREHOLDER WEALTH EFFECTS OF SPIN-OFFS

The abundant research studies that we reviewed focused on sell-offs and mainly included divestitures. The question arises whether spin-offs offer companies comparable positive shareholder wealth effects. We can look to the results of some research that specifically focused on spin-offs to help us answer this question. Cusatis, Miles, and Woolridge analyzed the returns on stock of both spin-offs and their former parent companies. Unlike many of the events studies that we have reviewed for sell-offs as well as for M&A announcements, this study examined the shareholder returns leading up to and including the announcement of the spin-off. In doing so the study tried to discern the long-term effects of spin-offs on the companies involved, not just the announcement period returns.

Cusatis, Miles, and Woolridge's research presents a favorable picture of the post-event performance of spin-offs. Both spin-offs and their parent companies showed positive abnormal returns over a period that ranged between 6 months before and 36 months after the stock distribution date.[8] They also noticed that the spin-off and the parent company *were more active in takeovers* than the control group of comparable firms who were not involved in such transactions. This involvement in takeover activity may help explain some of the positive shareholder wealth effects. When the firms that were involved in takeovers were removed from the sample, the returns are still positive but not statistically different from zero. This implies that spin-offs and their parent company are more likely to be involved in takeovers, and when they are, they will enable their shareholders to realize takeover premiums. When this is the case, then shareholders benefit. When companies return to their prior acquisitive ways in a manner that shareholders lose, they prove they may not have learned their lessons and may have to relearn them at shareholders' expense.

The Cusatis, Miles, and Woolridge results were also supported by other research studies conducted by J. P. Morgan. Morgan conducted studies on spin-offs in both 1997 and later in 2002. The 2002 study showed that spin-offs outperformed the market by an average of more than 12% over the first 12 months of their independent operation (see Exhibit 6.8).[9] These positive effects were greater the smaller

Exhibit 6.8    Shareholder Wealth Effects of Spin-Offs on Parent
Companies

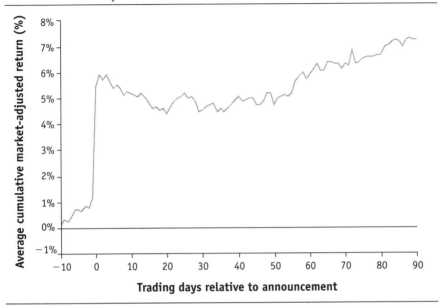

*Source:* J.P. Morgan Spin-Offs Study, 2002.

Exhibit 6.9    Shareholder Wealth Effects on Spin-Off Subsidiary

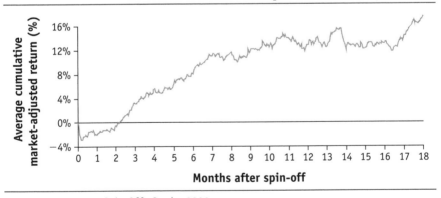

*Source:* J.P. Morgan Spin-Offs Study, 2002.

the size of the spun-off entity. In addition, the parent companies outperformed the market by an average of 6%. The positive effects were
greater the larger the spun-off entity (see Exhibit 6.9). Clearly, spin-
offs are a win-win situation for both the parent company and the company entity. It is no wonder why the market likes these transactions.

## CORPORATE FOCUS AND SPIN-OFFS

We have already discussed abundant research showing that diversifying deals and those that reduce corporate focus tended to erode shareholder value. Other research has shown that spin-offs that are used to increase focus enhance shareholder value. A study of 85 spin-offs over the period 1975 to 1991 by Daley, Mehrotra, and Sivakumar examined the relationship between spin-offs and corporate focus by comparing the performance of spin-off firms where the parent company and the spun-off entity were in two different SIC codes (cross-industry spin-offs) relative to instances where both were in the same SIC code (within-industry spin-offs).[10] Of their sample, cross-industry spin-offs constituted 60 of the total 85 transactions, while the remaining 25 involved a parent and a subsidiary that shared the same two-digit SIC code.

Daley, Mehrotra, and Sivakumar looked at the shareholder wealth effects of the different types of spin-offs, as well as looking at the financial performance of the entities involved. They found positive announcement period excess returns for both the within-industry group (1.4%) and the cross-industry group (4.3%), with the cross-industry group being significantly greater (see Exhibit 6.10).

Daley, Mehrota, and Sivakumar found improvements in various measures of accounting performance, such as the return on assets and net capital expenditures (ratio of capital expenditures to sale), for *cross-industry spin-offs* but not for within-industry deals. They did not just compare the pre-spin-off entity with that of the parent company after the spin-off because any effects they might detect could

Exhibit 6.10    Shareholder Wealth Effects: Cross Industry versus Own Industry Spinoffs

| Spinoff Type | Sample Size | Announcement Return | Excess Return |
|---|---|---|---|
| Own-Industry | 25 | 1.60% | 1.40% |
| Cross-Industry | 60 | 4.50% | 4.30% |
| Combined | 85 | 3.60% | 3.40% |

*Source:* Lane Daley, Vikas Mehrotra, and Ranjini Sivakumar, "Corporate Focus and Value Creation: Evidence from Spinoffs," *Journal of Financial Economics* 45 (1997): 257–281.

simply be a function of getting rid of a poorly performing entity without any other intrinsic changes in the performance of the company. They compared the pre-spin-off entity with their own consolidation of the financial data of the two separate post-spin-off entities. They found that when comparing the year before with the year after the spin-off, the median change in the return on assets for the cross-industry group was 3%, while there was no change for the within-industry group. They adjusted their results to take into account industry changes, and this had little effect. They also found improvements in profitability, as measured by the ratio of operating income to sales, for the cross-industry group while noticing minimal changes for the within-industry group. Their research also failed to find many differences in capital expenditures for either group.

The results of this research imply that spin-offs only create value when they result in an increase in corporate focus. These performance improvements seem to derive from companies removing unrelated businesses and allowing managers to concentrate their efforts on the core business while eliminating the distraction of noncore entities. So we see that merely doing a spin-off by itself may not generate positive shareholder wealth effects. The positive effects may come from the fact that the spin-off is one way, among other available ways such as an outright divestiture, that may allow a company to undo a prior move into an unrelated field that may be outside of its expertise or its strengths. After the cross-industry spin-off, the company may be better able to concentrate on what it does best. The market usually likes such moves, which is why we see the effects that Daley, Mehrotra, and Sivakumar found.

## PEPSI'S SPIN-OFF OF ITS FAST-FOOD BUSINESSES

The spin-off of Pepsi's fast-food businesses, a transaction briefly discussed in Chapter 2, is a good example of a company using a form of restructuring, a spin-off, to reverse some prior acquisition mistakes. Pepsi used acquisitions to try to reinforce its distribution chain. The company wanted to make sure that these important outlets for its soft drink products would be reserved for Pepsi. It was also a preemptive competitive strategy, where if Pepsi acquired these companies, they would no longer be available for its major rival—Coke. Pepsi thought the best way to achieve this goal was to acquire the fast-food chains of Taco Bell, Pizza Hut, and Kentucky Fried Chicken. Each had a major national presence, although each marketed very different foods. While the foods were different, they were marketed generally to similar consumers. More important, the different food chains each sold soft drinks marketed by companies like Pepsi and Coke.

While Pepsi believed in this acquisition strategy, over time, it found that acquiring these fast-food chains was an expensive alternative—and one that placed Pepsi's capital in a very different business. That industry was very different from the soft drink and snack business. New restaurants were regularly opened by rivals, and the business featured intense price competition. Eventually, Pepsi decided that the acquisitions were not necessary to achieve the company's goals and that a spin-off of these divisions could be implemented while still preserving the continuity of the distribution chain.

In 1997 when it concluded that it did not need to own fast-food restaurants outright to ensure that its soft drinks would be sold there, Pepsi recognized that fast-food business was very different from the soft drink business, and the former presented a very different degree of competition and potential returns. As a solution to this problem, Pepsi announced that it would spin off its fast-food businesses. The spin-off would put the Pizza Hut, Taco Bell, and Kentucky Fried Chicken chains, which had roughly $10 billion in sales, into an entity by the name of Tricon Global Restaurants. Under the spin-off plan, Pepsi shareholders would receive one share in the restaurant business for every 10 shares in Pepsi they owned. Tricon entered into its own financing plan, which allowed it to pay Pepsi $4.5 billion for the restaurants. This amount reflected some of the debt that Pepsi attributed to that business.

With the spin-off, Pepsi's shareholders would still enjoy the benefits of the investment in the fast-food chains, but shareholders in Pepsi would be holding a more pure play with their shares in Pepsi. One of the benefits of this transaction for Pepsi, however, was that it was able to still preserve its distribution link to these important outlets for its soft drinks without having to tie up its capital in these very different businesses. In addition, with the long-term deal implemented with Tricon, Pepsi was able to keep its chief rival out of these outlets. The market, however, was initially leery of this deal, as a similar spin-off of the Darden Restaurant business, which included Olive Garden and the Red Lobster chains, by General Mills in 1995 did not perform well. However, the deal was good for Pepsi because it allowed the company to concentrate on what it did best.

## EQUITY CARVE-OUTS

Equity carve-outs are still another sell-off alternative that a company can consider, along with a divestiture and spin-off. In an equity carve-out, a parent company makes a public offering of stock, which, in turn, brings in cash to the parent company. The investors who buy the issued shares receive stock in the newly formed entity that represents the division that is sold off by the parent company. In both a spin-off and an equity carve-out, a division is separated from the parent and becomes a stand-alone corporation. However, one of the key differences between a spin-off and an equity carve-out is that with an equity carve-out, the parent company receives a cash infusion from the sale of the shares, whereas with a spin-off, the division is separated from the parent company, and the parent company does not necessarily receive cash in exchange—new shares are issued to the parent company shareholders, and they hold shares in both entities after the transaction (Pepsi was an exception to that in the sense that the company did receive cash).

There are many examples of major equity carve-outs. When Sears, which was discussed in Chapter 2, decided to end its dismal diversification strategy, it decided to do a $.48 billion equity carve-out of its Discover Dean Witter unit and a $2.12 billion carve-out of its Allstate Insurance business. American Express did the same with its $1.16 billion carve-out of First Data Corporation.

Just as with spin-offs and divestitures, equity carve-out volume rose dramatically during the fifth merger wave (see Exhibit 6.11). Many companies found this option provided significant benefits that spin-offs and direct sell-offs did not provide. While total equity carve-out volume was $1.1 billion in 1990, by 2001 equity carve-out volume was $18.5 billion. In addition, equity carve outs become a higher percent of total IPOs as we went through the fifth merger wave.

Exhibit 6.11    Equity Carve-Out Volume

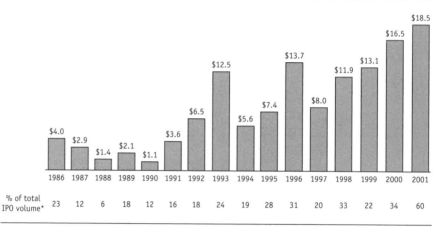

| % of total IPO volume* | 23 | 12 | 6 | 18 | 12 | 16 | 18 | 24 | 19 | 28 | 31 | 20 | 33 | 22 | 34 | 60 |
|---|---|---|---|---|---|---|---|---|---|---|---|---|---|---|---|---|

*Source:* J.P. Morgan Carve-Out Study, 2002.

## BENEFITS OF EQUITY CARVE-OUTS

Equity carve-outs share with divestitures and spin-offs the various strategic benefits of separating the division that no longer fits into the corporation's plan from the parent company. However, with an equity carve-out the parent company raises capital while with a spin-off it does not. In order to properly evaluate the equity carve-out option, a parent company needs to consider how it will invest the proceeds. If it can invest these proceeds and earn a return in excess of what the division would have provided, then this option can be attractive. If the company does not have good return options for the capital, then the company has to consider that there may not be as great an immediate gain, while shareholders may lose because of the loss of value of the division. When the division is not contributing much to the parent's wealth, or where it is even a drain, then this may not be an issue.

Clearly, equity carve-outs are better for some companies than for others. Allen and McConnell did a study of the financial characteristics of companies that underwent equity carve-outs. They analyzed 188 carve-outs over the period 1978 to 1993.[11] Their first interesting finding was that carve-out subsidiaries had relatively poor operating performance and higher financial leverage than their industry

Exhibit 6.12    Comparison of Pre-Carve-Out Firms with Industry Peers

| Performance Measure | Pre-Carve-Out Firms | Industry Peers |
|---|---|---|
| EBDIT/Interest | 2.29 | 5.42 |
| Long-term Debt/Total Assets | 0.260 | 0.220 |
| Total Debt/Total Assets | 0.331 | 0.285 |
| EBDIT/Sales | 0.070 | 0.103 |

*Source:* Jeffrey Allen and John J. McConnell, "Equity Carve Outs and Managerial Discretion," *Journal of Finance* 53, no. 1 (February 1998): 163–186.

counterparts (see Exhibit 6.12). The companies had not done well and they were relatively debt-laden with a lower ability to service debt, thus increasing their risk profile. Allen and McConnell then traced how companies that did the carve-outs used the stock sale proceeds. When they were used to reduce the company's overall debt level, such companies showed an average excess stock return equal to +6.63%. However, when the companies made other investments with the monies, then the average return was −0.01%.

## EQUITY CARVE-OUTS ARE DIFFERENT FROM OTHER PUBLIC OFFERINGS

There are certain similarities between equity carve-outs and other types of public offerings. In both an equity carve-out and a public offering, the company issues stock and receives funds in exchange. In both situations, the company receives a capital infusion. However, in a public offering, new shares in the parent company are issued, and this dilutes the equity-holding percentage of incumbent shareholders. Unless the return on the funds that are received more than offset this dilution, this can be an adverse event for shareholders. This is why the market sometimes reacts negatively to announcements of equity offerings by companies. However, in an equity carve-out, the company is parting ways with a unit that may no longer fit in its plans, and the company is receiving capital in exchange, thus liquidating the investment that may not be profitable. There are no equity dilution issues with an equity carve-out.

Schipper and Smith did a study of the stock price effects of 76 carve-out announcements. They then compared these responses with prior studies that measured the stock price reactions to public equity offerings.[12] They found that in equity carve-outs, shareholder wealth increased 1.8%. However, in the literature they received on other public offerings, they found an average shareholder loss of 23% for a subset of parent firms that engaged in public offerings of common stock or debt. The study's authors hypothesized that the source of these gains for equity carve-outs come from the various benefits that we have already discussed that relate to all forms of sell-offs.

## SHAREHOLDER WEALTH EFFECTS OF EQUITY CARVE-OUTS

Other, more recent, research has supported the work of Schipper and Smith, who found positive shareholder wealth effects for equity carve-outs. Vijh analyzed a sample of 628 carve-outs over the period 1981 to 1985.[13] He found that the carved-out companies performed favorably relative to various different benchmarks he used to compare their performance. When comparing carve-outs with initial public offerings over a three-year period after issuance, the carve-outs earned a return of 14.3% compared to a 3.4% for initial public offerings (IPOs). This contrasts with the initial listing day returns of IPOs that were 15.4%, compared to carve-outs that equaled 6.2%.

Another study of carve-outs was conducted by J. P. Morgan. It did a study of the benefits of equity carve-outs and found that the stock prices of companies doing these deals rose between 4% to 5% around the announcement of the deals (see Exhibit 6.13).[14]

While the stock market reaction to the parent company's decision was somewhat similar with both carve-outs and spin-offs, the performance of the entity that was carved out was different from companies that were spun off. Carved-out entities tended to lag behind the market following the creation of the company (see Exhibit 6.14). The Morgan researchers then tried to go beyond the aggregate statistics to determine which types of carved-out companies performed better than others. One distinction between carved-out companies that were able to keep pace with the market and those that were not was the liquidity of the company. Carved-out companies that had what J. P. Morgan considered high, or at least adequate, liquidity generally kept pace

Exhibit 6.13    Parent Company Stock Prices after Carve-Outs

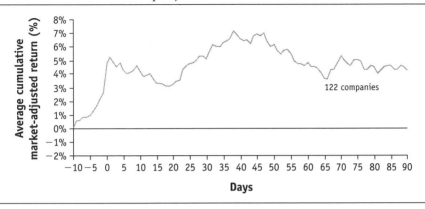

*Source:* J.P. Morgan Carve-Out Study, 2002.

Exhibit 6.14    Stock Performance: Carve-Out (a) versus Spin-Off (b)

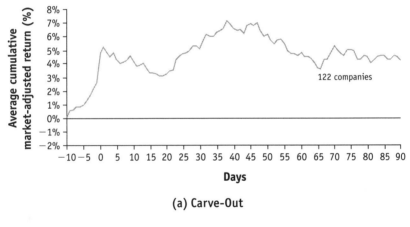

(a) Carve-Out

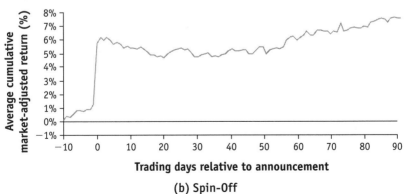

(b) Spin-Off

*Source:* J.P. Morgan Spin-Offs Study, J.P. Morgan Carve-Out Study, 2002.

with the market—sometimes a little above and sometimes a little below the market—with no major difference over a 374-month period following the public offering. However, they found that companies with less than adequate liquidity underperformed the market in a manner that steadily worsened over the same 374-month post-offering period.

From a strategy perspective, the outcome of the carve-out may or may not be a factor that a company selling off the division should consider. After the deal, the two companies are on their own. However, the lack of adequate capital is clearly a factor that affects the carved-out company. With this in mind, potential shareholders may want to explore the capitalization of the carved-out entity before purchasing their shares.

The J.P. Morgan study followed the carve-outs over a three-year period following the deal. One outcome was that they noticed that only one-quarter of the carve-outs remained in their original form over a three-year period after the public offering. One in four of the carve-outs were subsequently reacquired by the parent company—an outcome that clearly raises eyebrows. One in five were sold to a third company.

## UNDER WHICH SITUATIONS SHOULD A COMPANY DO A SPIN-OFF VERSUS AN EQUITY CARVE-OUT?

One of the main differences between an equity carve-out and a spin-off is the cash flow effects. Equity carve-outs result in a cash flow infusion from the proceeds of the stock that is sold in the new entity that is carved out. However, in a spin-off, cash flow does not change, but the spun-off entity is separated from the parent company and, in itself, may be a big benefit.

In trying to sift through the different effects surrounding both types of transactions, Michaely and Shaw conducted a study using transactions over the period 1981 to 1989. Specifically, they analyzed 91 master limited partnerships (MLPs) that were created during this time period. Michaely and Shaw found that the more highly leveraged companies chose to do spin-offs,[15] whereas bigger companies that had relatively less leverage tended to do carve-outs. These results imply that the decision of which option to pursue may be determined by the relative attractiveness of the companies involved. The stock of those companies that are less attractive to the market will have more limited options. Those entities that have better access to capital markets seemed to prefer carve-outs, whereas those that did not could not as easily pursue this alternative. Those companies that were less desirable to investors may not be able to enjoy the positive cash flows that come from carve-outs. These companies will more likely have to go the spin-off route.

The Michaely and Shaw study results are really more applicable to smaller and midsized deals and do not apply to the megadeals we have discussed, such as the AT&T and ITT transactions. These companies did their spin-offs for different reasons than many of the companies in the Michaely and Shaw study. Nonetheless, their findings are still relevant to the transactions that many companies may consider.

## SHAREHOLDER WEALTH EFFECTS OF TRACKING STOCK ISSUANCES

We have reviewed the shareholder wealth effects of various forms of sell-offs, including divestitures, spin-offs, and equity carve-outs, but have postponed the discussion of the shareholder wealth effects of tracking stock issues until after we discussed the effects of the various sell-offs. Now that we have covered them, we can complete our analysis by considering the shareholder wealth effects of tracking stock issues.

If a tracking stock is issued as a measure of releasing shareholder values that are being constrained by the corporate form with which they are held, then intuition would imply that the stock market reaction to such tracking stock announcements would be positive for the same reason it is positive when companies announce divestitures, spin-offs, and equity carve-outs. Elder and Westra examined the stock market reaction to 35 tracking stock announcements.[16] They found a mean abnormal return equal to 3% over a two-day window around the announcement date. Thirty of the 35 companies in the sample showed positive returns in response to the announcement of the stock issues. This result is intuitive if one believes that tracking stocks may achieve some of the benefits that other forms of restructuring provided. However, more recent research called into question some of the long-term benefits of tracking stocks.

A newer study by Billett and Vijh compared the performance of the stock of companies issuing tracking stock (TR shares) with what they referred to as general division shares (GD), which is "old stock." They analyzed 28 TR shares and 19 GD shares that were issued in the period 1984–1998. The greater number of TD shares is explained by the fact that some companies issued more than one class of tracking stock. They found that GD stocks underperformed the market before the issuance of the tracking stocks. This helps explain why the tracking stocks were issued in the first place. We assume that firms issue the tracking stocks to realize an increase in firm value, but Billett and Anand's research failed to find any evidence of that. Interestingly, however, they found that the performance of the tracking stocks was negative over the three-year period after they were first issued. Their research implies that tracking shares are usually not much of a solution to the problem of a poorly performing prior acquisition.

## CONCLUSION

We have approached this chapter with the assumption that a given merger or acquisition has been determined to be a mistake and is not contributing to shareholder value in a way that was anticipated when the deal was first done. The company must then decide if it should do a sell-off to reverse the error from the past, and if so, which route it should go: a divestiture, spin-off, equity carve-out, or tracking stock issue. Those are the alternatives to consider.

A review of all the different alternatives shows that the shareholder wealth effects are generally positive for all the board options that companies have at their disposal. These results have been the case over a variety of studies covering three decades of transactions data. Managers interpreting this data, however, have to keep in mind that the data are averages from results covering many companies. All companies do not conform to the average: Some perform above the average, whereas others yield lower results.

In a straight divestiture, the company sells off the business unit and receives compensation in exchange. It must consider the full range of effects of this transaction, including any tax effects it may have. This is also the case with other types of deals, such as spin-offs that can provide unique tax benefits for the company doing the spin-off. Spin-offs are often done to take advantage of the fact that they are often considered as a tax-free reorganization without the imposition of tax liabilities on the company doing the spin-off. Research shows that both the parent and the spun-off entity generally do well after the transaction. Other research shows that when spin-offs result in an increase in focus for the parent company, that company tends to perform better, as opposed to situations where there is no significant change in focus. Such situations fail to show benefits for the company doing the spin-off.

In both a spin-off and an equity carve-out, stock is issued in a newly formed company that is the business unit that is separated from the parent. However, with an equity carve-out the parent company receives cash in exchange for the shares that are offered to the public in a public offering. Thus, an equity carve-out results in a cash-flow infusion for the parent company, whereas with a spin-off the parent company does not receive cash but does part ways with the spun-off entity.

Under certain circumstances an equity carve-out may be the better alternative, whereas in others a spin-off or divestiture is the best option. There is some evidence, particularly for smaller and medium-sized companies, that companies that have lower debt and better financial performance to show the market may be better off pursuing an equity carve-out, which provides cash for the parent company. Many carve-outs fail to remain independent following the initial transaction. A significant percentage are reacquired by the parent company. Those that have better liquidity tend to perform better on the market than those that do not.

Tracking stocks are still another option that a company can pursue. Here a company creates a new stock that it sells to investors, which tracks the performance of a specific division. The dividends and capital gains of a tracking stock represent the gains and losses they may realize. Initially, as with the other more overt sell-off options, where the business unit is actually separated from the parent company, the market tended to respond positively to tracking stock announcements. However, these results include many of the earlier tracking stock issues. Many of these issues did not perform well and the market may be less receptive to such issue in the future. This may explain why later research failed to detect positive effects for issuing tracking stocks. This may also explain why there is a paucity of them on the market even when the market for new issues rebounded somewhat in the mid-2000s. Tracking stocks are a temporary solution to a company that may be reluctant to make the difficult decision and get rid of the company that no longer fits. Such companies can be assured that on average, companies tend to do well when they choose to do so.

In sum, we find that if a company has reached the conclusion that a prior acquisition or merger no longer fits with its strategy or has not performed up to expectations, it may be doing shareholders a significant benefit by separating the business unit from the parent company. In making this decision, management and the board need to be mindful of the abundant research evidence showing that shareholders may derive an immediate benefit when it announces such a sell-off. If the stock price of the potential seller has been depressed, possibly by the market not approving of the parent company continuing to operate the division, there probably is an easy case to be made that a sale where the company seeks to reverse the error is called for.

## ENDNOTES

1. Michael Porter, "From Competitive Advantage to Corporate Strategy," *Harvard Business Review* (May–June 1987): 43–59.
2. David Ravenscraft and Frederic Scherer, *Mergers, Selloffs and Economic Efficiency* (Washington, D.C.: Brookings Institution, 1987).
3. Steven N. Kaplan and Michael N. Weisbach, "The Success of Acquisitions: Evidence from Divestitures," *Journal of Finance* 47, no. 1 (March 1992): 107–138.
4. *AT&T Shareholders Newsletter,* Fourth Quarter, 1982.
5. James L. Bicksler and Andrew H. Chen, "The Economics of Corporate Restructuring: An Overview," *The Battle for Corporate Control* (Homewood, IL: Business One Irwin, 1991), pp. 386–387.

6. Charmen Loh, Jennifer Russell Bezjak, and Harrison Toms, "Voluntary Corporate Divestitures as Antitakeover Mechanisms," *The Financial Review* 30, no. 1 (February 1995): 41–60.
7. Prem C. Jain, "Sell–Off Announcements and Shareholder Wealth," *Journal of Finance* 40, no. 1 (March 1985): 209–224.
8. Patrick J. Cusatis, James A. Miles, and J. Randall Woolridge, "Restructuring Through Spinoffs: The Stock Market Evidence," *Journal of Financial Economics* 33, no. 3 (June 1993): 293–311.
9. "U.S. Spinoffs: Welcomed by Investors and Still a Significant Contributor to M&A Activity," J.P. Morgan Securities, Inc., Mergers & Acquisitions, February 12, 2002.
10. Lane Daley, Vikas Mehrotra, and Ranjini Sivakumar, "Corporate Focus and Value Creation: Evidence from Spinoffs," *Journal of Financial Economics* 45, no. 2 (August 1997): 257–281.
11. Jeffrey Allen and John J. McConnell, "Equity Carve Outs and Managerial Discretion," *Journal of Finance* 53, no. 1 (February 1998): 163–186.
12. Katherine Schipper and Abbie Smith, "A Comparison of Equity Carve-Outs and Seasonized Equity Offerings," *Journal of Financial Economics* 15 (January–February 1986): 153–186.
13. Anand Vijh, "Long Term Returns from Equity Carveouts," *Journal of Financial Economics* 51 (1999): 273–308.
14. "Equity Carve Outs: Market Reaction and Outcomes," J.P. Morgan Securities, Inc., Mergers and Acquisitions Research, April 22, 2002.
15. Roni Michaely and Wayne H. Shaw, "The Choice of Going Public: Spinoffs vs. Carve Outs," *Financial Management* 24, no. 3 (Autumn 1995): 5–21.
16. John Elder and Peter Westra, "The Reaction of Security Prices to Tracking Stock Announcements," *Journal of Economics and Finance* 24, no. 1 (Spring 2000): 36–55.

# Case Study

# DaimlerChrysler

In 1998, Daimler Benz and Chrysler merged in what was called a merger of equals; however, this deal was really more of a takeover of Chrysler by Daimler. The combination was one of the biggest industrial mergers in history, creating a $130 million automotive colossus. The new company was supposed to be run by co-heads—Jurgen Schrempp and Robert Eaton, the CEOs of Daimler and Chrysler, respectively. To call a transaction a merger of equals when it is really more of an acquisition is not that unusual, because even when the companies plan to pursue a merger of equals, the dominant organization and managers will rise to the top and soon take over running the company. In this deal, however, Chrysler was in a subordinate position with weaker managers right from the start. It appears that Daimler management sensed this and was not confident that they would be running the combined company quickly.

The merger created a combined company called DaimlerChrysler. It was a tax-free transaction that was entered into under a pooling of interest. Each Daimler shareholder received one share of the new company for each share of Daimler that they had. Chrysler shareholders received 0.547 shares of the new entity for each share of Chrysler they owned.

Daimler had pursued an aggressive M&A strategy as a main way to fuel its growth. Other companies in this industry, such as Ford,

General Motors, and Volkswagen, have also pursued such a growth through mergers strategy. In retrospect, this strategy has been highly questionable and, as far as DaimlerChrysler is concerned, was a failure. If one individual is responsible for this failure, it is the ego-driven Jurgen Shrempp—Daimler's chairman. His 1998 merger or acquisition of Chrysler was an unambiguous failure. One will never know how the company would have fared had it passed on this deal and sought to continue to grow the company internally.

The amazing aspect of the DaimlerChrysler disaster is that Daimler Benz was a company that already had a history of merger failures.

## DAIMLER'S PRIOR MERGER AND ACQUISITION FAILURES

The failure of the Chrysler acquisition/merger was not Daimler's first such failure—it was just its biggest. Daimler had entered into several prior deals that also performed poorly. However, this did not give Schrempp, or the board that was supposed to be monitoring him, pause before they agreed to enter into an even bigger flop. Another one of Daimler's failures was its investment in Mitsubishi Motors. The problems associated with this deal shared some similarities with the Chrysler failure. First, it was a part of Daimler's globalization strategy where Daimler, the number-one company in its segment of the auto market, acquired an interest in a nonleader in another geographical market. Mitsubishi was not the equal of some other Japanese auto makers. In general, Japan's car manufacturers have long been known for making high-quality cars. However, after Daimler's investment in Mitsubishi, the company began to register significant and troubling quality problems that further eroded its position in the industry. Daimler had hoped to benefit from Mitsubishi's expertise in making small, high-quality cars. It did not know it was buying a company that would soon become a source of quality-related problems. It was also a company that was "laboring under almost $14 billion in debt" while recording losses in the $600 million range shortly after its involvement with Daimler.[1]

---

1. "Conquest or Quicksand for Daimler," *BusinessWeek* (September 25, 2000).

Mitsubishi wasn't Daimler's only acquisition-related failure. The company already had registered major losses from its movement into the aerospace industry and its investment in Fokker. Fokker was a legendary name in the Netherlands, but it was in financial trouble when Daimler decided to purchase 51% of the company. The company suffered during the economic decline of the 1990–1991 period, and the Gulf War hurt overall demand for airplanes, and Fokker's 100-seat planes were no exception to this trend. By investing in Fokker, Daimler moved deeper into a cyclical industry and, once again, failed to pick a winner. Schrempp would eventually have to bite the bullet and not invest any more capital into this losing operation.

When we examine Daimler's M&A strategy, one pattern that becomes obvious is that its management has a great ability to find once-prominent companies that are just about to become big losers. Each of the three major investments the company made, Fokker, Mitsubishi, and Chrysler, became huge drains on Daimler because none was able to pay its own way. Daimler was good at finding soon-to-be losers. It was also good at manufacturing and marketing high-end luxury automobiles but was not content to continue to do what it did well and tried to move into other areas for which it had no ability to predict the outcome. Its management was not content to stick with what it did best, but in a hubris-driven frenzy to become a global industrial powerhouse, it dragged down shareholder values in the pursuit of a failed strategy.

We should not put all of the blame for Daimler's failed acquisitions strategy on Schrempp. He merely continued a bad program of poor acquisitions of his predecessor, Edzard Reuter. Schrempp wanted to better Reuter's dismal record and undo many of the failures Reuter engineered. Schrempp worked hard to extricate Daimler from many of Reuter's deals that were part of Reuter's diversification program of the 1980s. Unfortunately, while this attempt was commendable, Schrempp then went ahead with his own failures.

In trying to tackle the problems of the diversified Daimler that he inherited, Schrempp commissioned a study by Goldman Sachs that evaluated the 50 largest conglomerates. Goldman's study told him that holding companies such as Daimler were inefficient.[2] It is commendable that he commissioned such research before embarking on a major restructuring program, but the result of that study would hardly be considered novel to anyone who is familiar with the large volume of research in this area that was already available. It all told a similar story. It is unfortunate for Daimler shareholders that Schrempp's predecessor, Reuter, did not avail himself of such research because he could have saved his shareholders much money.

## ROLE OF THE DAIMLERCHRYSLER BOARD

DaimlerChrysler had, on paper, an all-star board of directors (see Exhibit A). It includes leading members of the CEO club from companies such as AT&T, Owens Illinois, Xerox, Deutsche Bank, and Bertelsmann. The fact that Robert Allen was former chairman and CEO of another major company that had made huge merger blunders is noteworthy. The board also included Joseph Califano, the former Secretary of Health and head of the National Center on Addiction and Substance Abuse at Columbia University. What expertise he had about overseeing an international automobile company has yet to be revealed. He certainly did not apply any such knowledge to hold back Daimler from doing poor deals. In retrospect, given that he has such little knowledge of this industry, he would not be in a good position to challenge an ego-driven, hard-charging CEO. This is one of the problems that Daimler shared with many other boards. It was filled with some leading names who did not bring any specialized abilities to their board assignment. It also included many other similarly situated leading corporate executives who can either choose to oversee the company for the betterment of shareholders, which is their assignment, or take a more passive stance and hope that other CEOs on their interlocking boards give them such wide rein.

---

2. Bill Vlasic and Bradley A. Stertz, *Taken for a Ride: How Daimler-Benz Drove Off with Chrysler* (New York: Morrow, 2000), p. 140.

## Exhibit A
### DaimlerChrysler Board of Directors

| Board Member | Affiliation |
| --- | --- |
| Hilmar Kopper | Board Chairman of Deutsche Bank AG |
| Robert E. Allen | Former Board Chairman and CEO of AT&T |
| Sir E. John P. Browne | Group Chief Executive of British Petroleum Company p.l.c. |
| Joseph A. Califano, Jr. | Board Chairman and President of National Center on Addiction and Substance Abuse at Columbia University |
| Dr. Martin Kohlhaussen | Group Board of Commerzbank AG Spokesman |
| Robert J. Lanigan | Owens-Illinois, Inc. Chairman Emeritus |
| Peter A. Magowan | Retired Board Chairman of Safeway Inc., President and Managing General Partner of San Francisco Giants |
| Manfred Schneider | Board of Management Chairman of Bayer AG |
| G. Richard Thoman | President and COO of Xerox Corporation |
| Bernhard Walter | Group Board of Dresdner Bank AG Spokesman |
| Lynton R. Wilson | BCE Inc. Chairman |
| Dr. Mark Wossner | Supervisory Board Chairman of Bertelsmann AG |

*Source:* www.media.chrysler.com/wwwpr98/2912.htm.

## MARKET PERFORMANCE OF DAIMLERCHRYSLER

The market performance of DaimlerChrysler has been dismal in the postmerger period. Almost from the time of the deal, the stock price of DaimlerChrysler declined. Looking back on the transaction approximately four years later, we find that the stock price fell approximately 50%! While the company continued to issue apologetic statements trying to explain its poor performance, the market was not fooled. While the market was down during this period, Exhibit B shows that the decline of the stock price of DaimlerChrysler was significantly in excess of that of the market, which also was weak during parts of this period.

## FAILED STRATEGY

Daimler's search for a U.S. acquisition/merger candidate was part of its globalization strategy. Each company was strong in geographical

**Exhibit B**

Stock Prices of DaimlerChrysler, October 1998 to September 2004

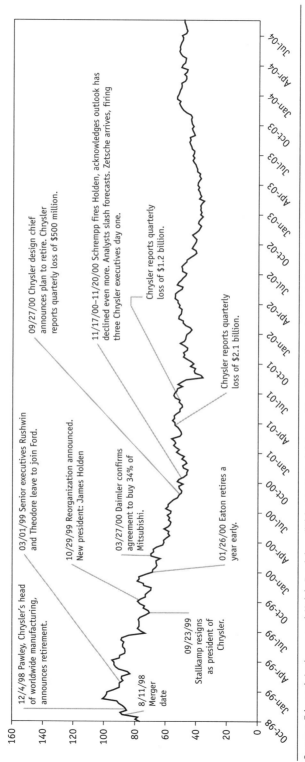

*Source:* Edmund Andrews and Keith Bradsher, "This 1998 Model Is Looking More Like a Lemon," *The New York Times* (November 26, 2000); and Finance. yahoo.com.

markets where the other was weak. Chrysler derived 93% of its sales from the North American market, while 63% of Mercedes Benz's revenues were derived from Europe.[3]

Before its acquisition of Chrysler, Daimler was already Europe's largest industrial company. Within its overall corporate umbrella was Daimler Benz Aerospace (DASA), Germany's largest aerospace company. Daimler sold its Mercedes cars throughout the world, including the United States. Buying the number-three U.S. auto maker would greatly enhance its presence in the U.S. market and possibly provide some ability to sell lower-priced cars manufactured by Chrysler throughout the world using Chrysler's but also Daimler's international sales network. Chrysler was not the first choice of Daimler as a U.S. merger partner. Daimler first set its sights on Ford, but both CEOs, Schrempp and Alex Trotman of Ford, agreed that Ford would not be a good fit because Ford and Trotman would not assume a subordinate position and allow Daimler to dominate the combination.[4] Robert Eaton, Chrysler's head, was more of a match for the domineering Schrempp. Thus, part of the basis for a proper strategic fit was in finding a personality and management group that Daimler could control as opposed to finding the best combination for the two companies that would yield the greatest profit and return for shareholders.

The ironic aspect of the Daimler–Chrysler merger is that both companies were profitable before the merger. They showed a combined profit of $4.6 billion in 1997. Chrysler was mainly a U.S. firm, although during the 1990s it became more internationalized,[5] while Daimler Benz was more of an international automobile company. Chrysler had established a reputation for successfully marketing low-cost trucks, minivans, and sport utility vehicles. Ironically, it had one of the highest profit-per-vehicle values in the auto industry. Daimler Benz was internally renowned as the leading automobile manufacturer of luxury cars, with a brand in that market that was second to none.

3. *BusinessWeek* (May 18, 1998).
4. Vlasic and Stretz, *Taken for a Ride.*
5. "Chrysler Corporation: Negotiations Between Daimler and Chrysler," Darden Business Publishing Case Study, UVA-F-1240, University of Virginia.

Its autos were known for their superb engineering. In the year before the merger, 1997, Daimler sold 715,000 Mercedes-Benz cars, which was a new sales record. Daimler wanted to expand further into the U.S. market but faced a relatively limited ability to do so within the confines of the luxury segment. It saw Chrysler as the key to that entrance. The only problem was that it was in a different segment of the market—one in which Daimler had not demonstrated success.

Chrysler's North America operations were divided into two divisions: Dodge and Chrysler/Plymouth/Jeep. One of its leading products was the minivan that Chrysler claimed it had invented. The company had sold 7 million of these minivans between 1984 and the year of the merger.[6] In addition, Jeep was one of the leading sport utility vehicle brands in the world.

Several questions should have stood out boldly before the merger:

- *Were there any significant synergies between these two companies?*
- *What would happen to the combined entity if the economy turned down?*
- *Would the auto styles that the companies marketed maintain their popularity in the postmerger period?*

It seemed that there were few meaningful synergies to be enjoyed from the union of Chrysler and Daimler. Daimler, which was known for high-quality production, was supposed to share its expertise in this area with its U.S. partner, thereby enabling it to enjoy advantages over its two major U.S. rivals. Instead of enhancing Chrysler's quality production, Daimler's own product quality declined during the postmerger period. Daimler also would be able to provide capital to Chrysler, which it could use to aggressively take market share from Ford and GM. Instead, Chrysler reaped big losses and required Daimler capital to stay afloat. Rather than use Daimler resources to aggressively pursue competitive advantages, DaimlerChrysler had to use its resources to try to fix the problems at its troubled units. Instead of benefiting the bidder, the deal's problems presented opportunities for competitors to take market share from the distracted

---

6. Chrysler press release, December 11, 1998.

acquirer, who is trying to fix the results of the poor deal.[7] This is not an unusual outcome in a failed merger.

## DISTRACTION AND DETRACTION FOR DAIMLER

When Chrysler began to record staggering losses in 2001, Daimler shifted its gaze to its troubled U.S. unit. In 2000 Daimler fired Chrysler president James Holden, an American who had been in that position for only 14 months, and put in place German management led by Dieter Zetsche. Unfortunately, he failed to come up with any quick fixes. Chrysler's problems ran deep and could not be alleviated by short-term managerial changes. However, while Daimler focused on Chrysler's problems, cutting costs, and emphasizing specific vehicles that showed promise, it seemed to lose its own force. A series of quality problems for Mercedes vehicles materialized during the post-merger period, which is a sore spot for such a high-end, high-quality product like a Mercedes. The problems were apparent in the J. D. Power ratings for the E- and M-class sedans. Mercedes began to receive complaints for faulty transmissions. In addition, Mercedes encountered strong competition from its long-term, high-end rival—BMW. Mercedes tried to use its C-Class smaller sedans to compete with BMW's successful 3-series models. However, BMW, which was not held back by such a major project as the failure of the Chrysler merger, seemed to take advantage of its distracted rival to mount a stronger challenge. The Chrysler merger failure is a classic case of a company doing a major bad deal, and then having to devote great monetary and managerial resources to try to make it work while its normal competitors used this distraction as an opportunity to gain ground. Here we can see that not having to deal with postmerger integration problems, as well as problems stemming from a failed strategy, can be a great advantage to undistracted competitors.

The distraction of dealing with the postmerger problems was compounded by cultural differences between the two companies. Chrysler marketed autos in a competitive U.S. market. The premerger

---

7. Thomas Grubb and Robert B. Lamb, *Capitalize on Merger Chaos* (New York: The Free Press, 2000).

Chrysler aggressively reacted to the moves of its rivals when they put out a new product or introduced a new incentive program. The Daimler-dominated business moved more slowly and was not as quick to react. "Under the Germans, management meets only every two weeks, essentially preventing Chrysler from acting quickly in between."[8] It seems the Daimler way of marketing did not work well for lower-priced, more competitive markets, although it worked fine in the luxury market, where they were more insulated from aggressive competition. Even within this segment of the market, however, they had to work hard to maintain themselves in the sales of the lower-priced segment of the luxury market.

## HUBRIS AND DAIMLER'S CEO

Daimler's CEO, Jurgen Schrempp, is an ego-filled, hard-charging, heavy-smoking manager who seems to dominate his subordinates. When Chrysler's losses began to mount while Daimler registered its own problems, calls for Schrempp's resignation rose, but he refused to step down.[9] Daimler's largest shareholder was Deutsche Bank, which held 12% of the company—a shareholding that greatly suffered during the postmerger period. Deutsche Bank was in a position to impose pressure on Daimler to have a change at the wheel, but it failed to do so.[10] Here we have a case of a hubris-driven CEO of an auto company not living up to his fiduciary responsibilities, but also a large shareholder, Deutsche Bank, which failed to take the necessary and difficult steps it needed to realize a better return for its shareholders. Schrempp wanted to build a global auto goliath and was not satisfied to be merely the premier luxury auto company in the world. In the pursuit of this ego-driven dream, he pulled down shareholder values and could not ever admit that his strategy was a failure.

---

8. CarsDirect.com, CBS Market Watch, January 29, 2001.

9. Edward Andrews, "No Apologies From Stuttgart," *The New York Times* (December 2, 2000): C1.

10. Gail Edmondson and Hathleen Kerwin, "Stalled: Is the DaimlerChrysler Deal a Mistake? Many Say Yes—and Call for Shrempp's Head," *BusinessWeek* (September 29, 2003): 56.

## LESSONS OF THE DAIMLERCHRYSLER FAILURE

There are several lessons we can take away from the DaimlerChrysler debacle. Their failures can be tied to a hubris-driven CEO and the company's overall poor track record in M&As:

- *Beware of the hubris-driven CEO.* CEOs with bountiful hubris and strong personalities need to be held in check by a strong board. Board members must protect shareholders from the strategies that such leaders would put forward. The stronger the CEO, the stronger the board needs to be. This does not mean strong CEOs are not good; they just need to be monitored by comparably strong boards.

- *Companies need to learn from prior merger failures.* When a company has had a track record of prior merger failures, it needs to be extra cautious of further deals. At a minimum it needs to learn from its prior mistakes. Companies, in general, should learn from the mistakes of other companies. However, when the company already had a track record of failed deals as Daimler had, then this should give management and the board pause before it considers any new deals. Boards must make sure that management presents a strategy that is extra convincing when serving on the board of a company that already has a history of prior failed deals.

- *Admit a failure and move on.* As of 2004, years after the failed marriage between Chrysler and Daimler, both companies continue to coexist. DaimlerChrysler is still being run by Jurgen Schrempp, and he is reluctant to admit that the merger was a failure. As a result, the company cannot move on and go in a different direction. Daimler would be better off admitting that Chrysler was a failure and going back to what it did best.

# 7

## Joint Ventures and Strategic Alliances: Alternatives to Mergers and Acquisitions

In this book we have looked at some of the various reasons why some M&As have failed and why others have succeeded. Most of the companies that initiated what turned out to be failures probably wished they had never completed the transactions. However, the deals were obviously supposed to further certain business purposes (hopefully these are not the advancement of the CEO's own financial gain). The question that arises is whether a less drastic alternative to an outright merger or acquisition could have accomplished the same goals. Sometimes this alternative is a joint venture or strategic alliance. In this chapter we will explore these options and see why under some circumstances they may accomplish what a company wants to achieve at a fraction of the costs of a merger or acquisition. In other circumstances, they will not accomplish what a merger or acquisition would and are not really viable options.

As with our discussions of other types of transactions, we will review the shareholder wealth effects of both joint ventures and strategic alliances. This information is useful because it allows us to compare what we know about the impact of M&As announcements. Does the market tend to react more positively when companies announce a joint venture or strategic alliances than when they announce a merger or acquisition? If this is the case, is it uniformly true or do these effects vary by type of business?

## CONTRACTUAL AGREEMENTS

Before we begin the discussion of joint ventures and strategic alliances, we should recognize that another less drastic alternative than either of these arrangements is a simple contractual agreement between the parties. If the goals of the relationship are specific and can be readily set forth in a contract between the parties, then this may be the least costly and most efficient solution. For example, companies make agreements with suppliers to provide them with certain products all the time. They may not need to create a strategic alliance or a joint venture to get a supplier to commit to providing them with specific products and services. However, when the products in question are not readily available and require a specific development commitment on the part of the supplier, a contract may or may not suffice. If the process is even more complicated and involves the parties exchanging valuable and proprietary information as well as a buyer providing funding for the supplier to engage in a long-term and uncertain development process, such as what often occurs between biotechnology and pharmaceutical firms, then a contract may not be enough and either a strategic alliance or a joint venture may be needed if not an outright merger or acquisition. We would expect to have a contractual agreement with a strategic alliance or joint venture, but most contracts between businesses are not strategic alliances or joint ventures. Thus strategic alliances and joint ventures involve agreements that go beyond the usual contractual relationships with businesses. They are more complicated and require more detailed roles and commitments between the parties.

Exhibit 7.1   Comparative Level of Commitment Flow Chart

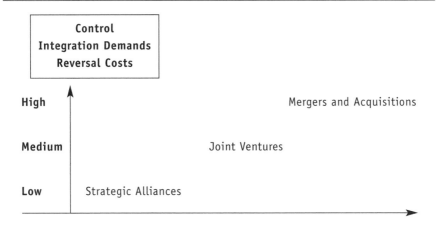

## COMPARING STRATEGIC ALLIANCES AND JOINT VENTURES WITH MERGERS AND ACQUISITIONS

Strategic alliances feature less involvement between the alliance part-ners than joint ventures, which, in turn, are also a lesser commitment than a merger or acquisition. In terms of investment of capital, con-trol, and the cost of reversal, Exhibit 7.1 shows that strategic alliance is the lowest on this scale, followed by joint venture and then M&A.

## JOINT VENTURES

In a joint venture, two or more companies combine certain assets and work toward jointly achieving a business objective. Usually the time period of this combination is defined and limited in duration. This is another difference between joint ventures and M&As, because the latter involve an indefinite period unless it is a specialized deal where a company is acquired with the planned goal of selling it within a limited time period. An example would be a leveraged buyout (LBO), where the deal makers acquire a private company with the goal to improve it and sell it to another private buyer or take it public again in what is called a reverse LBO.

The companies involved in the joint venture maintain their own separate business operations and continue to exist apart as they did before the joint venture. This venture is then formally created as a business entity such as a separate corporation or partnership. A formal agreement among the venture participants sets forth the extent to which they each will exercise control over the venture's activities and will participate in the entity's profits or losses. Presumably this will be a road map that each can follow to assess the venture's progress toward achieving its goals.

Joint ventures can be used for a wide variety of business purposes. Perhaps two companies have specialized resources that when combined can be used to create or market a specific product. For example, one could be a traditional pharmaceutical manufacturer while the other might be a biotechnology firm. The pharmaceutical company may want to utilize the R&D resources of the biotech business to develop a particular drug for the treatment of some ailment. If this is the goal, buying the biotech business, which may be involved in many other areas in which the drug manufacturers are not interested, may be an expensive way of gaining the research capability it needs to develop the drug. The drug manufacturers may have in place a widespread marketing network that would be able to rapidly capture market share when the product is eventually developed. In this case, both parties bring resources to the table and, for this one particular venture, both can gain from the other's resources. The solution may be a joint venture in which the two businesses come together for this one activity and may not necessarily do anything else together in the future. Of course, if this venture worked out well, they may pursue other joint efforts.

Joint ventures may be a way of two potential merger partners assessing how well they work together. Cultural differences between two companies may become apparent when they are involved in a joint venture or strategic alliance. If these differences are problematic, the business dealing can usually be curtailed at comparatively lower costs in a joint venture or strategic alliance compared to a merger or acquisition that may erode shareholder value.

## MOTIVES FOR JOINT VENTURES

If we consider that a merger or acquisition is a combining of the resources of two different companies, then a joint venture is a different process that, to some extent, may achieve the same goals. The motives for joint ventures are varied, but the following list provides a few examples that often occur:

- *Enhance research and development capabilities.* A company, such as a pharmaceutical company, may enter into a joint venture with another business that has some specific capability that it needs to further its R&D process.

- *Gain access to key supplies.* Two or more companies may form a joint venture so they can have a better source of supplies for their production process. Such supplies could range from joint exploration for oil by petroleum companies to joint training programs for workers.

- *Enhance distribution systems.* Two companies may enter into a joint venture agreement that will enable one or both of them to have an enhanced distribution network for their products.

- *Gain access to foreign market.* International joint ventures may enable companies that operate in different countries to work together to achieve gains in one or more countries. A U.S. company, for example, might initiate a joint venture with a Russian firm in the hopes that it will use that Russian firm's expertise to help market products in Russia.

An example of such a Russian investment was General Motor's joint venture with the troubled Russian automaker AvtoVAZ in 2000. GM contributed capital while AvtoVAZ provided its production facilities. The two companies wanted to establish a plant to produce an off road Chevrolet Niva and an Opel Astra. AvtoVAZ was established in the Russian market and would help GM gain access to this developing economy. Unfortunately, one needs to make sure you have the right joint venture partner. AvtoVAZ had a history of financial and quality control problems. GM's choice of a Russian joint venture partner was poor but this was consistent with many of the company's international joint venture decisions.

## REGULATION AND JOINT VENTURES

Simply because two companies form a joint venture instead of doing a formal merger or acquisition does not exempt them from some of the same regulatory scrutiny they might face if they merged or one was acquired by the other. This is definitely the case for antitrust laws. The anticompetitive provisions of the Sherman Act and the Clayton Act can also be applied to joint ventures, where the effect of the venture on the market is to reduce competition. The cases of the Justice Department or the Federal Trade Commission challenging joint ventures are less common than their challenges of M&As. However, in theory the same laws look at the business combination and its impact on the degree of competition in the market. Keep in mind that when a company enters into a joint venture or a strategic alliance, it cannot be doing so to circumvent antitrust laws, and those laws still apply. Another point to also remember is that if the antitrust authorities find a venture to be anticompetitive, it can usually be terminated at a lower cost than a merger or acquisition of a business that has been fully integrated into the parent company.

## SHAREHOLDER WEALTH EFFECTS OF JOINT VENTURES

In Chapter 3, as well as elsewhere, shareholder wealth effects of corporate combinations were examined. It was found that the market responses to acquisition announcements are often not positive, and target shareholders often do not do well. When target shareholders receive their premium, assuming it is not in stock and they do not hold those shares for an extended period, they have measurable gains. If there are some similarities between M&As, then the logical question that arises is "How do shareholders do in joint ventures?"

McConnell and Nantell did a study of 136 joint ventures involving 210 U.S. companies over the period 1972 to 1979.[1] The joint ventures were in a variety of industries, with the most common being real estate development (18/136) and television and motion pictures (14/136). The study was an announcement period, short-term-oriented study that compares with many of the event studies that have been conducted for M&A announcements. It is important to bear in mind, however, that when we say short-term-oriented, the market is adjusting to the announcement in the short term, such as during an event window of three days before and after a joint venture announcement, but this adjustment reflects the market anticipation of the long-term effects of the benefits and costs of the venture. The reaction occurs in a short time period, but it is attempting to reflect or forecast long-term effects. This is different from a long-term study, which looks at the financial impact of an event after the fact, when we have had the benefit of the passage of a number of years.

The McConnell and Nantell study showed that shareholders in companies entering into joint ventures enjoyed announcement period returns of 0.73%. They found similar results when some of the industries such as real estate were removed from the sample. They also found that the gains were fairly evenly distributed across venture participants. When the authors tried to convert that seemingly small percentage return to a dollar amount, they found it corresponded to an average value of $4.8 million. Their results were also similar to the combined returns for companies involved in acquisitions (remember these are referring to combined returns, which may include a negligible or even negative returns for an acquirer and a higher return for a target, which also may be smaller than the bidder.)

The McConnell and Nantell study supports the idea that, when considering the shareholder wealth effects, joint ventures are a viable alternative to a merger or an acquisition. Whether they may accomplish what a company wants to achieve with an M&A is going to be determined on a case-by-case basis. However, while it also varies depending on the circumstances, one cannot argue that joint ventures lack some of the aggregate positive shareholder wealth effects that M&As provide. One thing that a joint venture will not provide, and for acquirers this is a good thing, is a large buyout premium for target shareholders. Without that premium, the opportunities for management to make bad decisions by overpaying may be more limited. They may still be able to negotiate poor terms for their own companies, but the opportunities for large financial rewards *may* be more limited.

The McConnell and Nantell findings of positive shareholder wealth effects for joint ventures were supported by the research of Woolridge and Snow, who analyzed a sample of 767 announcements of strategic investment decisions involving 248 companies operating in 102 industries.[2] These strategic investment decisions included joint ventures as well as R&D projects and major capital investments. Their methodology featured an examination of the stock market reaction to the announcement of these decisions. In general they found positive stock market responses to these various announcements. When the sample was divided into subsamples for the different types of announcements, they were able to determine that the shareholder wealth effects were positive for joint venture announcements. These results are consistent with the McConnell and Nantell findings.

## SHAREHOLDER WEALTH EFFECTS
## BY TYPE OF VENTURE

While the McConnell and Nantell study looked at the shareholder wealth effects by type of industry, it did not differentiate these effects by type of venture. Johnson and Houston analyzed a sample of 191 joint ventures over the period 1991 to 1995.[3] They divided their sample into vertical joint ventures (55%) and horizontal joint ventures (45%). They defined *vertical joint ventures* as transactions between buyers and suppliers. *Horizontal joint ventures* are transactions between companies that are in the same general line of business and that may use the products from the venture to sell to their own customers or to create an output that can be sold to the same group. The results showed average positive gains from joint ventures equal to 1.67%. For horizontal joint ventures, it appears that the gains are shared by the venture participants. The average returns for vertical joint ventures were somewhat higher—2.67%. However, what is particularly interesting when they looked at the vertical sample was that the gains did not accrue to both parties. Suppliers gained an average of 5%, with 70% of the returns being positive, while buyers received an average return of only 0.32%, which was not statistically significant and of which only 53% of the returns were even positive. For vertical joint ventures, the biggest winners were suppliers, who were able to capture the bulk of the gains, while the market did not see major benefits for buyers.

Johnson and Houston recognized that when two companies entered into a joint venture, especially a vertical venture that showed the greater gains, the venture participants could have entered into a contract as opposed to a joint venture. Why did they choose the venture alternative? Johnson and Houston analyzed a sample of announcements of contracts and also found positive shareholder wealth effects with such announcements. However, they found that companies enter into joint ventures, as opposed to contracts, when transaction costs are high. They describe some of these transaction costs as "hold-up hazards." This could occur, for example, if a supplier had to make buyer-specific investments, such as investments in certain machinery and capital goods needed to produce the buyer-specific products. Although a contract may provide some temporary protection to the supplier over the contract period, once this period is over, the supplier may be vulnerable unless this capital equipment could be redeployed to another buyer. For these types of transactions, Johnson and Houston saw benefits for joint ventures that mere contracts could not provide.

## RESTRUCTURING AND JOINT VENTURES

Sometimes a company may be able to pursue restructuring or a sell-off through the use of a joint venture. Consider a company that wants to divest itself of a division but is having difficulty finding a suitable buyer for 100% of the company that would provide a sufficient value to make the company sell off the division. One alternative would be to sell off part of the company and, in effect, run the division as a jointly owned entity. If the goal of the company doing the partial sale is really to be able to do a 100% sale, it may negotiate terms with the partial buyer, whereby that buyer would be able to purchase the remaining shares in the division at some point in the future based on the occurrence of certain events. Such events might be the division achieving certain performance goals. If this occurs, the seller would, in stages, have found its buyer. That buyer is able to utilize the capabilities of the business unit without, at least initially, having to do a 100% acquisition. If it buys control of the target, it may be able to enter into whatever agreement it needs while saving on the costs of a 100% acquisition. If it finds that the relationship is rewarding, it may then want to be a 100% shareholder and not have to share in the ownership of the company. The seller may also be able to add terms to the original agreement that states that if certain targets are met, the buyer is bound to complete the purchase and buy the remaining shares as of some date.

## POTENTIAL PROBLEMS WITH JOINT VENTURES

Many potential problems can arise with joint ventures. They are certainly not a cure for all of the ills of M&As. This is obvious from the fact that we continue to do so many M&As, and if joint ventures were the solution, we would see more of them instead of M&As. The potential problems with joint ventures are as varied as the types of ventures. They may fail because the venture partners do not work well together. There can be disagreements between the participants, which may get in the way of accomplishing the venture's goals. The venture may require participants to share intellectual property or other proprietary knowledge, and they may be reluctant to do so as one venture partner may be using such information in a way that was not intended by the other venture participant. The participants may not see themselves as fully committed as they might if the activities of the venture were part of the overall business. This lack of full commitment may prevent the venture from achieving its goals. Other problems may be that the venture simply does not accomplish what it was set out to accomplish. We will see that many of these same problems can occur with strategic alliances as well.

## STRATEGIC ALLIANCES

Strategic alliances are less formal associations between companies compared to joint ventures. In a joint venture, a separate entity is often created, whereas in a strategic alliance the agreement and the relationship is less formal. Such alliances are common in various different industries, including the pharmaceutical, airline, and computer industries. Airlines that serve different geographic markets often form alliances or airline partner agreements. Under such agreements, they remain separate airlines but share routes. This enables them to be able to keep a customer who wants to fly beyond the range of a given airline route. Each airline alliance partner can market the entire route, and the same flights may be marketed under different numbers for each partner. With such alliances, the various partners may be able to provide customers with a global network. In addition, as various companies in an industry form such alliances, this puts pressures on competitors to follow suit so they are not at a disadvantage because of a smaller network.

Enhancing research and development is a major reason why companies form strategic alliances. Robinson reports a National Science Foundation study that indicated that one company in ten that was involved in R&D financed such work outside of the company.[4] Robinson and Stuart also report a survey from the Pharmaceutical Research and Manufacturers of America, which suggested that approximately "25% of the $26 billion in U.S.-based, industrially financed, pharmaceutical R&D that occurred in 2000 took place in over 700 collaborative agreements with outside organizations."[5] As an example of such an agreement is the alliance between Novartis, a Swiss-based pharmaceutical company, and Vertex, a biotechnology research company, whereby Novartis made various payments, including an initial payment of $600 million and additional payments of $200,000 staggered over six years, in exchange for the rights to market various pharmaceutical products. With such agreements, pharmaceutical companies can gain access to technology provided by biotech firms that may not be available to the drug companies. As technological change accelerates in the pharmaceutical industry, the methods of developing drugs also change. In recent years, the way in which pharmaceutical companies created new drugs has changed, and many of these companies lacked some of the capabilities and expertise to conduct more modern research. Drug manufacturers need access to research capabilities that biotech companies have and that they may not be able to develop quickly in the time frame they need to stay competitive with other drug companies, which may have such capabilities in-house or through other alliances with biotech companies.

## GOVERNANCE OF STRATEGIC ALLIANCES

When a company acquires another company, the governance process is hierarchical in the sense that the acquirer pays for and receives the right to control the target. It governs the target—hopefully in a manner that facilities growth of the wealth of the acquirer's shareholders. The governance of strategic alliances is bilateral and is determined by the agreement the alliance partners enters into as well as by factors such as the nonlegal commitment of the alliance partners to make the alliance succeed. In entering into such an agreement, the alliance participants seek to lower some of the various costs that might exist if they had a looser arrangement. This does not mean that they will not have opportunities for strategic behavior. Depending on the type of alliance entered into, a significant degree of trust may be needed between the partners. If the success of the alliance requires that they share confidential information, then the parties must be confident that this valuable intellectual property will not be used inappropriately. If this proves to be a concern, it may inhibit the success of the alliance because the parties may be reluctant to share what needs to be shared in order to have complete success.

There has been much discussion in the economic and financial literature on the assignment of control rights in joint ventures.[6] This assignment is important in alliances involving the development of new technologies. Aghion and Triole point out that two factors should govern the allocation of control rights:

- The degree to which there may be an underinvestment of either party that could have an adverse effect on the success of the alliance

- The relative bargaining parties of the two partners

We can add another factor as follows:

- The extent to which one party may engage in opportunistic behavior, which can have an adverse effect on the outcomes

Lerner and Merges describe a case study involving pharmaceutical company Eli Lilly and the Repligen Corporation, a biotechnology company. They worked together on a project involving monoclonal antibody treatments of inflammation:

> In the negotiations there were three areas where control rights were in dispute. The first was the management of clinical trials: which drugs would be pursued and when. A second was the control over the marketing strategy, an area in which Lilly had extensive experience and Repligen only a slight acquaintance. Finally, both parties wished to undertake the process development and ultimate manufacturing of the drug. Repligen, in fact, had recently acquired a cell culture facility and the key personnel that went with it.

The final agreement appeared to assign control rights to the parties with the greatest discretion to behave opportunistically. Repligen was allowed a great deal of flexibility in developing the lead product candidate (where it had the greatest experience), but tangential product development activities would only be supported when precise milestones were reached. Lilly was assigned control over all aspects of marketing; while Repligen was assigned all manufacturing control rights, unless it encountered severe difficulties with regulators.[7]

Lerner and Merges did an empirical study of 200 contracts/alliances between biotechnology companies and sponsoring firms. They found results that were consistent with the previous case study they described in their paper. They found that, in general, control rights were assigned to the smaller alliance partner as an increasing function of their financial health. It seems that in the drug development industry, it may be optimal for control rights to be assigned to the smaller company, but the limiting factor may be its own financial condition. Smaller companies that are in better financial condition are in a stronger bargaining position and also are less risky alliance partners. Larger pharmaceutical companies may be less able to force their terms on a financially sound smaller biotech company. They also may have more confidence in a well financed sound but smaller biotech company and may worry less about it being able to do what it agreed to do.

## SHAREHOLDER WEALTH EFFECTS
## OF STRATEGIC ALLIANCES

Just as we have with joint ventures, we will look at the shareholder wealth effects of strategic alliances. Chan, Kensinger, Keown, and Martin looked at the shareholder wealth effects of 345 strategic alliances over the period 1983 to 1992.[8] Almost one-half of their sample involved alliances for marketing and distribution purposes. For the overall group, they found positive abnormal returns equal to 0.64%. This is somewhat comparable to what was seen with the research of McConnell and Nantell for joint ventures. The Chan, Kensinger, Keown, and Martin study also found no evidence of significant transfers of wealth between alliance partners. This implies that there was no evidence that one partner was gaining at the expense of another. This result supports strategic alliances as an alternative to M&As—*in the limited circumstances where it is appropriate.*

## SHAREHOLDER WEALTH EFFECTS BY TYPE OF ALLIANCE

Chan, Kensinger, Keown, and Martin looked at how the shareholder wealth effects varied by type of alliance. They separated their sample into horizontal and non-horizontal alliances. They defined horizontal alliances as those involving partners with the same three-digit SIC code. They found that horizontal alliances that involved the transfer of technology provided the highest cumulative abnormal return—3.54%. This may help explain why strategic alliances occur so often between technologically oriented companies. Nonhorizontal alliances that were done to enter a new market provided a positive but lower return—1.45%. Other nonhorizontal alliances failed to show significant returns. Another study conducted by Das, Sen, and Sengupta also looked at the types of alliances that might be successful, as reflected by their initial announcement shareholder wealth effects.[9] They were able to show how the announcement effects varied by type of alliance as well as by firm profitability and relative size of the alliance participants. They discovered that technological alliances were associated with greater announcement returns than marketing alliances. These are two of the more common types of alliances. In his research of 4,192 alliances, Hagedoorn has previously shown that, as expected, technological alliances were more common in high-growth sectors, whereas marketing alliances were more common in mature industries.[10] Das, Sen, and Sengupta also showed that the abnormal returns were negatively correlated with both the size of the alliance partners and their profitability. We see that the market is concluding that larger and more profitable partners will capture fewer of the gains from the alliance. Stated alternatively, the market sees greater benefits for smaller and less profitable businesses to partner with larger and more profitable companies. The smaller and less profitable companies seem to have more to gain from strategic alliances. This does not imply that the partnerships are not also good for larger companies. Given that they are bigger and their profits are greater, it would be reasonable to expect that when such companies partner with smaller firms, they have less to gain because the impact of that alliance will have a smaller impact on the overall business of the larger company. That larger company may enter into several such alliances, and the aggregate effect of all of these alliances may make the difference less.

## WHAT DETERMINES THE SUCCESS OF STRATEGIC ALLIANCES?

What factors determine whether a strategic alliances is going to be a success or not? Which types of alliances are more likely to be successful and which will be more difficult to pull off? A study that focused on this issue was conducted by Kale, Dyer, and Singh.[11] They analyzed a sample of 78 companies who reported on 1,572 alliances that had been established for at least two years. As of the study date, approximately 12% of the alliances were already terminated. The researchers surveyed managers within the firm, who responded to questions designed to elicit responses on the degree of success of the alliances. They found that firms that had more experience with alliances were more likely to be successful in future alliances. This means that there is a learning curve, and companies do better at alliances the more they do them. This result is intuitive. They also found that companies that had a dedicated alliance function, such as a department and department head dedicated to overseeing alliances that the company entered into, were more likely to be successful with their alliances. An example would be companies that have a vice president or director of strategic alliances position. They found that Hewlett-Packard and Eli Lilly, for example, had such positions. It would also be reasonable to assume that if a given company established such a position, it would be more likely to engage in alliances than other companies that did not have one. The reported success rate of companies with a dedicated alliance function was 68%, compared to a 50% rate for those without these positions. Interestingly, the market reacted more positively for alliance announcements for those companies that had such dedicated alliance functions (1.35%

compared to 0.18%). The other interesting product of this research is that it shows a consistency between the initial market response and long-term results—in this case as applied to alliances. This is one of many pieces of evidence that allows us to take the results of studies of the short-term announcement effects for various events, such as mergers, acquisitions, joint ventures, and alliances, seriously because they seem to correlate well with long-term research results.

## POTENTIAL FOR CONFLICTS WITH JOINT VENTURES AND STRATEGIC ALLIANCES

The potential to have conflicts between the partners in a joint venture or a strategic alliance is always present and very different than what would occur if the deal was an M&A. With an outright acquisition a bidder takes clear control of the target and there is less opportunity for conflict. One does not eliminate conflict with M&As as we can always have internal discord. However, with a joint venture or strategic alliance, the partners remain independent and each has their separate corporate strategy. Over time markets, the economy change while companies evolve—sometimes in very different directions. Since both companies remain independent, each has only a limited ability to control the other. This became clear with the long running battle between the New Jersey medical products giant, Johnson and Johnson, and California biotech Amgen. The two companies reached an agreement in 1985 for the marketing of erythropoietin (EPO), which is a drug that helps the body produce red blood cells. Amgen, far smaller than Johnson and Johnson, developed and patented EPO but needed Johnson and Johnson to fully tap the large market for the drug. The agreement between the two companies gave Johnson and Johnson the larger market, approximately $3.7 billion, which it sold for chemotherapy treatment. Amgen was then left the smaller market for anemia patients on dialysis. In addition, the companies never agreed on how the gains from follow-on products would be divided. This gave rise to years of litigation. The outcome was a 1998 arbitration ruling which allowed Amgen to market a newer and longer lasting version of EPO, called Aranesp, in competition with the markets which were previously the domain of Johnson and Johnson. The problems of the joint venture between Amgen and Johnson and Johnson arose early on in the relationship. The parties were in conflict and became competitors. Neither seemed to trust the other and the relationship soured quickly.

Johnson and Johnson's experience with Amgen contrasts sharply with its very successful 1989 joint venture with New Jersey pharmaceutical giant Merck. Merck developed and manufactured Pepcid AC, an over-the-counter heartburn treatment, while Johnson and Johnson assumed the responsibility for marketing and sales. The combination worked well and Pepcid AC quickly became the market leader. In this successful venture, both parties understood and agreed to their very defined roles. There was also a clear plan for how the gains would be shared. The drug did not have separate applications which would leave one partner much richer than the other—thus creating distrust and envy. When partners consider their input into a venture to be equal but one realizes much greater gains than the other, a conflict is likely to arise. When the gains can be allocated in a manner that each partner would agree is commensurate with their input, conflicts may be less likely. When roles and responsibilities are clearly defined, then there are fewer opportunities to have disagreements. We have to be aware that all agreements between companies, whether M&As, joint ventures or strategic alliances, are ultimately agreements among people. The uncertainty inherent in human nature will always leave an opportunity for problems and conflicts. Therefore, another part of the due diligence process is to know the people you are doing business with. Are they problematic types? Have they had a history of litigation with prior business partners? If so, then this is a risk factor that needs to be incorporated into the decision making process.

## CROSS STOCK HOLDINGS AS CONFLICT INSURANCE

One step that companies sometimes take to try to reduce the potential for conflict is to create an equity-based linkage between the venture or alliance partners. In such an agreement each company would hold shares in the other. Thus, each would be a significant shareholder in the other company and thus would gain when their partner profited.

This can be done using voting or nonvoting shares. Nonvoting shares allow each company to receive the benefits of financial gains in the other without exchanging control. However, such cross holdings are no assurance that conflicts will still not arise. This was clear in the successful 1993 international joint venture between LVMH and Guinness PLC. They had formed the combination to expand their international alcoholic beverage marketing and it had provided benefits to both companies. However, Guinness was not enthusiastic about Bernard Arnault's luxury expansion strategy outside of the drinks business. This is one problem with cross share holdings as each company is now more involved in the other's business strategy. This became even more problematic in 1997 when Guinness announced its $19 billion merger with Grand Metropolitan PLC. LVMH initially opposed the merger based on its belief that the combination would take away from LVMH and Guinness' joint efforts. LVMH fought the combination for five months and finally settled for a $405 million payment while also agreeing to add Grand Met drink brands, Smirnoff vodka and Baileys Irish Cream, to their joint beverage marketing agreement.

Cross stock holdings provide only limited insurance against conflicts. In some ways they can even increase the potential for conflict as the force the partners to be even more involved in the other's business beyond what they would with a more limited joint venture or strategic alliance.

## CONCLUSION

Joint ventures and strategic alliances can be a less drastic and less expensive alternative to a merger or acquisition. Sometimes a prospective acquirer may really only want to control certain aspects of a potential target's business. If it can get the other company to form a joint venture with it or if it can get that firm to enter into a strategic alliance, then it may be able to achieve all its goals without the costs of a merger or acquisition. Usually such arrangements can be discontinued with less effort and costs than reversing a merger or acquisition. However, joint ventures are more formal arrangements than strategic alliances and may feature a greater level of commitment.

When we review the research literature on joint ventures and strategic alliances, we see that the announcements of such ventures and alliances tend to be associated with positive shareholder wealth effects for the participants. Vertical joint ventures showed higher gains than horizontal ventures. Research has also showed that for horizontal joint ventures, shareholder gains are shared by the venture participants. However, for vertical deals, this was not the case. In vertical joint ventures, the bulk of the gains went to suppliers, while buyers did not realize many of these gains.

Strategic alliances also show their own positive shareholder wealth effects, so they also are a favorable alternative. Horizontal alliances yield positive shareholder wealth effects while non-horizontal alliances show negative returns. In addition, technologically-oriented alliances yielded positive returns while marketing alliances often showed negative returns.

Certain companies seem to do better with strategic alliances than others. Companies that have had significant experience with such alliances seem to do better with them than those that have not. Similarly, companies that have a dedicated alliance position or department do better than those that do not have such a position.

Before approving a merger or acquisition, management and the board of directors need to make sure that either of these two less drastic alternatives would not accomplish the same goals at a lesser cost. When this is the case, the deal planning needs to be redirected in this direction.

## ENDNOTES

1. John J. McConnell and Timothy J. Nantell, "Corporate Combinations and Common Stock Returns: The Case of Joint Ventures," *Journal of Finance* 40, no. 2 (June 1985): 519–536.

2. J. Randall Woolridge and Charles C. Snow, "Stock Market Reaction to Strategic Investment Decisions," *Strategic Management Journal* 11, no. 5 (September 1990): 353–363.

3. Shane Johnson and Mark Houston, "A Reexamination of the Motives and Gains in Joint Ventures," *Journal of Financial and Quantitative Analysis* 35, no. 1 (March 2000): 67–85.

4. David Robinson, "Strategic Alliances and the Boundaries of the Firm," Working Paper, Columbia University, Graduate School of Business, November 2001.

5.  David Robinson and Toby Stuart, "Financial Contracting in Biotech Strategic Alliances," Working Paper, Columbia University, Graduate School of Business, February 2002.

6.  Phillipe Aghion and Jean Triole, "On the Management of Innovation," *Quarterly Journal of Economics* 109 (1994): 1185–1207.

7.  Josh Lerner and Robert P. Merges, "The Control of Strategic Alliances: An Empirical Analysis of Biotechnology Collaborations," NBER Working Paper No. 6014, April 1997.

8.  Su Han Chan, John W. Kensinger, Arthur Keown, and John D. Martin, "Do Strategic Alliances Create Value?" *Journal of Financial Economics* 46, no. 2 (November 1997): 199–221.

9.  Somnath Das, Pradyot K. Sen, and Sanjit Sengupta, "Impact of Strategic Alliances on Firm Valuation," *Academy of Management Journal* 41, no. 1 (February 1988): 27–41.

10. J. Hagedoorn, "Understanding the Rationale of Strategic Technology Partnering: Interorganizational Modes of Cooperation and Sectoral Differences," *Strategic Management Journal* 14 (1993): 371–385.

11. Prashant Kale, Jeffrey H. Dyer, and Harbir Singh, "Alliance Capability, Stock Market Response and Long-Term Alliance Success: The Role of the Alliance Function," *Strategic Management Journal* 23 (2002): 747–767.

# Case Study

# AT&T

AT&T has a history of failed megamergers that no other company can match—a dubious distinction. Its history of merger failures is analogous to an NBA team—the Los Angeles Clippers. It seemed that each year the Clippers, who for a long time were one of the worst teams in the league and thus the annual recipient of one of the highest draft choices, would be talked into trading away this valuable asset for some over-the-hill veterans. The track record of these deals and the repeated bad position of the team every year got so bad that there was talk that the league would prohibit the team from entering into any deals to trade away its valuable draft choices. Although AT&T has a rich corporate history, unlike the Clippers, it shares its incompetence in doing deals.

## AT&T HISTORY

In order to understand why AT&T made some of its merger blunders, it is helpful to understand its history as a monopoly and regulated company. At one point, AT&T was the largest company in the world. Its securities, such as its corporate bonds, were the standard to which all others were compared. The AT&T bonds were the bellwether bond, representing the lowest-risk bond while all others were assumed to have higher risk. AT&T can trace its roots back to Alexander Graham Bell, who invented the telephone in 1876. In the following year, he founded the Bell Telephone Company. The company fueled its growth through mergers from very early on in its history, when it acquired the Western Electric Company, the largest manufacturer of electrical equipment in the United States, in 1882. Bell Telephone then created the American Telephone and Telegraph Company, which was created to facilitate the growth of the long-distance telephone business. The company was by far the dominant firm in this growing industry. However, it suffered when the economy turned down after the turn of the twentieth century and its debt levels mounted. J. P. Morgan and other investment bankers moved in to take control of the company, as it had with many other companies it combined during the first merger wave. J. P. Morgan put Theodore Vail in charge and acquired Western Union—the largest company in the telegraph business. However, this raised antitrust concerns, and in 1913 AT&T was forced to divest this company. As part of this antitrust agreement, it had to agree to let local phone companies connect to AT&T's long-distance network, even though it still had a monopoly on the long-distance business.

While AT&T dominated the telephone business, it continued to foster innovation. It invented the transistor just after World War II, and this led to tremendous developments in the electronics business. It launched Telstar as the first orbiting communications satellite in 1962. However, as antitrust enforcement picked up at the end of the 1940s through the 1950s, AT&T became the target of various antitrust lawsuits. As a result, AT&T was prohibited from entering unregulated businesses so it could not use the tremendous cash flows derived from its monopoly position in the telephone industry to dominate other industries. Regulators also eliminated AT&T's monopoly on telephone equipment while allowing microwave-based long-distance companies to access the AT&T network.

The Justice Department maintained its antitrust pressure on AT&T and filed two lawsuits in 1974. The Justice Department wanted to dismantle the telecom giant, but AT&T was able to drag the lawsuit on for years while enjoying huge cash flows from its dominant market share. Its profits rose above that of any other company, putting further pressure on government regulators to do something about a company they believed was enjoying monopoly profits while stifling competition. Merely ruling that other companies could compete against AT&T was not sufficient in light of AT&T's incredible financial might. The Justice Department wanted AT&T to separate the equipment business as well as to break the link between the long-distance business and the operating companies. AT&T, for its part, was not satisfied with its great profitability and wanted to enter more exciting businesses, such as the computer business, but was prohibited by regulators from doing so. It saw the loss of the operating companies as a price well worth paying in order to be able to become more of a diverse company. Needless to say, this strategy was simply terrible.

In 1984, AT&T was finally broken up. The company spun off its 22 operating companies into seven large holding companies. These holding companies, known as the Baby Bells, included Ameritech, Bell Atlantic, Bell South, Nynex, Pacific Telesis, Southwestern Bell, and U.S. West. There was criticism of AT&T for parting with the regional telephone companies, but this did not give management pause because it was too eager to forge ahead into more exciting pastures. Ironically, these companies would eventually evolve through M&As and come back to take major positions in the U.S. telecommunications business. Meanwhile, AT&T, which was unaccustomed to being a mere fraction of its former self, sought to grow the business back to its dominant position. The problem was that coming from a culture of being a dominant company in a regulated industry, it did not know how to be an aggressive competitor, but it still had impressive financial resources that it could wield in any battles with rivals. While its resources were still impressive, its management proved to be its undoing.

## AT&T'S ACQUISITION OF NCR

As a result of the breakup of AT&T, the company was released to enter other industries such as the computer industry. AT&T had agreed to part with the boring regional phone companies, to be able to enter more exciting fields. In addition, the technology of telecommunications was changing, and the telecom industry was becoming more computer-like while the computer industry was moving closer to the telecom business. Robert Allen assumed the position of CEO in 1988 and wanted to transform AT&T into more of a technology company, and he saw the computer industry as a way to do that. AT&T tried to succeed on its own in the computer industry when it formed its own computer business. For example, it manufactured and marketed high-quality and high-priced personal computers in a market that was packed with competent rivals. Companies like ITT, Panasonic, and many others unsuccessfully marketed personal computers in an industry that proved to feature cutthroat competition. AT&T manufactured and sold high-quality products, but with its bloated overhead structure, it could not compete with more efficient rivals. Its movement into the computer industry was a failure. AT&T sought to acquire a computer company that could come in and help it succeed in that business. It set its sights on NCR, which had some compatible product lines and was stronger in networking than AT&T. In addition, NCR had more of an international computer business than AT&T.

NCR did not want to be acquired, but AT&T would not accept no for an answer. It seemed that price was no object to the rich AT&T. A hostile takeover battle that lasted six months ensued, but in the end AT&T acquired NCR in an all-stock transaction valued at $7.5 billion. This 1991 deal was the biggest acquisition in that year and was the largest computer deal up to that date. The market disliked the deal right from the beginning, and during the six-month-long negotiations, AT&T saw its market value decline by between $3.9 billion to $6.5 billion as the market concluded that AT&T greatly overpaid for the computer company.[1]

The post-acquisition performance of the merged computer business was poor. AT&T initially retained the name of NCR, but this was eventually changed to AT&T Global Information Solutions. NCR

---

1. Thomas Lys and Linda Vincent, "An Analysis of the Value Destruction in AT&T Acquisition of NCR," *Journal of Financial Economics* 39 (1995): 353–378.

senior management, its CEO, and president, who had many years of computer experience, left the company following the takeover. AT&T had a management void and struggled to succeed in a business it had worked so hard to enter. It paid a very high price in the form of the loss of the regional phone companies and the equipment business to enter the computer arena. When it was initially unsuccessful in this business, it then overpaid for NCR and proceeded to erode its value. As corporate strategists, AT&T was proving to be terrible. However, it continued to pursue bad strategy for years to come.

## AT&T RESTRUCTURING

AT&T continued to plow ahead with its misguided strategy, but the market remained down on the company. Pressure on management mounted, and it tried to present an image that senior managers knew what they were doing, using a special language called CEO speak. This is really a combination of words, body language, and a good overall presentation that is designed to create the image (in this case a false image) that management knows what it is doing and that it is following a grand plan drafted by senior managers who are all-knowing and confident. The market, however, had heard this language before, and it was not convinced that the post-divestiture management group at AT&T had a clue.

The stock price weakened and pressure on management mounted (see Exhibit A). The strategy was not working, and management finally had to make major changes. On September 30, 1996, AT&T announced that it was issuing stock in its equipment division — Lucent Technologies. The offering netted the company $30 billion. In January 1997, AT&T spun off NCR by giving shareholders 101.44 shares of common stock in NCR. This ended its failed computer strategy. As part of that spin-off, however, AT&T disclosed that it had pumped $2.84 billion into the troubled computer division over the period 1993–1996.[2] The net result of the restructuring was that AT&T

---

2. Bart Ziegler, "AT&T Discloses Details of Plan on NCR Spinoff—SEC Filing Reveals Parent Pumped $2.84 Billion to Help Sustain Unit," *The Wall Street Journal* (September 27, 1996): B6.

**Exhibit A**
AT&T Stock Trends before First Restructuring

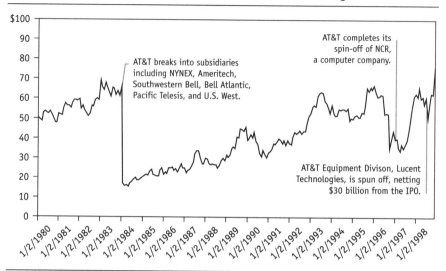

*Sources:* Deborah Soloman and Nikhil Deogun, "AT&T Board Approves Breakup Proposal,"
*Wall Street Journal* (October 25, 2000); and finance.yahoo.com.

was split into three units: the long-distance, computer, and equipment
businesses. While its acquisition strategy had been atrocious up to this
point, the market would have to put up with even more failed acquisitions from AT&T, because this company would never let failure slow
it down from making big merger mistakes.

## AT&T'S LATER ACQUISITIONS

AT&T entered the wireless telephone business in 1994 when it acquired
McCaw Cellular for approximately $12.6 billion in stock. McCaw had
3.9 million customers and was the nation's largest provider of cellular
telephone service.[3] The unit would become AT&T Wireless Services.
AT&T could now offer not only long-distance services but also wireless communications. When they eventually parted ways with their
wireless division, they would at least be able to say that the McCaw deal
provided good returns even though that acquisition was also part of
a failed strategy.

---

3. AT&T Press Release, September 1994.

AT&T was never satisfied with its traditional telecommunications business. In fairness to AT&T, this business was changing, and it correctly believed that it needed to change with it. AT&T had been losing market share in the long-distance market for many years as aggressive competitors, such as WorldCom, eroded its market shares. It could not hold its ground against these competitors, and instead of getting better, it tried to become different. The Telecommunications Act of 1996 deregulated the telecommunications industry, and as with many deregulations, it created opportunities for management to stray from what it did best and move into areas that it did not know well.

In June 1998 AT&T announced that it would pay approximately $48 billion to acquire Telecommunication, Inc. (TCI) (Mergerstat valued the deal at $52.5 billion), which was one of the largest cable television companies in the United States. At the time of the deal, AT&T's CEO, Michael Armstrong, announced that it "would bring to people's home the first integrated package of communications, electronic commerce, and video entertainment services . . . and we will do it with the quality and reliability that people have come to expect from AT&T."[4]

TCI was providing cable television service to approximately 7 to 11 million households. The 4 million household range is large but important. TCI actually had 7 million households but had affiliate cable companies, which had another 4 million households. The only problem was that TCI did not control them, and this was an important difference.[5] AT&T valued TCI because it believed that it may have been able to use these cable lines to provide not just cable but also telephone service. Anyone familiar with the company's not-too-distant history might find this pretty amusing because AT&T had eagerly parted with the greatest direct access to customers through the operating companies it gave away. Now it was willing to pay a hefty price to get back to where it was, but that was part of the problem.

---

4. *www.businessweek.com.*

5. Leo Hindrey, *The Biggest Game of All* (New York: The Free Press, 2003), p. 67.

It saw this merger and others as a way to reacquire direct access to telecommunications consumers, but it did not do its homework and did not end up purchasing what it thought it was buying.

In order to expand its cable network and be a truly dominant player, in 2000 AT&T bought Media One for $43.5 billion.[6] Media One, a Denver-based company, had 5 million subscribers and major market shares in some of the best markets in the United States, such as Atlanta, Boston, and Los Angeles. AT&T combined its acquired cable businesses and called them AT&T Broadband. The company could now be in a position to fulfill CEO Michael Armstrong's grand strategy. Armstrong came to AT&T in 1997 having been CEO of Hughes Electronics. His strategy was to offer consumers long-distance, cable, and wireless service as well as eventually local telephone service. However, there were a few major problems with Armstrong's strategy. One of the most fundamental of these was the fact that the cable lines that AT&T had acquired through its cable deals could not support the demands of modern telecommunications. The company would need to make a major investment to get these lines modernized to compete with other local telecommunications providers. Ironically, as hard as it is to fathom, it seemed that Armstrong knew little about what it would take to get TCI's cable lines to do what he wanted them to do. It also seemed that his eager investment bankers did not provide him with valuable advice that would have either caused him to back away from the deal (which would cause them to lose fees) or pay a lower price that would allow for the fact that AT&T would have to make a major financial investment in line improvements.

AT&T made unrealistic projections about the cable business's future cash flows. "They were extraordinarily, and unrealistically, optimistic."[7] Readers are encouraged to read TCI and AT&T Broadband's CEO Leo Hindrey's account of his experience with AT&T deal making in his book, *The Biggest Game of All*. In that book he recounts how Armstrong pushed TCI deal makers to do the transaction faster, while knowing little about the cable business and not taking time to

---

6. Houlihan Lokey, *Mergerstat Review*, 2004.
7. See note e, p. 91.

do his homework. He greatly overpaid for TCI and its programming arm—Liberty Media. Hindrey says the following:

> Since John (Malone) and I were on the sell side, we were happy to accommodate AT&T's request to seal the deal quickly. Faster is always better when it come to selling—less time for second thoughts, cold feet, and due diligence. But it was a huge tactical error on AT&T's part. The deal stood to fundamentally change AT&T forever. It was also a huge selling price. AT&T should have taken more time to do proper due diligence, because once it is signed on the dotted line there is no looking back. (Rule 1: Do more homework than the other guy.)[8]

Once again it was AT&T megamerger failures at their finest. Truly no company can match AT&T's record for doing merger flops. It does everything on a grand scale, and doing bad deals is something it has perfected. Its senior managers have perfected the art of CEO speak to superior level, where they can with a straight face tell markets one day they are unveiling this great but costly strategy only to come back a relatively short while later and announce that they were undoing that great strategy to move in the opposite direction.

Many have been critical of Armstrong's strategy. It basically gambled $100 billion to create a bundled set of telecom services that consumers showed little desire for. Shareholders also suffered mightily for this misguided strategy (see Exhibit B). In describing AT&T's strategy, Larry Bossidy, former chairman and CEO of Honeywell, said the following:

> AT&T's strategy was disconnected from both external and internal realities. It didn't test critical assumptions and it had no alternative plan for what to do if one or more of them proved wrong. The company did not take into account its organizational inability to compete against aggressive rivals in a fast-moving marketplace. Its culture, which was not much changed from the old monopoly days, could not execute well enough or fast enough to make the plan work soon enough.[9]

---

8. See note e, p. 93.
9. Larry Bossidy and Ram Charan, *Execution: The Discipline of Getting Things Done* (New York: Crown Business, 2002), pp. 181–182.

**Exhibit B**
AT&T Stock Price History in Its Second Restructuring Era

*Source:* finance.yahoo.com.

On October 25, 2000, AT&T announced that it would restructure itself—again. Its one-stop shopping strategy had been a failure. In 2001 AT&T Wireless was spun off and began operations as a separate company. The breakup of the remaining parts of the company was approved by shareholders in July 2002. The cable business would be merged with Comcast, the nation's number-one cable operator. Called a merger, that deal can be considered a takeover of AT&T Broadband, then the number-three cable operator, by Comcast. Michael Armstrong initially was named chairman of that entity, but in May 2004 he stepped down. In his defense, Armstrong complains that AT&T was faced with unfair competition from rivals like World-Com that were "cooking their books." He states:

> What we didn't know was that WorldCom was fraudulently cooking their books for $6 billion in the year 2000." . . . Qwest was federally investigated, individuals criminally charged, and it has restated billions in financial reporting.[10]

---

10.   Rabecca Blumenstein and Peter Grant, "Former Chief Tries to Redeem The Calls He Made at AT&T," *The Wall Street Journal* (May 26, 2004).

Armstrong is proud that he and his fellow managers did not stoop to the level of criminals in order to effectively compete in this difficult industry, but this does not explain his terrible strategy decisions. The questionable nature of the strategy he proposed to enhance the number of services the company would offer consumers was underscored in 2004 when the company announced it was leaving the consumer market! The number of 180-degree turns that this one company can make is truly amazing. The failure of AT&T's strategy is underscored by the decline in its market capitalization which came at a time when the regional telecoms were registering impressive growth.

## LESSONS FROM AT&T'S FAILED MERGER HISTORY

Unfortunately for shareholders, AT&T has a rich history of M&A failure that one can learn from. A few of the many lessons we can take away from AT&T's failures are:

- *If you have failed many times before be extra careful.* This is such an obvious point but was apparently not one that AT&T could appreciate. The company never seemed to accept that it had a troubled history in this area and each new CEO would seem to disassociate himself with past failures while then proceeding to do even bigger flops.

- *When moving into new areas, be extra cautious and seek out the best expertise.* While AT&T knew the telecom business, you need to be extra careful doing big deals in new areas. AT&T did not know the cable business but pushed huge deals like the TCI acquisition forward while dealing with shrewd sellers who knew their business well.

- *Do your homework.* The bigger the deal, the more homework you need to do. This is what management gets paid for. The board also needs to do its own homework. The bigger the deal, the more research and evaluation the board needs to do.

- *M&A is not for everyone.* If you are really bad at M&A, then maybe it is not for you and you should try to grow other ways. However, in rapidly evolving businesses, you may not be able to avoid M&As. If that is the case, then you need to make sure that the upper management in place is capable of doing successful deals.

In January 2005 the long saga of AT&T took another defining turn when AT&T agreed to be acquired by its former division—SBC Communications, Inc. for $16 billion (subject to regulatory approval). SBC was a successful regional telephone company that had previously acquired Pacific Telesis—also offspring from the AT&T breakup. SBC was a relatively conservative telecom company that seemed to have a good sense of its proper strategy. It is ironic one of AT&T's less well known "children" would end of taking over its former parent.

# Index